"Mastin Kipp doesn't just suggest the possibility that we could live a better life; his very presence seems to demand that we do so! *Claim Your Power* invites us to meet an infinitely creative universe with an infinite willingness to receive its gifts."

— **Marianne Williamson**, six-time *New York Times* best-selling author and internationally acclaimed spiritual lecturer

"For a long time I've been a big believer in Mastin Kipp, and if you read *Claim Your Power*, you will be too."

— **Mike Dooley**, *New York Times* best-selling author of *From Deep Space with Love*

"Mastin wrote a timeless legacy harmonizing safety, inspiration, and direction, allowing me to slice through fear and ego. I was able to explore, understand, and release my multiple traumas of sexual abuse, physical abuse, and PTSD in order to claim my power. Forever grateful!"

— **George Bryant**, former United States Marine and *New York Times* best-selling co-author of *The Paleo Kitchen*

"With *Claim Your Power*, Mastin Kipp has done for personal growth and healing what *The Virgin Diet* did for nutrition—created an innovative, researched, and time-tested system that creates lasting results, fast."

— **JJ Virgin**, four-time *New York Times* best-selling author of *The Virgin Diet*

"I first met Mastin Kipp at 5 A.M. in the gym. He was tirelessly pounding away on the treadmill while writing a book and working on e-mails. I knew right away that this guy not only had an amazing work ethic, but was also extremely passionate about something. Later, I discovered his deep and unique wealth of knowledge on little-known tactics for removing the hidden obstacles that keep us stuck in life, and finding our life's true purpose. I find this guy completely fascinating, and I think you will too. Enjoy his work. It will change your life."

— **Ben Greenfield**, Ironman triathlete and *New York Times* best-selling author of *Beyond Training*

"Liberation of spirit is the greatest gift anyone could give another. Mastin Kipp has developed a process to rid the root cause of human suffering that holds us back from living the best version of ourselves. It's brilliant."

— **Dr. Jeff Spencer**, Olympian and creator of the Champion's Blueprint

MASTIN KIPP'S

CLAIM YOUR POWER

ALSO BY MASTIN KIPP

Daily Love: Growing into Grace

The above is available at your local bookstore,
or may be ordered by visiting:

Hay House USA: www.hayhouse.com®
Hay House Australia: www.hayhouse.com.au
Hay House UK: www.hayhouse.co.uk
Hay House South Africa: www.hayhouse.co.za
Hay House India: www.hayhouse.co.in

MASTIN KIPP'S

CLAIM YOUR POWER

A 40-Day Journey to Dissolve the Hidden
Blocks That Keep You Stuck and Finally Thrive
in Your Life's Unique Purpose

HAY HOUSE, INC.

Carlsbad, California • New York City
London • Sydney • Johannesburg
Vancouver • New Delhi

Copyright © 2017 by Daily Love Media, Inc.

Published and distributed in the United States by: Hay House, Inc.: www
.hayhouse.com® • **Published and distributed in Australia by:** Hay House
Australia Pty. Ltd.: www.hayhouse.com.au • **Published and distributed in the
United Kingdom by:** Hay House UK, Ltd.: www.hayhouse.co.uk • **Published and
distributed in the Republic of South Africa by:** Hay House SA (Pty), Ltd.: www
.hayhouse.co.za • **Distributed in Canada by:** Raincoast Books: www.raincoast
.com • **Published in India by:** Hay House Publishers India: www.hayhouse.co.in

Cover design: Amanda Strutz • *Interior design:* Nick C. Welch

Cataloging-in-Publication Data is on file at the Library of Congress

Hardcover ISBN: 978-1-4019-4954-9

10 9 8 7 6 5 4 3 2 1
1st edition, September 2017

SUSTAINABLE
FORESTRY
INITIATIVE

Certified Sourcing
www.sfiprogram.org
SFI-01268

SFI label applies to text stock only

Printed in the United States of America

CONTENTS

THE PATH BEFORE YOU

We have not even to risk the adventure alone
for the heroes of all time have gone before us;
the labyrinth is thoroughly known;
we have only to follow the thread of the hero-path.
And where we had thought to find an abomination,
we shall find a god;

where we had thought to slay another,
we shall slay ourselves;
where we had thought to travel outward,
we shall come to the center of our own existence;
where we had thought to be alone;
we shall be with all the world.

– JOSEPH CAMPBELL

FOREWORD

When I first met Mastin a few years ago, he was puffy, noticeably over-weight, and came across as a kind human being almost intensely looking for a deeper connection. He was still searching. We had a meaningful dinner conversation with a couple other leaders in the personal development field. At the end of the dinner, I still remember how Mastin looked at his dining companions and said, "I really want to be your friends. Will you guys actually do it? I really care about you." What was striking was the earnestness and truth in his statement. He really does care about you at a deep level even if he just met you.

I didn't know him when he was a much younger, couch-surfing co-caine user and party animal, but a few crumbs of that old Mastin were still with him, revealing themselves throughout our conversation. Since that time, as he connected deeply with the work you'll read about in *Claim Your Power*, I stood witness as he shed his physical weight and really connected with his purpose. As his body got lighter, his spirit did too. It was like watching the sunrise get brighter every minute as dawn approaches, and it's been an honor to be his friend as he dialed in to his true purpose and figured out a method to help countless others do the same thing. He has walked this path, studied it, lived it, and put up signs to make it easier going.

Finding your purpose is scary, because if you are a rational person trained in engineering like I am, admitting that you might have a purpose opens a can of worms. If you came here with the purpose, who gave it to you? You might have to ask yourself some difficult spiritual or religious questions. On the other hand, if you can suspend your disbelief and do the work to connect to your purpose—no matter where you believe it comes from—you will find that everything you do gets easier.

This book can save you hundreds of thousands of dollars and years of work. I don't say that lightly. In my own quest to find my purpose, I was fortunate to find patient spiritual people who convinced me that it was at least possible that I might have a purpose. Then I combed the ends of the earth, from ancient shamanic ayahuasca ceremonies with shamans in Peru (way before it was cool), to Holotropic Breathwork™ workshops with Stan Grof, the almost 90-year-old psychiatrist who treated 10,000 patients with LSD in the 1960s, only to replace drugs with breathing exercises, creating the field of transpersonal psychology along the way. From learning meditation from the masters in remote parts of Tibet, advanced yoga, and breathing exercises from India, and with almost 20 years of hooking EEG brain-wave monitoring equipment to my head to help me meditate more deeply, culminating in the 40 Years of Zen neurofeedback program, I've spent more than four months of my life with computers connected to my head in order to figure out and reprogram what was in there. *Claim Your Power* is your shortcut to finding your purpose and removing traumas, because most of us don't have the time or resources to comb the ends of the earth for answers.

Along this path, as I connected more deeply with my purpose and edited out my own traumas, my effectiveness as a human being at work and at home improved in almost unimaginable ways. Starting my company Bulletproof only five years ago didn't feel like a chore or like work—it was joyful because it is a part of my purpose. Today, the company is worth more than $100 million, and it consistently attracts the most amazing and influential people who can sense that it is mission driven. People like Mastin, who figured it out when they met me before it was successful.

I imagine what would have happened had someone put this book in my hands when I was 22 years old instead of 44, the age I am as I write this. All of the struggle, all of the suffering, all of the time I spent searching for ways to get out of my own head and turn off the critic that sat on my shoulder . . . it wasn't necessary. There are shortcuts. This book would have helped me stop running away from failure and start running toward things that matter.

It's not that running away from failure doesn't work—I made $6 million when I was 26 years old because I was terrified of failure. I also lost that same $6 million when I was 28 years old because I was afraid of failure. Fear is a terrible motivator. What I learned on my own path, and what Mastin's book explains eloquently, is that your deepest fears are invisible, and they guide your behavior every day without you knowing it. It's not because you're weak; it's because we are wired that way. There is plenty of science to verify this—and Mastin has researched it to come up with such an effective program.

Getting around that wiring can be a lifetime of work if you don't know how to do it. The Claim Your Power process is innovative, shockingly efficient, and fast. When you get to the root causes of the things holding you back, you can actually remove them. You can stop spending so much of your energy trying to think your way out of failure.

If you want to experience exponential growth in your relationships, and your career, or just in your life, there is nothing more important and more pressing than healing hidden traumas. I've had the great pleasure to coach billionaires, hedge fund managers, CEOs, and celebrities—some of the most successful people on the planet. Every single one of them has behaviors that stem from hidden traumas, and every single one of them has benefited from healing the traumas. It's a part of the human experience no matter who you are, what you do, and how good you think you are (or are not).

The hardest part of this work is that your body will fight to hide it from you. That's why this book is genius. It's not a conscious decision you're making—it's an unconscious decision your body made without your knowledge or awareness. When you read this book, you'll get clear on what is going on. *The world will keep smacking you until you figure it out. Everything gets easier when you get out of your own way.*

Read this book not for yourself, but for all the people you'll touch from this day forward. The more you work toward your purpose (once you know what it is), and the more you work from your higher self instead of invisible trauma-induced habits, the better you'll make every person you touch for the rest of your life, from grocery store clerks to your most cherished family members.

Use this book to do more than survive. Be way more than enough.

So take a deep breath, set out your favorite pen, and commit to do some real work in *Claim Your Power* every single day for the next 40 days. The world will thank you, and so will I.

Dave Asprey
CEO, Bulletproof
Founder, 40 Years of Zen
New York Times best-selling author of
Head Strong and *The Bulletproof Diet*
Victoria, BC
2017

INVOCATION

A day will come when you will be stirred by unexpected events. A part of you will die, and you will begin to search for the elixir that will bring this part of you back to life. You will seek the elixir in friends, lovers, enemies, books, religions, foreign countries, heroes' songs, rituals, and jobs, but no matter where you look the treasure will evade you. All will seem lost, and you will lose all hope that this magic potion even exits. This will be the darkest of nights, and the promise of certain death will lead you to the abyss of despair. But staring into the abyss you will see the dim light of your own illuminated Soul. Your radiance will transform the abyss into the elusive elixir of life, and for the first time you will realize that all the while it was your own Light that you've been searching for.

READ THIS FIRST

"You may not control all the events that happen to you, but you can decide not to be reduced by them. Try to be a rainbow in someone else's cloud. Do not complain. Make every effort to change things you do not like. If you cannot make a change, change the way you have been thinking. You might find a new solution."

– MAYA ANGELOU

This book is a love letter from my Soul to yours. It's also a no-B.S. map of life from the trenches.

As a Functional Life Coach™, I work with people to accelerate their success and create lasting change. To do that, the coaching interventions I facilitate are at the deepest level. In a shallow world, I am a disciple of depth. I go places with my work that many cannot, or will not, go—to the root cause of human suffering. So when I say that this book is a map of life from the trenches, I mean it. If you haven't been getting results up until now, it's probably because you've been focusing on the symptoms of what's keeping you stuck but haven't gotten to the root. I created Functional Life Coaching™ with one intention—to help you rapidly discover the root cause of why you're stuck and help you dissolve it for good. When you do this, anything is possible.

While you may have been spending a lot of your time focused on your goals, your dreams, and where you want to go, until you discover and dissolve the root cause that's keeping you stuck, you'll just keep running in circles. For you to go to the next level in your success, we've got to take you to the next level of your healing. So, if you're stuck, buckle up—we've got some healing to do.

While I am a six-four white man from Kansas who grew up in an upper-middle-class home, I have the honor of "going there" with my clients. Together, we go to that place that many spend a lifetime running from. After facilitating hundreds of interventions, I've had the privilege to bear witness to the profound ranges of the root causes of suffering. And we've been able to heal my clients' causes, which allows them to bring their Purposes to life.

Now it's our turn to team up and go deep.

If you've been feeling like something is missing and you aren't quite sure what it is, let me tell you plainly: it's your Purpose. Together, we are going to help you answer the most important question there is: "What is my life's Purpose?"

Let me explain.

If things haven't been working out the way you wanted them to, or if you're wondering, "How the heck did I get here, again?"—you're in the right place.

Here's the good news: abundance in all its forms is the by-product of discovering and bringing your Purpose to life. The only difference between people who are truly abundant and thriving spiritually, emotionally, romantically, financially, and professionally and those who are stuck, stagnated, and feeling they are missing out and living the same boring, depressed, and small life is that those who are truly abundant know their Purposes and are living them daily.

It doesn't matter if you don't know what your Purpose is, if you think you knew what it was and then lost it, if you don't believe that you have a Purpose, or if you have an idea of what your Purpose is already. There's always a next level, and it's not too late. You didn't miss it. You are exactly where you're meant to be. Your Purpose is here, right now, waiting for you to find it—and when you do . . . Well, my friend, everything changes; your whole life improves. Discovering your Purpose is the most significant thing you will do in your life, and you, your loved ones, and the world will be better off because you went on this journey.

When you bring your Purpose to life, you connect to dormant energy and power. Doors open. Things turn around. You go from being stuck, confused, and pining for something more to stepping into the greatest expression of your life that you can imagine. You don't have to aimlessly chase money—money will abundantly follow you. You don't have to change yourself or stress about finding soul-mate love—your soul mate will be where you're going. If you have an adversarial relationship with food or feel shame about your naked body when you see it in the mirror, when you bring your Purpose to life, you step into a life of health and well-being and make peace with food and your self-image. Your Purpose will guide you to the career or business of your dreams. No more soul-sucking job, no more talking about starting your business—your Purpose will see that those days are behind you.

Perhaps the most exciting thing about discovering your Purpose is that when you do, you are no longer held back by the past. Any trauma, hurt, victimization, betrayal, injury, or injustice—poof, it's gone. Your Purpose transforms trauma into power and finally sets you free from any person or circumstance that caused you pain.

If this seems too grandiose or far-fetched, I get it. I am the captain of the skeptics club when it comes to any kind of religious-, spiritual-, or self-help-type claims of such magnitude. I've also found that sometimes skepticism can be a way to hide from living your Purpose.

So, if you're thinking that this Kipp guy is off his rocker and that this Purpose thing seems like some magic wand, let me put you at ease. Bringing your Purpose to life is real work. And it's hard.

Here's some real talk: this book is a wake-up call. We've most likely come together because you feel that you have a calling within you that is ready to be answered. You have a deep knowing that there is something greater for you to bring forward, and you're ready to finally figure out what the heck it is. So grab your journal and a pen or pencil—tools to assist you on this journey.

To get to the Promised Land of your Purpose, you've got to wander through the desert of your traumas. We've got to get to the root cause of what's kept you stuck. We've got to be more honest than you have proba-bly ever been. We've got to face your biggest fear, call BS, and find the part of you that is far greater than this fear. This is serious work that pays off the highest rewards this life has to offer. It will not be easy, you will want to quit, and you will make lots of mistakes. That's just how it goes. It's going to be messy and scary and you might feel like you should "already be there." That's okay. Don't give up—hang with this process and see it through. You are going to have your mind blown.

Everyone has a Purpose. Most people don't even know they do, and they live the worst kind of shallow life—a life on semiconscious autopilot, at the whim of whatever happens to them. A shallow life where connec-tion comes from how many people "like" them online. A life of shallow relationships, because they have better relationships with their mobile devices than they do with actual human beings. Constant distraction fueled by the neurotic overconsumption of the lowbrow attention ecosystem (social media, sensational/violent headlines, and binge-watching show after show). When you don't know you have a Purpose, you become addicted to the shallow and need a hit every minute or so. Did they like my post? I need to know. Did they text me back? I must know. Did you see what happened on the last episode? How many followers do I have today? (Better be more than yesterday.) How many views? A life without Purpose is lived on the surface, and this is how most people live today.

A smaller number of people have some sense that they have Purpose, but they aren't living it. This can sometimes be worse than living the distracted life, because when you get a sense that your life has a Purpose, it's waking up from the trance of the shallow and feeling disconnected from something important. This can cause depression, anxiety, and a general sense of feeling like an alien in a world you can't relate to. If you go long enough with having a sense that your life has Purpose and you don't get to the Promised Land, you can suffer the worst kind of pain: being consciously separated from who you really are and—as a result—your Purpose. This can cause all kinds of coping mechanisms. Eventually you go from being an optimistic seeker and wanting to make the world a better place to a burned-out, jaded, and close-hearted person; you turn into a skeptic with a Ph.D. in why things didn't work out for you.

So, make me a promise, okay? Don't be that person. For the rest of our time together, just table the skepticism, all the stories you've convinced yourself are true about why you can't have what you want. Tell the voice of insecurity in your head to pack up and go on vacation for the next 40 days.

After working with thousands of people from all walks of life, I have seen time and time again that having an open mind and a curious spirit and being a student of life are the foundations in creating success. You can't discover your purpose and experience all the great stuff that comes along with that if you are going to start your journey by staying focused on all the stories of limitation and lack, life being unfair, and why you can't have the life that you want. News flash: no matter what you've been through, someone else (and most likely millions of other people) has gone through it or is going through it right now. Your problems, your past, your hurt, your trauma are not what make you special. What makes you special is your ability to discover and thrive in your Purpose in spite of all those things.

You have a powerful, resilient, and infinite spirit within you that is unstoppable. To access it, you've got to get out of your own way and decide that from this moment forward you are going to earn a Ph.D. in results and in creating the outcomes you truly desire.

What Is "Purpose," Anyway?

Purpose is one of the most overused words in the world of religion, self-help, and personal growth. It's been used so often that it's almost lost its meaning.

At the same time, discovering your Purpose is the most important work you can do in this life. Your Purpose helps you answer questions like the following:

Why am I here?
What was I made for?

Technology connects us in ways that just a couple of decades ago seemed unfathomable; new advancements seem more and more like magic. But one thing is likely still missing from this world today. Your *Purpose*.

Your Purpose resides where it has always been, within you. And yet it eludes you. You feel the lack of its presence as a small twinge of fear at first. Then the feeling grows into anger, resentment, unworthiness, and exhaustion. Finally life hits you with a crisis you cannot ignore. I call these moments your Divine Storms. I wrote about my own Divine Storms in my last book, *Daily Love: Growing into Grace*, but this book is about yours. A Divine Storm (or "shit storm," as some of my clients call it) is a moment in time when life, God, and The Universe all seem to be against you. What used to work no longer does. What used to feel certain now feels uncertain. All your power and Purpose is gone. And if you're not careful, you'll never get them back.

The Power Required to Make Changes

We've talked about Purpose, but what is *power* exactly? And how does it relate to your Purpose? I define *power* as your ability to make your Purpose real on earth, taking the unseen and making it a reality. The whole point of experiencing a Divine Storm is because your Creator is trying to get your attention to wake up and live your unique and special life's Purpose.

The good news: we all have Divine Storms.

The bad news: if you don't get the message your Divine Storms are trying to send you, the future is only downhill—or a plateau of stagnation at the very best.

One of my biggest aha moments as I was beginning my transformation. I was going through a breakup with my then girlfriend, and our whole relationship was based on drugs, addiction, and Hollywood nightclubs.

One night I was driving back from her house in Sherman Oaks to my house in Santa Monica. It was toward the end of our relationship, and I had already moved out, but we still saw each other now and then. And on this night, we'd just had a big fight, which was why I was driving home.

I had a pretty substantial-size bag of cocaine underneath my driver's seat. It was really late at night (so late it was early), and no one else was on the street as I turned onto Ventura Boulevard. Somehow I cut off a police officer—the only other car around—who was coming down Ventura.

He pulled me over under the suspicion of drunk driving, and thankfully I wasn't—that time. I was under the influence of drugs but not alcohol. I'd had an awareness for a while that it was time to stop doing drugs. But I always told myself I'd stop later. And now I was on the side of the road with cocaine in my system and directly below me in my car, being questioned by the police.

I was only 22, and I had just landed my dream job. I was very aware of how bad it would be if I were to be arrested for cocaine. My mind spun: *You're a good kid from Kansas. You were raised by good parents. This is not how your life should end up.* In that moment, I started bargaining with God: "If you let me go, I'll stop."

I truthfully told the officer that I was tired, I'd just had a fight with my girlfriend, and I was driving home. He let me go.

I had taken previous warnings for granted, but this moment was sobering. When I got home, I brought the bag of cocaine inside. Somewhere toward the end of the week, I had the urge to use again at 3:00 a.m. The funny thing about addiction is that when you are sober you tell yourself you're going to do one thing, and when that craving hits, all logic, promises, and integrity tend to go out the window. I'd since lost my dream job, been drinking a lot, was in massive emotional pain from my breakup and the job loss, and I felt so down that I wanted to do the whole bag.

But a visceral knowing came over me as I was cutting up the cocaine . . . I literally could not move. I just couldn't do it, almost as if I wasn't in control of my body. Maybe it was Jesus, or the Divine, or my intuition—but something wouldn't let me continue to hurt myself. In fact, this knowing knew that if I did one more line, I'd die. So, in an act of what I can call only Grace, I found myself flushing it all down the toilet right then and there.

The next morning I decided I wanted to feel as good off the drugs as I did on them. And it was all thanks to a late-night traffic stop—a Divine Storm.

The key was, of course, that I was just sober and scared enough to pay attention.

My guess is you probably wouldn't have picked up a book called *Claim Your Power* if everything was rocking in your life. Perhaps you're in the midst of a tremendous Divine Storm too. Perhaps you're in search of an answer to the question "Why did this happen to me?" Or you may simply be feeling stuck, depressed, sad, or anxious, or like someone else holds all your power and you don't know what to do about it. Maybe you don't have a clue about what your Purpose is, you thought you did but then lost it, or you aren't quite convinced that you have a Purpose. That's quite fine.

You can think of this book as Purpose 101. We are going to use it to get your power and Purpose back. Because when you're living your Purpose, you are fully in your power.

Your Purpose Won't Make You Broke

One of the biggest irrational fears I hear from my clients regarding this work is: "If I live my Purpose, it will cost too much, either financially or emotionally. I'll be broke, my family will suffer, and I'll hurt the people I love." These seem like valid concerns at first. Who would want to take a step forward if you knew your family would suffer?

The problem is that this belief is a fear-backed lie. Following your Purpose *won't* make you broke. Living your Purpose *won't* cause your family and friends to suffer. In fact, if anything is going to cause you or your loved ones to suffer, it's the possibility of you staying stuck in the exact same place you are now for the next 10 years, continuing to be unfulfilled, and existing just out of reach of your Purpose. Remember: abundance is a by-product of living your Purpose. And, no, you won't harm your family or make them poor by doing what you were created to do.

The truth is that when you step into your Purpose, everything becomes better and everything increases—your finances, your health, and your relationships. And when you improve one area in your life, all areas are improved, everything changes, and there's a wealth to your life that wasn't there before. Also know that deciding to live your Purpose does not make you selfish. It does require that you become a little *self*-ish, but this decision will allow you to fill up your cup. From that place you can serve others even more.

My therapist once told me that all the problems in my life had one thing in common: me. *Ouch!* That stung for a bit, but I realized it was true. I also realized it was the same equation for my successes. Every success in my life had one common denominator—me! And once I discovered my Purpose, my life began to shift in a new and exciting direction.

I went from couch surfing, not having a business, not having energy, and not having a relationship to having a successful business that has inspired millions of people, having an incredible soul-mate relationship, and having plenty of energy to do everything I need to do each day. It didn't happen overnight, of course, but as I continued to take steps forward, in spite of the fear and uncertainty I felt, new opportunities arose. Unexpected finances came to me. I began to feel physically stronger and more alert. And I was more aware of signs in my life that were leading me in the right direction. All of this allowed me to contribute to my loved ones even more.

Now I don't believe that if you put something on a vision board, you'll automatically get what you want. Having a vision alone doesn't make you "healthy, wealthy, and wise." It takes action. It takes work. Most important, it requires that you find courage on a daily basis. But there is a rich reward for doing so. As you go along this path, you won't disappoint the people you love; you'll become more for those people.

There's also some great news about your Purpose. No matter what your background is, you have the opportunity to find your Purpose and experience abundance in all areas of life. When you connect to your Purpose, you connect to something larger than yourself, and that power breathes in you and moves through you. And it always has.

What Keeps You Stuck, and Why It's Important to Break Free

What's stopping you from stepping into your Purpose? What's keeping you from moving forward? What nearly imperceptible blocks keep you playing small when your Purpose is so big?

Trauma.

We are all traumatized to one degree or another, and the brain registers the pain the same, regardless of the actual event. The dictionary defines *trauma* as a deeply distressing or disturbing experience, emotional shock, a physical injury, or a stressful event.

In ancient Greek, *trauma* literally means "wound." Interestingly enough, *Traum* is the German word for "dream." The most common definition of *dream* is a series of thoughts, images, or emotions occurring during sleep. And a *nightmare* is a frightening dream that often wakes the sleeper.

Based on that, my definition of *trauma* is: *a nightmare of thoughts, images, and emotions based on past wounds that creates unconscious and irrational stress in the body that suspends awareness of our Infinite nature.*

It's easy to see now how a trauma can affect our dreams—both during our sleeping and waking hours. When we are traumatized, we are asleep to our true nature. The emotions of trauma are stored in our bodies, and regardless of how long it has been since the traumatizing event, our bodies always remember. In fact, we relive our "nightmares" until we realize that we are the dreamers and can wake up.

In short, we continue to hurt ourselves until we heal ourselves.

In addition to keeping us stuck in a living nightmare, a frequent side effect of trauma is to take on the victim mentality.

Victim or Victimized?

Let's talk for a moment about the difference between acting like a victim and being victimized. Every day human beings are victimized. There are victims of unjust wars, sexual assault, racism, sexism, religious persecution, unjustified police brutality, greedy politicians, and bad parenting. It could be that you sustained life-altering injuries from a car crash caused by a drunk driver. Maybe your peers publically turned on you. I wish I could say that this cycle of victimization is going to stop soon, but chances are it's going to get worse before it gets better.

My clients have shared incredible stories of trauma and survival in my seminars that captivated an entire room full of attendees:

- *"I am a victim of multiple acts of molestation, including my brother, my cousin, several other family members, and even co-workers."*

- *"My mother struggled with mental illness, and beginning when I was three years old, she would throw heavy objects at my head and strangle me."*

- *"I was blocks away from the World Trade Center on 9/11 and witnessed the tragedy firsthand, getting showered by debris as the second tower fell."*

As you can imagine, these individuals were living in a continuous identity of trauma as victims—even decades after the traumatic event. Once we acknowledged the trauma, we were able to shift their perceptions and allow them to see that they could step out of the victim identity, give the trauma a new meaning, and move forward to live their Purposes.

- The client who'd endured multiple acts of molestation realized that to be an example of strength, love, and determination would ensure that the perpetrators' actions would not negatively affect her children. If she shut down and decided not to live her Purpose, those who hurt her were still winning.

- The client whose mother was mentally ill realized that her mother's poor behavior was a catalyst for her growth, allowing her to be a wonderful, loving mother to her own kids and not pass on generational trauma.

- The client who'd witnessed 9/11 had shielded a friend with his own body, and he was finally able to see himself as a hero who acted with love in the midst of an act of unknowable hate and evil.

Being a victim is an identity with a corresponding emotional state. If you take on the identity of a victim, you put yourself into a trance, and that's how you see the world. It's like saying, "I am my wound." And the rest of the world will agree with you! You'll find other people who are also wounded who will justify your wound-based identity, and you'll remain together—wounded and stuck indefinitely. But the tragedy is you will also cut yourself off from your Purpose. You'll make innocent people your enemy by associating them with your past wounds, rally against them, and in some ways you'll become the very thing that hurt you.

Being victimized, on the other hand, means you were wounded but the wound does not define who you are. Just because you have been victimized, it does not mean you are a victim. There's a big difference between "*I am* my wound" and "*I was* wounded." So, in order to jump out of being a victim at the level of identity and saying you were victimized, you must say the following:

1. I have felt like my identity was my wound.

2. I realized that that is not totally true.

3. What's actually true is I was wounded.

4. I can find new meaning in that wound, which will set me free.

5. Then I can live my Purpose.

When you are victimized, there is a natural grieving and healing process that must occur. And history is full of people who have been victimized and not remained in victim consciousness: Viktor Frankl, Nelson Mandela, Jesus Christ, Gandhi, Martin Luther King, Jr., Immaculée Ilibagiza, Malala Yousafzai, and thousands more.

The most extreme examples of people who endured victimization and rose above it have all come to the same conclusion: *I am not defined by my past, no matter what's happened to me.* You don't have to ignore it. You don't have to agree with it or pretend it didn't happen. And forgiveness doesn't mean you're condoning what happened. But if you don't forgive and get free, the people who hurt you are *still winning.*

Taking on the identity of a victim is something we do in the aftermath of victimization. It makes total sense. When something traumatic happens, the body goes into fight-or-flight mode and creates beliefs, emotions, stories, and behaviors designed to prevent further trauma.

The true tragedy here is that, if left unchecked and unresolved, you can turn a moment of trauma into a lifetime of acting the victim and therefore never living your Purpose. If I'm in that state, living my life based on my past trauma, I'm not living in the present. And, again, when you do that, *the person who victimized you wins.* That is the ultimate tragedy.

Part of my Purpose is to help those who have been victimized break free from victim consciousness and go on to claim their power, connect with their Souls and Purposes, and become beacons of light. This not only heals those who have been victimized; it creates a tidal wave of healing where before there was pain.

In this book we're on a journey of Purpose, but we're also on a journey to heal the past. And as you'll see, your wounds lead you to your Purpose. Regardless of the hurt you've endured, and the negative beliefs you believe about yourself, you'll soon realize the opposite is true—you are worthy, you are loved, and you are exactly where you are supposed to be in order to take your next step.

The Drain of Disconnection

What does it feel like to be disconnected from your Purpose? Stuck. Stagnated. Frustrated. You feel like you are missing out on "something" and you're not quite sure what that something is. You get jealous of people who are successful, or you judge others for doing what you secretly want to do—but haven't. You feel like you have to push your life up a never-ending hill. You live on what I call the "horizon," where you think that "one day" you will "make it." But no matter how hard you work, how far you go, how much you sacrifice—the horizon never gets closer. That "one day" never comes. And, if you're not careful, you'll arrive at the end of your life and realize that horizon has turned into a cliff and you can't get out alive.

Sounds miserable, doesn't it? Thankfully it doesn't have to be this way. So let's trade the comfortable life for the life of Purpose.

Make a Commitment

Accelerated times call for accelerated measures, so before we go any further, I have two questions for you: *Are you truly committed to discovering, living, and prospering in your life's Purpose? Or are you only committed to thinking about the many "what-ifs" for the rest of your life?*

People talk about wanting to live their Purposes all the time, often like they are the exact opposites of their current lives. But here's the simple and difficult truth: you are exactly where you want to be. You may say, "No. That's not true. I don't want to be stuck in this dead-end job." Or "No way! I never signed up to be in such an unfulfilling relationship as the one I'm in now." But the fact that you're still in that exact situation says that you've accepted this as your fate for the time being. You have settled for less than what you desire. But for whatever reason you haven't taken the steps to make a change. You have become comfortable with a less-than-fulfilling life, always looking for distractions.

In fact, this book could be yet another distraction. You may read it, have a few "aha moments," and then go on your merry way. Then several weeks or months later you'll pick up the next book, watch the next TV show, take the next online course or seminar, hoping and praying for the moment when it all happens, it all makes sense, and your path becomes clear.

I call this *spiritual entertainment*, which boils down to taking in all the spiritual content you can and then *doing nothing with it*. Life is still passing you by. You need inspiration, sure. But what you really need is to dive into the area of your life where you are most frustrated, stare at it, feel the pain, learn the lesson, and get free. That requires taking great action on your part, rather than consuming endless ideas about *what you could do.*

Yes, it can be scary to take the plunge—to make these big changes in your life. And it's not usually easy to do. It's much easier to skip along and onto the next thing, ignoring the pain of being stuck.

But here's what's awesome: God has already done most of the work for you.

God Who?

Wait. *Pause.* Are you and I mature enough to use the word *God* and know what we're talking about? Let's not let the next evolution of your life depend on something as unimportant as a word.

I honor your tradition. It doesn't matter what you call your Creator: Allah. Buddha. Jesus. Ra. Nanak. Yahweh. Dao. Spirit. Source. Higher Power. When I say "God," "Spirit," "Source," or "the Divine," just fill in the name you believe in. The sun, by any name, gives us life. As does our Creator.

Now look around you. Creation exists. We've been given a chance to do something with these lives that we did not create ourselves. You did not create your heart; yet it beats. You did not create your lungs; yet they breathe. You did not create your skin; yet it protects you. You didn't create the sun, the oxygen you breathe, or the food that sustains you. You didn't create water, and yet it is there for you to drink.

What did you do? You chose to come here, at this moment, in this space and time, and to give your unique gifts to the world. You, right now, have the radical opportunity to claim your power by discovering and living your Purpose—and then using all your hurt, your stuckness, and your pain to help other people get free. You see, when you come home to your Purpose, you become a beacon of what's possible for others.

I need you—no, *the world* needs you to wake up, find your Purpose, and serve. Why? Because if you don't, there will be less light in the world, less healing, less joy, and much more pain. There are people you don't know right now who are waiting for you to get going and get your act together. *Because they can't do it without you.* They aren't reading these words. They aren't seeking like you are. They haven't had a Divine Storm yet, or they may be so deep into it that they can't see their way out. And they need you to be ready, willing, and able to help them when they surface.

Emerge as a Leader

I'm writing this book for you, but ultimately I'm writing this book for those you'll touch as a result of embodying what this book teaches. I do not want to create a bunch of followers. I want to create a bunch of leaders: Souls who have claimed their power and then, in their own way, help others do the same.

So, I ask you again, *How committed are you to going on this journey with me?* Because I intend to take you on a journey, a hero's or heroine's journey, that will take you from a Divine Storm to your life's Purpose, from stuck to powerful, from lost to found so that you never again have to wonder, *Why do I feel like something is missing from my life?*

The world is full of dabblers, people who talk about, dream about, and vision-board about changing their lives. Now it's time to go further. The world needs you to rise up in courage and action and make claiming your power a way of life.

How?

By diving deep. There's a new model of personal growth emerging— the Heart model. Let's start by taking a look at the old model—the head model—and its flaws, so you can better understand why this Heart model is needed to fully claim your power and live your Purpose.

The Head Model Is Keeping You Stuck

We've been told that changing our lives by changing our thinking is the name of the game. While there is truth in this, it's kind of like saying that to change the direction your car is going, you simply have to turn the steering wheel. The problem is that depending on the situation, turning the steering wheel can be very hard. And if you're out of gas, it won't make much difference anyway.

My friend, we are out of gas. We are tired and stuck. We have affirmed ourselves into oblivion, and we're *still* stuck.

Think about it: Have you ever been in the midst of a positive affirmation like "I love myself," and almost before you were done saying it, another part of you jumped in and screamed, "BS!"? You probably said to that part of yourself, *Thank you for sharing, but be quiet,* and continued with your positive affirmations. But the nagging voice didn't go away. You judged yourself and you have probably judged others who have heard the same voice.

We've all gotten caught up in a massive superstition that positive thinking is the answer. If I think a positive thought, I will get a positive result. If I think anything negative, I will attract disease, poverty, and unhealthy relationships. We've become like helpless toddlers tossed into a pool of thought, trying to keep our heads above water with all this positive thinking and visioning, even though we can't swim. It's no wonder we tend to sink and drown.

As a result, we all too often do something that kills our dreams. When all our positive thinking doesn't lead to the positive results we're looking for, we make it personal. We say, "Something's wrong with me," "It wasn't meant to be," "I'm not good enough," and on and on. Even if you can get past those self-blaming narratives to give changing your thoughts another chance, success can seem like just a distant wish, something for the gurus or privileged people—but not for you. Your sad story about your life becomes a self-fulfilling prophecy. The inevitable uncertainties of life come, and you use these moments as an excuse, as confirmation of why you're stuck and why you're going to stay that way. Claiming your power, living your Purpose—it all just becomes a bunch of wishful thinking.

Or perhaps you've turned to talk therapy. You've spent thousands of dollars over many years creating a massive case file about your life: who hurt you, who held you back, how your parents didn't give you what you needed, and so on. You've psychoanalyzed the whole of your life, and in the end you find you're still left asking, "Why did this happen to me?"

Perhaps you want to change an addiction. The head model would tell you to think thoughts of sobriety and happiness. Yet too often those thoughts take hold for only a short while, and then it's back to your normal set point. So you take pills, hoping you won't feel the pain of your failure as acutely. You may listen to those who tell you you'll always have your *disease* of addiction, and you need to accept your lot in life. But all the while there's something else calling you. Something subtle. A whisper coming from deep inside. And it's getting dimmer and dimmer and dimmer.

No amount of chemical healing agents can fill the void of your Purpose. If you are spending your time numbing feelings that should be felt and released, you are keeping yourself stuck.

No matter what old-model methods most of us have tried, from positive thinking to therapy, we still suffer from this sense of feeling stuck. We still are left wondering if there isn't more to life. In short, we suffer from what I call P.D.D., or Purpose Deficit Disorder.

Head Model Beliefs That Lead You to Suffer from P.D.D.

1. You can change your life based solely on the level of thinking is enough.

2. Negative thinking is bad.

3. Fear is the opposite of love.

4. You can attract what you want without any work.

5. Not getting what you want is a sign that it's not meant to be.

6. Once you've had a breakthrough you don't have to do any more work.

7. Medication is sufficient and it's all you need to fix a spiritual problem.

8. Something is wrong with you that needs to be fixed.

Why We Need a Heart Model

We need a Heart model because these head models never served us well. Yes, they have worked for some, but for many they provided a temporary Band-Aid that got ripped off at the first sign of failure. Guilt quickly took over, and the search for Purpose was abandoned yet again.

On the contrary, using a new, more Grace-filled model, I've seen clients carrying decades of trauma go from being too paralyzed to talk about it to genuinely laughing about it in a span of just 20 minutes.

I've seen survivors of rape and incest overcome these evil acts to become beacons of healing for others who needed their unique perspective.

I've seen clients go from making $37.50 an hour to $16,000 in a week.

I've seen clients whose therapists told them to get a divorce reconcile and then go on to have children together.

I've seen gay clients courageously come out to their families and be embraced when they thought they would be shunned.

I've seen a client who tried to commit suicide while pregnant admit that it was scarier to be her true, vulnerable self than it was to try to take her own life. Both she and her son are thriving today.

Acknowledge Your Divine Spark

This world is full of infinite potential, so there shouldn't be so many of us feeling so stuck. *Infinite potential. Yeah, right.* But it's true.

Suspend your disbelief for a moment and hear me out: You are not just a human being. You *inhabit* a human being, but at your core you are a Divine Spark of the Creator. You are a Soul who chose a body and lessons to learn in this lifetime. Your true identity is Divine. And your Soul learns through contrast.

What does that mean?

If your Soul wants to learn forgiveness in this lifetime, then you must also experience betrayal. If your Soul wants to learn self-love in this lifetime, then you must also experience self-hatred. Without your difficult experiences, you wouldn't be able to learn, grow, and transform in the way your Soul desires. Pain is a teacher. But we also have infinite possibilities to choose love as our go-to reaction.

This lesson in opposites may sound contradictory, but it's true. When you begin to take on this new perspective and belief system, everything changes. Questions like "Why did this happen to me?" are easily answered. You find out how much the opinion of others truly matters, and how much power you've been giving away to your family, friends, tribe, celebrity, and so on. You see that what you thought was the goal of life wasn't it at all. You see that there is great meaning in the seemingly insignificant "coincidences" in your life.

Einstein has said that you cannot solve a problem from the same level of thinking that created it. The head model served us by giving us the basic understanding that we do indeed create our own reality. But some of the unintended consequences of the head model are the following:

- Blaming yourself for your failures

- Turning "aha moments" into reasons to feel guilty and ashamed

- Buying into the superstition that negative thoughts attract a negative reality or make you sick

- Feeling like you can never fully arrive

- Believing that self-love is something you can perfect

- Giving up when you meet resistance or fear

- Turning God into a vending machine based on your vision board

- Thinking that sharing your truth and emotionally vomiting on someone are the same thing

- Trying to only identify with your Soul or Divine nature and ignoring your humanness—even worse, thinking your human thoughts and emotions are wrong

- Believing that your teacher, guru, pastor, preacher, or mentor has all the answers or better answers than you do inside

In your journal, write additional unintended consequences of the head model that have occurred in your own life.

Using the Heart Model to Prosper in Your Purpose

I'm a present-moment kind of guy, but I don't want to discount all the work you've done in the past. I want to celebrate it—quickly—and then get right to the business of closing the gap between where you are and where your Soul desires for you to be—to live your true Purpose. To do that, I want to share with you the Heart model of personal growth, because it will make you think differently and probably challenge some long-standing rules and beliefs you've had about how this game of life works.

Here are three things that are true within this Heart model of transforming your life:

1. Intense emotion + belief + action = result.

2. You live within circumstances (and patterns) you have created.

3. Your circumstances (and patterns) can be changed at any time.

Patterns are learned at young ages as coping mechanisms, and while I don't think they ever completely go away, I think the frequency gets turned down, and they lessen over time. I hear it all the time from clients when they encounter patterns: "I thought I worked on this. I thought I fixed this already, and now all this stuff is coming up." But that's a short-sighted way of seeing it. The real truth is that when a Survival Pattern™ (SP) continues to come up again and again, that's your work now.

One of my SPs is comparison. That's my work now. One of my SPs is procrastination. That's my work now. One of my SPs is neglecting and not nurturing myself. That's my work now.

It's not like you work with an SP once and you've got it under control. It's information and a manual that shows you who you are. The patterns will be the same throughout your life; they'll just manifest in different situations.

Remember, you cannot solve your current situation from the same level of thinking that created it, so if what I'm suggesting here sounds strange or new, celebrate! We are going to work on creating new patterns within you that will create new outcomes in your life as a whole.

Heart Model Beliefs

1. You must change your life on the level of emotion, not thought.

2. Negative thinking and emotions are calls for awareness, invitations to break patterns that no longer serve you.

3. Fear is a sign you are living your Purpose.

4. Hard work is still required.

5. Persistence is still required.

6. Not getting what you want is spiritual redirection.

7. There is a Divine reason for every experience you have.

8. A breakthrough is a starting point to begin the real work. This must become a lifestyle.

9. Chemical drugs can solve short-term problems or chemical imbalances, but for sustained happiness, eventually, when the time is right, you want to choose Purpose over pills whenever possible.

10. There is nothing wrong with you. All you need is to change a pattern or two.

Don't Just Survive—Thrive!

I am going to assume that there has been some degree of victimization in your life. It could be small (Dad was late picking you up at school when you were six years old), or it could be large (sexual or physical assault). Either way, I know there is a part of you that has created certain patterns to protect yourself and keep you safe. And that's great—those patterns brought you this far. But from now on, you are going to have a higher standard for your life.

Now, you want to do more than just protect yourself and survive. You want to thrive. That means yesterday's medicine is today's poison. You can't heal trauma or step out of victimization from using your mind alone; it's got to be emotional. You've got to *feel* something. You see, trauma is stored in the body. The problem with trying to only think your way into healing is that you ignore the very thing that needs to heal—your body. So, we've got to go deeper than that and feel our way from pain to freedom, from hurt and resentment to forgiveness, from small to unleashed. This transformation happens at the emotional level, not the level of thinking.

To do this, you must allow yourself to feel any and every emotion necessary. And you've got to change your view on what those emotions mean. Understanding the power, relevance, and profound wisdom in *all* your emotions is the key difference between the head and Heart models because they are what are going to point the way toward our transformation.

The biggest leap in belief I'm going to ask you to take as you read this book is this: on some level, you chose this life and your current circumstances—and everything that's happened in it—for the sake of your own Soul's evolution toward your life's Purpose.

On the level of human logic, this makes little sense. But human logic is not what is going to set you free.

You've got to learn to tap into the paradoxical and nonlogical Divine mind. You see, human beings crave a God who operates by their belief systems. But it is unwise to try to fit your Creator into your current level of awareness. God does not operate by your rules or your sense of justice. There is a much bigger picture happening here. Souls are learning lessons over many lifetimes, so we must take an expanded view of our current circumstances to truly claim our power.

I will help you understand and adopt this expanded view of your circumstances over the course of this entire book, but what's important to understand right now is that all pain comes bearing lessons, all suffering has meaning, all unjust actions have a karmic debt, and all roads lead back to love. When we stop trying to understand our lives through the lens of human logic and instead surrender to the fact that we are a part of something greater, we can truly and forever get unstuck.

A Word about Fear (Your New Best Friend)

One of the great superstitions and lies that the New Age has installed in our minds is that fear is the opposite of love. And where there is love, there can be no fear.

Let me be clear—this is wrong. Dead wrong. At least in the human experience.

I'm sure that Heaven or the Spirit World is a place of perfect love. But we chose to come here. So we have chosen to separate from our spiritual home and to experience this life through the lens of a human body. And the human body experiences fear practically all the time.

The sophisticated seeker may call it something else. *Stress* is the fancy word many people use today for fear, but it's still fear. The point is, if you have a brain, you experience fear. Why? Because you have a limbic system in your brain—the fight-or-flight place—that is always on, detecting threats and producing fear in your body.

Here's why the superstition that fear is the opposite of love is wrong: to live your Purpose, you must begin to live a courageous life. Which means you must risk making choices *that will scare you.*

Been in a relationship way too long and know you should leave? There's a courageous choice to make.

Want to start your own business but scared of where the money will come from? There's a courageous choice to make.

Want to speak up about a past trauma but scared of being judged? There's a courageous choice to make.

Want to protect your country from forces that are trying to annihilate it? There's a courageous choice to make.

Want to say, "I love you," for the first time? There's a courageous choice to make.

In the new era of spiritual pursuit, courage is the primary virtue that we must embody. When you're stuck, it's because you lack courage. It's that simple. Having the courage to follow your intuition and make the right choice can be massively rewarding, but it's also terrifying at first. And yet you've been told this great big lie that you shouldn't be afraid, or that being afraid is not spiritual.

In our fast-paced world of instant gratification, there is no courage app. Finding the courage to claim your power and live your Purpose has got to be done the old-fashioned way—through taking a risk, leaping into the unknown, and feeling like you are going to die in the process.

Good news: you won't die.

But it will feel that way at first. You'll find that one of the most important acts of courage you must take to get unstuck is to fully feel the negative emotions you've been avoiding for most of your life. Feeling your negative feelings and learning the lesson they carry is the name of the game. P.D.D. is perpetuated through a lack of courage, through an avoidance of negative feelings and the lessons they bring.

Your Soul speaks to you through your Heart, which is why the root of the word *courage* is *coeur*, the French word for "Heart." The true demonstration of courage is learning to take direction from your Heart, no matter what your brain says.

If you're wondering how to listen to your Heart, worry not. I've got you covered. You'll learn all about that in the coming days, but for now just know that things are about to change. If you really trust your Creator, it's time to get courageous. What if you really *don't* trust your Creator? Time to jump in headfirst anyway. The courageous, the bold, and the persistent will not suffer from P.D.D. for long. In fact, courage is the antidote to your depression, anxiety, lack of fulfillment, and stuckness.

But we don't want you leaping just to randomly leap. First I need to teach you how to take risks that are Soul guided. To do that, I need to teach you about the two types of fear.

The Two Types of Fear

The broad statement "fear is the opposite of love" creates massive confusion and keeps well-intentioned seekers stuck. The Bible says that "perfect love casts out fear," which is true—but typically not until you've gone through hell.

When you live your Purpose, you will be tested over and over again. You will come face-to-face with your deepest fears right before you transcend to the next level of your emotion. Why? Ultimately so you can be shown that your worst fear has no power over you. When you face your fear, you transcend it, and that is how you cast out fear.

We've got to change our understanding about fear and the fight-or-flight response. What are your triggers? The news. Social media. Traffic. Your spouse. Your kids. What other people think. Past trauma that is unresolved. Unexpected bad news. Flight delays. Lost luggage. Being rejected. Taking a stand. And many other stimuli that affect us each and every day.

Technology is expanding at an exponential rate. Each year we are making faster and faster progress, and this means greater and greater pressure on the human nervous system. Our technology helps us, but it also stresses us out and wears us down. With all this stress, it can be hard to tell what's really worth being afraid of and what's not.

Let me help clarify. There are two types of fear:

1. Irrational fear (which I call Survival Patterns™ [SPs])

2. Necessary fear (which I call Survival Instincts)

First let's talk about necessary fear, which includes things like being afraid of someone pointing a gun at you, being afraid your toddler will choke on a small object, being afraid in an abusive relationship, being afraid in battle, and so on. These necessary fears protect us. They keep us alive. And staying alive is a good thing. But that part of the brain where fight or flight exists is binary, meaning it's "On" or it's "Off." It gets triggered in the same way, whether our fears are necessary or irrational.

On the other hand, 98 percent of our fears today fall into the irrational category. I called irrational fear SPs. These are irrational patterns of fear that keep us stuck and not living our Purpose. When a client of mine is stuck, they are stuck for one reason. When we get down to the bottom of it, they believe that if they take action in the area where they are stuck, they will die. This is an SP and it goes something like this:

- I'm scared to get a divorce because I'll never find another partner, so I'll just be alone my whole life, and that loneliness will kill me.

- I'm scared to start my business because no one will buy my product, and then I'll go broke and I'll die.

- I'm scared of getting my heart broken again, because if I do, I'll die.

- I'm scared of being abandoned by the person I love most, because if they leave me, I'll be alone and then I'll die.

- I'm scared to lose this weight and show my real self to the world, because if I show my real self, no one will love me and then I'll die.

- I can't delegate any of the tasks in my business to someone else, because they might mess up, and if they mess up, my business will crash and I'll be broke, and then I'll die.

- I can't go to sleep when I want to because there's more for me to do, and if I don't do it right now, everything will fall apart and then I'll die.

You get the point. Here's the truth: *you're not going to die when you take risks on behalf of your Purpose.* When you risk, you'll feel like you're dying, but that is actually the feeling of something greater being born within and through you.

There are predictable SPs; in fact, I've been able to create a list of the top 11 SPs I've seen after working with thousands of clients:

1. Putting yourself last

2. Trying to control other people

3. Perfectionism

4. Playing small

5. Always assuming the worst

6. Doubting your Higher Wisdom

7. Addiction

8. Procrastination

9. Staying in toxic relationships

10. Needing the approval of others

11. Confusion (saying, "I don't know" all the time)

Here's some real talk: If you bought this book, you almost surely have enough food, clothing, and shelter. You are resourceful and live in an abundant world. *You will not die.* Does this mean that you should just not care and throw caution to the wind? No. The previously listed concerns are valid concerns, but they should not stop you from taking courageous action guided by your Purpose.

It's prudent to be prepared and to know the road ahead so that you can be successful. It is not prudent to fail to begin because you are afraid that following your Purpose will lead to your ultimate and untimely death. The bottom line in fear is this: if you're not afraid, you should be afraid; do something to make yourself experience fear. If you *are* afraid— too afraid to begin living your life—you don't need to be afraid. Fear is a sign that you are living your Purpose. The more fear, the more you should celebrate, not cower!

Here is my fear maxim: *Unless you're in mortal danger, fear is a compass showing you where to go.*

If you aren't facing fear, you are most likely in a crisis. What is the purpose of a crisis? To reveal the SP(s) that need to be interrupted in order for you to live your Purpose.

In this book we are going to learn to follow your fear. We've been taught to follow our bliss, but before we can do that, we must first follow our blisters. The good news is the area of your greatest frustration is the doorway to your Purpose and your bliss. You can't follow your bliss without first following your blisters.

> ## Unless you're in mortal danger, fear is a compass showing you where to go.

Following Your Blisters or the Anatomy of Transformation

I've had the privilege of working with thousands of clients from all walks of life, belief systems, socioeconomic backgrounds, and age ranges. What I've found is that when it comes to getting unstuck, finding our Purposes, and living a life led by our Souls, getting there is the same process for all of us. It doesn't matter if you're a single mother, a rich billionaire, a middle-class teacher, a health coach, a politician, or an artist; we all have the same internal anatomy that keeps us stuck or helps us break through.

My Anatomy of Transformation is a simple five-part system that will help you immediately understand why you're stuck. The layers descend from the most superficial to the deepest. Here they are:

5—Behavior

4—Story/Thoughts/Mental Level (how you describe your circumstances)

3—Emotion (hardest layer to crack)

2—Beliefs (meanings created from past trauma)

1—Original Incident (OI) (trauma)

What you'll notice is that the majority of personal growth work being done today deals only with the top two layers. We look at the behavior and then try to change our lives (our stories) based on our mental capacity to understand what's happened. The problem with this is that there are three deeper layers that must be visited, understood, and, most important, *felt* before you can create lasting transformation.

The third layer, the layer of emotion, is the hardest one to crack because we will do almost anything to avoid feeling our negative feelings. They rise up, and we quickly try to get rid of them. We do the opposite of what we should do; we disassociate rather than dive into them.

This disassociation of emotion creates our stuckness. We become experts in stories and behaviors that keep us stuck and prevent us from feeling, and then we surround ourselves with people in similar situations and stay stuck together. This is why misery loves company. You can stay stuck, comfortable, and numb together and justify it through social proof, surrounding yourself with people who validate your negative experiences and commiserate with you about how *life is unfair.* This is also why your ability to claim your power threatens so many people around you who are choosing to stay stuck in their SPs.

How do we dissociate from negative feelings? With all sorts of behaviors that are considered normal today, like distracting ourselves with social media or binge-watching TV; ignoring difficult conversations; overeating; all addictions; not leaving a relationship that's toxic; playing small so others are not threatened; taking care of others instead of ourselves; praying God will do for us what we should do for ourselves; and many more.

I'm a believer in therapy. I'm a believer in yoga. I'm a believer in visualization. But none of these modalities are going to be worth a single cent of spiritual power until you tap into how you are feeling, learn the lesson of your emotion, revisit painful moments of your past, and see them from the point of view of your Purpose.

Why must it be this way?

The late neuroscientist and pharmacologist Dr. Candace Pert said in her book *Molecules of Emotion* that emotions are "God talking to you." Pert goes on to say:

> My research has shown me that when emotions are expressed—which is to say that the biochemicals that are the substrate of emotion are flowing freely—all systems are united and made whole. When emotions are repressed, denied, not allowed to be whatever they may be, our network pathways get blocked, stopping the flow of the vital feel-good, unifying chemicals that run both our biology and our behavior.[1]

---

1   Candace Pert, *Molecules of Emotion* (New York: Simon and Schuster, 2010).

I'm going to say it a bit differently. Positive emotions are a sign that you are aligned with your Purpose. Negative emotions are a call for awareness, a sign that you need to get back into alignment. Instead of negating or suppressing our negative emotions, we must liberate them in a healthy way so that we can understand why they are there. You feel what you feel for a good and valid reason. When you understand that reason, you will experience bliss.

Joseph Campbell said that "every feeling fully felt is bliss." But we don't often allow ourselves to go there. Our world is still ruled by our mental capacities, as well as our social expectations, and so we are ignoring the genius of our emotions and our bodies.

Think of it this way: your head is Darth Vader. Your body and your emotions are Yoda. You need your mental capacity and logic. However, your mind must become the servant of your Purpose, instead of the slayer of your Purpose. This cooperation happens in conjunction with your emotional body and your Heart.

Have you ever considered that depression and loneliness are a deep cry from your Purpose asking you to connect back to it? You cannot numb your Purpose with drugs, alcohol, or medication. It is still there. It has always been there, and now we've got to get back to it.

We've got to follow your blisters to get there.

Here's How We'll Work Together

You're about to go on your own hero's journey. I've based the structure of this book on Joseph Campbell's model of the hero's journey, which means there are going to be four parts:

Part I—Separation
Part II—Initiation
Part III—Ordeal
Part IV—The Journey Home

All four stages are crucial to transforming your life.

Before you can discover your life's Purpose, you must *separate* from your comfortable and ordinary world. Then we will *initiate* you into a new way of being. In doing so, we will consciously evoke an *ordeal* or *death* of old patterns, beliefs, and ways of living that will lead to a powerful breakthrough. Finally, you will *return* from your journey to incorporate this new way of being into your everyday life and go on to share what you've learned with the world. Remember, you're going on this journey so that you can ultimately serve others. No journey is complete until we share what we've learned and, in doing so, improve the lives of those around us.

Each chapter in this book represents a day in your hero's journey. I'm going to encourage you to take each chapter one day a time. Of course, you could rush get through this book right away, but I've found that breaking big ideas down into bite-size pieces of information creates quicker, lasting results. Plus, it feels good to make continual, bit-by-bit progress toward a goal. It creates new momentum in our lives and allows us to make big shifts through small wins.

There is a spiritual reason why I've chosen 40 days for our journey together. Forty is a number that appears in all sorts of spiritual texts. It's best known in the Christian tradition, when Jesus spent 40 days and 40 nights in the desert. It also takes a minimum of 40 days to change a behavior—not 21 days like we've heard so many times before. So get ready to truly dedicate yourself to this process for a full 40-day period. And then to make the biggest impact, you must commit to turning your life around and sticking with this new life for *at least six months*. That seems like a long time now, but when you're living in the excitement and possibilities that you've manifested, those six months will fly by.

Choose a beginning and an end date. If after 40 days your life hasn't changed, then by all means go back to your old way of thinking. But I know that if you are truly dedicated for the entire journey, that won't be the outcome.

If you miss a day, just pick up where you left off the next day. However, if you miss more than three days, I suggest you start over from the beginning. That's how important it is that you focus on this process for the specified period of time.

It's also a great idea to go through this process with friends and other like-minded people. An energy is created when you share the experience of transforming with others, but it's also totally okay to do it by yourself. The process works either way.

This 40-day journey is also accompanied by a free online component so that I can be your personal coach during the process. If you haven't already, please go to www.ClaimYourPowerBook.com/40 and opt in for this free training. This book is a coaching process, so each chapter will be interactive. We'll work together, coach to student, to create instant progress.

Don't just read this book; use it. Throughout you'll find questions and journal prompts to answer in your own physical or electronic journal. I hope you'll underline passages, dog-ear pages, and do whatever will help make the material come alive for you.

Are you ready? We have no time to waste. Your Purpose is waiting, and so are those whom you're meant to touch. So let's start claiming your power right now.

Part I

SEPARATION

"If the path before you is clear, you're
probably on someone else's."

– JOSEPH CAMPBELL

No matter how hard you try, you'll never get your past back. It is a hard, sobering, and redeeming truth. And in order for you to move forward on your path of Purpose, you must look with new eyes, a refreshed Heart, and an open-minded curiosity about what's next.

Campbell marks the first part of the journey as "Separation" because you must detach yourself from what you've known up until now. Because this Separation is a form of death, many of your SPs will try to abort your progress. Don't give them that kind of power anymore.

You are about to transform before your very eyes; let me speed up your process by giving you a map of what's to come.

All transformation has three phases. They are:

1. Excitement

2. Fear and Resistance

3. Mastery

Right now, you're excited. Filled with hope. Ready for the adventure. And that's great. So am I! But I'm going to be real with you: that excitement will wear off, and soon enough you will find yourself coming up against your old SPs. You will want to turn back. You will want to quit.

Yet your destiny is determined by how well you handle the moments of frustration and setback.

The first thing I do when I feel frustration is to allow myself to feel it. And then I immediately ask myself, *What does this mean?* And within seconds I find an empowering meaning. *It means I'm learning and growing. It means something better is on the way. This is the contraction before the expansion.* I work the problem and try to mine whatever I'm supposed to be learning from it. It can be very painful, but my meaning is: *this is how you grow.*

It's easy to have faith when all is well. It's easy to be excited when you haven't come up against the terrified part of your personality that will stop at nothing to make sure you keep the status quo. It's easy to get psyched up for a moment. But you must first commit to a path of mastery before you begin.

What does mastery look like? First, a master is a beginner who kept beginning, and that is who you must become. Keep beginning. Quantum moments, where everything happens all at once, are a result of years of beginning. When you see someone "come out of nowhere," she hasn't. She has been working diligently, each and every day, when no one else was watching. She was committed to a path of mastery, and it led to her success.

Of course, there will be obstacles. There always are. Here are three thoughts that will fight to hold you back:

1. I've heard this all before.

2. Actually, someone else told me that's not true.

3. It's easy for you—you're successful.

Before we begin our journey, let me address these.

First, "I've heard this all before."

The most successful people in the world keep a childlike approach to life. Note: not childish . . . childlike—there's a difference.

Childlike means you are open to any possibility. You remain open to miracles, to synchronicities, and to hearing a truth that you've heard before. It's vital to stay open as you begin your journey because, let's face it, you're stubborn. Just like me. And maybe you have to hear the same truth 1,001 times before it *finally* sinks in.

Plus, knowledge can be easy to forget. We get caught up in the hustle and bustle of life. We get interrupted, and we default back into our old SPs. So while you might mentally understand concepts you will read in this book, *do you truly know them?*

The difference between understanding and knowing is in results. You can understand the basic concepts behind losing weight, but you only know how to do it if you've gotten the result. You might understand how to meditate, but you only know how to meditate if you've gotten the result.

So stay open-minded, okay?

Second, "Actually, someone else told me that's not true."

In our world of information overload, you will find millions of pieces of advice that will contradict one another. Just because you read something on the Internet or in a book doesn't make it true. It's true if you feel it in your Heart. Truth is Truth.

To get the most out of this book, set aside everything you've heard and let yourself be a blank slate. Consider this: Your best thinking got you here. Your best thinking also got you stuck. So it's time to change your thinking, starting with everything you think you know about transforming your life.

Give me 40 days and then you can have your old beliefs back, if that's what you decide. Until then, be a blank page.

Third, "It's easy for you—you're successful."

This is the thought of someone who doesn't understand how I, or anyone else who has created success in their life, got there. Successful people are those who have been through trial after trial after trial, who committed to a path of mastery and stuck with it. Like my dad says, "Success is what happens after you've survived all your mistakes."

You weren't there back in 2004 when I was living a crazy life and working in the entertainment industry and I almost overdosed on cocaine.

You didn't see me fall apart, quit my job, and couch surf for two years while trying to start my Heart-centered business.

You didn't see me contemplate taking my own life when all seemed lost, only to be saved by the intuition that if I took my own life, I'd just have to go through this again later.

Likewise, I haven't seen everything you've gone through to get here. But I know we're both here together for such a time as this. I don't believe it's a coincidence.

People who say "it's easier for successful people" use that story as a reason not to try. Because trying means they could fail. So let's put aside the idea that it's easier for successful people, because it isn't. A master has failed more times than a dabbler will ever try.

Your aim is to dedicate yourself to mastery, to take personal responsibility for your reaction to your circumstances, and simply begin each day. When you fall, get back up. When you want to quit, keep going. You never know what tomorrow will bring. Time will pass, but the effort, no matter how small, will have an eternal effect on your destiny. Jesus said it best in Matthew 6:4 (Aramaic Bible): "Your Father who sees in secret will reward you in public."

With that said, you are now ready to consciously induce separation from the life that you've known up until now and begin your journey.

DAY 1:
WHY ARE YOU DEAD?

"The big question is whether you are going to be able to say a hearty yes to your adventure."

– JOSEPH CAMPBELL

You're a living, breathing miracle of life. Capable, unique, and powerfully made. Your lungs are ever expanding and contracting to keep you alive; your heart beats 60 to 100 times per minute to pump blood through your body. Your logic says, "I'm very much alive."

Yet if you're falling short of your potential, you will feel stuck. And feeling stuck often feels like death. Yes, you're alive, technically. But you *feel* dead.

The word *dead* is a bold word to use. But we're taking bold actions from here on out. So from now on, during our time together, instead of using the word *stuck,* I'm going to use the word *dead.*

Why? Because it will evoke more emotion from you, and we need that emotion to change your life.

So, stuck = dead. *That which does not move is dead.*

We know from basic physics that objects in motion tend to stay in motion, and objects at rest tend to stay at rest. The same applies to transforming your life. Areas of your life that are dead tend to stay dead. Areas of your life that are alive tend to stay alive. Going from dead to fully alive is our aim here. While at first it will take courageous action, and it might feel like you're pushing a one-ton boulder up a steep mountain, once you've gained some momentum, it will become a heck of a lot easier to keep that momentum going.

What's so cool is that when you connect back with your Purpose, instead of pushing, you will invoke a different energy. You will be pulled by your Purpose. Instead of trying to make things happen, miracles and synchronicities will happen all on their own, and they will be better than your mind could have ever imagined.

So, why are you dead in certain parts of your life? Because you lack courage in those areas. Within those areas, there are negative emotions you haven't felt or learned from yet. But let's not get ahead of ourselves. Today all we're going to do is get real about why you're dead and discover which areas of your life are affected.

The primary feelings of being dead are *powerlessness, contraction,* and *frustration.* I'd bet you're experiencing all three of these feelings in one or more areas of your life.

Here's a cosmic irony about fear: *When you are afraid to take action because there is an outcome you're afraid of, not taking action produces the outcome you are afraid of.* So you are living within a self-fulfilling prophecy. And here are some examples to jog your awareness:

Scared of being hurt in a relationship? You pick someone you know you don't have to let in, and he ends up hurting you.

Scared of not having any money? You withdraw, become scared, and stop taking risks, which results in no new opportunities and a lack of abundance.

Scared of people abandoning you? You twist yourself into someone you're not in order to satisfy what other people want. Then, when you show your real self, they are surprised and leave you.

The area of your life where you're dead is your own creation. You may have been victimized in the past, and if you have, my heart is with you. However, the time has come to step out of victim consciousness and begin the courageous process of resurrection.

Telling the Truth

It's honesty time. You know how they say the truth will set you free, but first it will piss you off? That's not entirely accurate. Better stated: the truth will set you free, but first it will terrify you.

The areas where you feel dead are the areas where most of our work must be done. It is in these areas where you have the least amount of faith in your Creator, as well as in yourself. You see, your Creator loves you more than you can possibly know, and there is more in store for you than you can possibly imagine.

To tap into that Love, we must take our faith out of the world *in front of our eyes* and place it in the world *behind our eyes.* Your Creator knows all that you need. If you could see how protected you are by your Creator, you would not be dead in these areas of your life. However, up until now, the places where you feel dead have been your greatest challenge. Thankfully, dead areas of our lives provide the greatest opportunities for personal and spiritual growth.

One courageous action in a dead area of your life is more powerful than 1,000 therapy sessions, 100 bottles of green juice, and all the yoga you can twist yourself into.

Our aim during the course of our time together will be to bring more of your Purpose into the areas of your life where you are dead, so that you can become undead and fully alive. But you don't have to worry about all that right now. You don't have to worry about changing anything yet. All you have to do is be honest with yourself.

Where are you dead in your life? These are areas where you are most frustrated, annoyed, resigned, or stuck. You cannot change your life without first admitting this to yourself. So list the areas in your journal:

1. _____

2. _____

3. _____

4. _____

5. _____

Now take a few moments to reflect on the dead areas of your life above by answering the following questions:

1. What Survival Patterns™ (SPs) have kept you from admitting you were dead in the past?

2. When was the first time you can remember feeling dead in each one of these areas?

3. How has remaining dead in these areas actually benefited your survival?

4. Are there any relationships in your life that support your being dead in these areas?

What I've found with many of my clients is that the areas where they feel dead seem so familiar and so comfortable that they feel like home.

However, something deeper is calling for change. It's time to connect back to your Purpose and, in doing so, to your Creator. We are going to break open your protective shell and inch you forward toward your destiny one day at a time.

The key on this first day is to not beat yourself up for being dead. By looking into what's holding you back, you may start to feel guilt, shame, and self-doubt. On another day, we will talk about how to really feel these emotions so you can work through them, but that is not our goal for today. So for now, just know that these emotions are totally normal and natural, but that they do not serve your greater Purpose. Instead, focus on our aim for today, which is simple honesty. Being honest with yourself is the first step toward claiming your power.

In admitting where you are dead, you are taking a courageous first step toward your growth. Celebrate this as your first win.

You cannot transform your life when you lie to yourself. You cannot transform your life if you hide from the truth. Today, allow yourself to come out of your shell and reveal your truth in these pages.

Today's affirmation: I am capable of reaching my full Potential.

Today's prayer: Creator, please help me see clearly the areas of my life where I am dead, and help me forgive myself for holding myself hostage. I am ready to be honest with myself. Show me how to move forward into my Purpose.

DAY 2:
WHY IS NOW THE RIGHT TIME TO CHANGE?

"Remembering you are going to die is the best way
I know to avoid the trap of thinking you have something
to lose. You are already naked. There is no reason
not to follow your heart."

– STEVE JOBS

I'm a present-moment kind of coach. Many of my clients talk about what they are "going to do." Some even talk about what they're going to do as if they already did it. But then a strange thing happens. They never . . . quite . . . do it.

They put off leaving the job or relationship they feel stuck in. They say they'll start a health and wellness program tomorrow. They say they will start their business in three months. They have a million reasons why now is not the right time. Something else has to happen first. To bring certainty. To make it safer.

My question for you is: *How quickly do you want your transformation to come?* One day I prayed for patience, and I thought that would speed things up, when it actually slowed things down. But I can also say that the speed at which your transformation occurs depends on your courage. When I've been courageous, things have happened quickly. I've also delayed transformation.

The hard part is coming to terms with the little voice in your head that says, *You should be further along by now.* When that thought pops up, I respond, "Based on what?" We can't hold ourselves accountable to anyone else's timeline.

How fast your life changes will also be determined by your belief system (more on your beliefs later). You can easily plug into the belief that you need to wait for X, Y, or Z reasons. Or you could plug into the belief that now is the time, and you must begin immediately.

I was recently with a client who shared with me all the benefits of not filing her divorce papers. One of the reasons was because her husband was still paying her each month, so we got clear about the fact that she was staying for the money. She was honest about it, and I respect honesty. But then she said something that I need to share with you. She said that if she filed the papers, she would be missing out on the certainty of money coming in regularly for her and her children. When I heard that, I asked her a question that made her pause: "What are you missing out on by *not* filing?"

You see, The Universe hates a vacuum. When you make a change, you create a vacuum. And when you create a vacuum, something new will come along to fill it. This is law. You can only create something new with space.

We are scared of creating a vacuum because that space, or momentary sense of not having safety, triggers our SPs. That's why we resist change. Change triggers our fear of possible or impending death, so we put it off, and put it off, and put it off.

All the while, however, your Soul is watching. When you lack courage, life tends to get messy, and you get closer and closer to a Divine Storm. The crises in your life, the stuckness, the frustration, the powerlessness, these things are Divinely sent. They happen because you won't make a move until you're in too much pain not to make a move.

Most humans learn through pain. We can also learn through joy, but learning through joy requires us to be spontaneous and take risks no matter what's at stake. That's much harder to do.

Why change now? Because if you don't, the intensity of your Divine Storms will only get worse. I'm not saying this to scare you. I'm saying it because it's true.

So I ask you: *When would now be a good time to begin?*

That's right—right *now*.

It's your time. You can't wait another year, another month, another week, day, hour, or minute. It's come down to right here, right now. It's time to commit to change.

But why?

Creating Clarity

We need to get clear about why *now* is the right time to change. Each day our work together will require absolute honesty, so let's take some time to really think about this. Think about all you've missed out on by playing small, trying to be perfect, procrastinating until your next life, or by putting others first. Think about all the times your Soul has nudged you to leave a relationship, start a business, let the right one in, to truly trust yourself, to take care of your body, to quit your job, to do what you love even though you have kids, and to let yourself truly live.

The truth is, you have missed out. You've missed out on love. On passion. On joy. On excitement. On adventure. You know this deep in your Heart.

I don't say this to shame you. I say this because truth creates the emotion needed to inspire change. So don't fret. After our time together, you will be set free, and you will experience more than enough love, passion, joy, excitement, and adventure. But right now it's time to get real about what you've been missing out on.

What Am I Missing?

Be honest with yourself and spend some time writing in your journal about what you've missed out on because you have let fear win—until now.

- When it comes to romance, I've missed out on:

- When it comes to my work, career, or business, I've missed out on:

- When it comes to my health and well-being, I've missed out on:

- When it comes to my connection with my Creator, I've missed out on:

- When it comes to my connection with my family and friends, I've missed out on:

- When it comes to my finances, I've missed out on:

- When it comes to contributing to others, I've missed out on:

- The good I've prevented from entering my life is:

Awesome.

I know that writing out these answers can be challenging, but trust the process. If you feel you weren't entirely honest, please go back and try again. You can't transform without first being real with yourself.

Life has a tendency to slip by you. You can't always feel it, but a day can turn into a week, a week into a month, and a month into a year. The next thing you know, a year has turned into a decade, and you never quite got around to transforming your life.

No more. You will no longer allow even one more moment to pass without taking courageous action toward your Purpose. Now is your time. Not tomorrow. Not next week. Now. Right here. Right now.

So much has been missed already in this life. You can't wait one more day to change. You don't want to miss one more moment of joy, connection, excitement, love, or adventure. You have no idea what wonderful things your Creator has in store for you once you commit to trusting your true Purpose.

Why is now the right and only time for you to change? Declare to yourself, to me, to your Soul, and to your Creator why you won't wait one more moment to change.

Make a list in your journal of all the things you want to feel, do, be, have, give, and love in this life. All these things and more are waiting for you to decide that now is your time.

I commit to changing now because (be detailed):

Now answer the following questions in your journal:

1. What's the worst thing that will happen if I don't change now?

2. What's the worst thing that will happen if I decide to change now?

3. Of the above two questions, which outcome is worse?

4. Recently, how has my Creator tried to get my attention to change? What signs have I seen?

Today's affirmation: I commit to positive change now, as I step into my full Purpose with faith and courage.

Today's prayer: Creator, be with me and give me courage as I decide to change now. I put full faith and trust in Your hands. I am now Your humble servant. I will faithfully follow the signs that You send me. My whole life is in Your hands. I am ready for change, so please show me the way.

DAY 3:
IDENTIFY THE LIMITING BEHAVIORS
AND STORIES THAT HOLD YOU BACK

"Behaviour arises from the level of one's
consciousness."

– MAHARISHI MAHESH YOGI

Yesterday you decided that now is the right time for you to change, so let's dive right in. Without much introspection or understanding about the art of transforming your life, of moving from feeling dead to filled with Purpose, you might think it's simply a matter of creating a new behavioral pattern.

Want to stop being an alcoholic? Easy! Just stop drinking.

Want to lose weight? Simple! Just stop eating sugar and carbs, and work out more often!

Want to make more money? Simple! Just visualize it!

Want to fall in love and live happily ever after? Simple! Just pick someone who is needy and relies on you more than you rely on them.

Just kidding about that last one, *but only slightly.*

It's an oversimplification to say we can change our lives on the level of behavior. What's more, it's a sentiment that truly lacks compassion or true understanding for the human condition.

We see this en masse every January 1 at gyms across the world. Well, more like January 5, because it takes a few days to recover from the holidays. That's when a whole bunch of people sign up for new gym memberships.

Why does this happen? Are people not disciplined enough? Do they not want it enough? Are they just lazy? That's not what I've found.

What I've found is that people genuinely want to better their lives, but they don't have a proper map showing them the way, and they don't know what they are up against. They don't understand that in trying to better their lives, they are going up against a *lifetime* of behaviors, stories, emotions, and beliefs. Not only that, they are going up against the rules and value system of their current peer groups. Without the proper mind-set and determination, they're destined to fail.

It's the same with our lives. We can create a never-ending cycle of guilt, shame, and regret, not knowing what is keeping us stuck.

Overcoming Your Own Worst Enemy

Transforming your life challenges your SPs, which sends your whole nervous system into fight-or-flight mode. When that happens, you end up battling against yourself to change. That is why the greatest barrier to claiming your power is yourself.

I don't say this to shame you or blame you. I say this to prepare you. So get ready to meet all the terrified parts of you that don't want to change, because only then can you transform your life in the areas where you are dead.

How do we get there? We've got to descend down the Anatomy of Transformation ladder. Let me reiterate it for you here.

5—Behavior
4—Story/Thoughts/Mental Level
3—Emotion
2—Beliefs
1—Original Incident (OI)

You see, if you just try to change just on the level of your behavior, then there are still four other layers that will keep you stuck. Now that doesn't mean you have to worry about all the layers all at once. We are going to do this in baby steps. So today, I want to focus on just the fifth and fourth levels: the behaviors and stories that hold you back.

Listing Your Limiting Behaviors

Let's start with limiting behaviors. You know what these are. These are the behaviors you desperately want to understand and change, like procrastination or self-sabotage. You come up against them in those moments when you ask yourself, "Why am I doing this *again*?"

Early on, my self-limiting behaviors included overeating and not eating at all. Staying in a job that didn't serve me. Blaming women I was dating for crap I was doing wrong. Withdrawing from being seen. And most of the time, all these behaviors brought me was a feeling of being numb.

In your own life, these behaviors might manifest as bingeing, relapsing, and pushing away what's good. They are the behaviors you beat yourself up about over and over again, and yet can't seem to find a way past. And you have at least five of them. Everyone does.

In your journal, list the five behaviors that hold you back:

1. _____

2. _____

3. _____

4. _____

5. _____

These behaviors will feel like old, familiar friends—friends you love to hate. Identifying them might make you want to swirl off into guilt and shame land, but hold steady. We are on a journey of self-discovery, and before we can get to the good stuff, we've got to find out what's in the way.

Today is just about awareness. We will get to the negative emotions that come with this awareness soon enough. For today, let's just stay with this new awareness of your limiting behaviors.

Stopping the Self-Fulfilling Stories

What I've found is that all behavior is driven by a story you tell yourself. You don't just do things randomly. Thoughts create behavior. Every behavior was first a thought, or, as we'll call it here, a story.

Your story creates your behavior. We've been told in the past that if we just change our stories, our lives will change. I've found that that doesn't work. Remember, changing your life on the level of thought alone is an old-model idea. That doesn't mean that thoughts aren't important. We're still going to uncover your true thoughts, or the story that drives your behavior, but once we do, we are going to go deeper. But that, too, is a subject for another day, so let's stick to your story for now.

There are all kinds of stories that can hold you back. Common ones I've seen are the following:

"The world is not a safe place."

"I'm too old."

"I'm too fat."

"I don't have enough time."

"I don't have enough money."

"I'm too young."

"I'm powerless to change."

"Life will never get better."

"This is all I'm worth."

"It's always been this way."

"Other people always come first."

"It's not safe for me to be my true self."

"I have to wait until the kids are older."

"My children's happiness is more important than my own."

"My parents won't approve of who I really am."

"Life won't support me any other way."

"This works for other people, but not for me."

You may see your story above, or you might have a different one. I want you to pause now and ask yourself a question: What stories am I telling myself that create my limiting behaviors? It helps if you say it out loud.

If nothing comes to mind, sit with the question for a moment. Most of us aren't consciously aware of the limiting stories we tell ourselves. We inherit them from our peer groups, our families, and the cultures we grew up in. So think about your parents, your peer group, and your culture. What are their expectations of you? What stories do they tell you about what's possible in your life?

The expectations of your peer group can give you insight into how far you will be able to go in life. Why? Because your peer group has collective stories they tell themselves, which get passed on to each person in the group. For example, in Australia they have a phenomenon called "tall poppy syndrome." If someone gets too big for his britches, they chop him down. People tend to be uncomfortable with success and honesty and form unconscious agreements to keep it safe, keep it vague, and keep it mediocre. In these unconscious agreements, the group remains safe and secure. But it's time for you to break free from that perceived safety and find out who you really are.

So let's do that now. Let's start by writing down the top five stories you tell yourself that create your limiting behaviors:

1. _____

2. _____

3. _____

4. _____

5. _____

Don't get caught up in needing to find the perfect answer here. Just trust what comes. If you find yourself struggling to be perfect, maybe you should add that to the list of stories you tell yourself, which create limiting behaviors: "Things have to be perfect before I move forward."

Looking at your limiting behavior and the stories behind them is like holding up a big mirror to the darkest parts of your life. I know this isn't easy, but this is the path required to claim your power. I respect you for having the courage to stay the course.

Digging Deeper

At the moment, your limiting behaviors and stories seem like the status quo. Just how things are. The way the "real world" works. This way of thinking and behaving is normal for you and normal for your peer group or family. Any action or thought that questions your particular brand of normal can seem strange, inappropriate, or egotistical. But for now just trust me when I tell you that it's not.

You have to accept that you're upping your game and changing the rules, and not everyone you know is going to be okay with that. These limiting behaviors and stories can and will change into empowering behaviors and stories. Our journey together will show you how. But for now let's just sit with the awareness and ahas of Day 3. Take a few deep breaths if you'd like. That was hard work.

Now let's try to identify where your stories came from. As you do this, remember not to beat yourself up. Be kind and gentle with yourself as you look at the hard parts of your life, and trust the process. Go back and read what you wrote about the stories you tell yourself. Allow yourself to soak them in. Don't push them away.

Then ask yourself, *When is the first time I remember hearing this story?*

Say this question out loud to yourself a few times. This jars the nervous system, forcing your brain to come up with an answer.

Where do my clients get the stories they tell themselves? Here are some of the usual suspects:

- Their parents

- Their significant others

- Their religions

- Their bosses

- Their brothers or sisters

- The media

- Bullies in school

- Their friends

- Their extended families

- People they look up to

- Role models

- The negative voices within

Now it's your turn. Ask yourself one more time: *When is the first time I remember hearing this story?* Identify the top five sources of the stories you tell yourself and list them in your journal.

1. _____

2. _____

3. _____

4. _____

5. _____

Great! There's nothing more to do today. All you have to do now is sit in the awareness of your limiting behaviors, the stories behind them, and the origins or sources of those stories.

This is not easy work, so I want to congratulate you on having enough self-love and courage to do it. It's not for the faint of heart, but trust that we are well on our way to claiming your power.

Today's affirmation: I am an infinite Soul connected to my Divine Creator, moving forward in self-love and courage.

Today's prayer: Dear Creator, please help me see who I am in Your eyes. Help me love myself as You love me. Help me see beyond my limiting behaviors and stories. Show me who I really am in Your eyes.

DAY 4:
DISCOVER THE NEGATIVE EMOTIONS UNDERNEATH THE STORIES THAT HOLD YOU BACK

"Every feeling fully felt is bliss."

– JOSEPH CAMPBELL

I'll give it to you straight: today is going to feel like you are pushing an ancient splinter out of your Soul. In fact, if you are feeling resistance to going further right now, I totally understand. I have much compassion for you.

In this very moment, your SPs are saying, "Don't go any further or you'll die!" Don't listen—it's a flat-out lie.

I have lead thousands of people through this process, and not one has died yet. *Not one.* Your stories and behaviors from the past might make you want to run away and hide, take comfort in a safe box of caramel corn, or stay in bed for a month, but now is the time to have courage. Remember, as Joseph Campbell says, "Every feeling fully felt is bliss."

Campbell got a lot of flak for saying, "Follow your bliss," and some people used that as an excuse to continue in their unhealthy patterns of additions and abuse. Someone could easily say, "My bliss is cocaine." But that's not at all what he meant. The emotion that you want to feel—free, joy, happy, nurtured—must be sustainable long term.

There's a big difference between feeling long-term bliss and hedonism, which is the pursuit of pleasure and self-indulgence. Hedonism can include drugs and alcohol, frequent sex with multiple partners and no commitment, overeating, and bingeing. But Campbell was referring to finding a long-term and sustainable bliss, which can be found only by doing the inner work, overcoming our patterns and excuses, and finding our true cores.

Before we go any further, I want to set your expectations. When I take my clients through this part of the journey, they readily admit that they would rather do almost anything else than feel their negative feelings. I mean *anything else*. I've had clients admit they'd rather commit suicide than go there. They'd rather stay in a toxic relationship than go there. They'd rather bury their faces in a pan of brownies than go there. Bottom line: they want to go back to the safe and the familiar.

You know what? That's totally normal. Totally human. If that's how you're feeling, then know that you are in good company. Remember why you're doing this—not just to heal yourself but to help heal others as well.

On every journey, the heroes or heroines have an impulse to turn around and say no to their adventures. Bilbo didn't want to leave the Shire. Harry Potter was scared to come out from under the staircase. Luke Skywalker didn't want to leave Tatooine. But they did, both for themselves and for the greater good. And so must you.

Before you can claim your power, you must go through the eternal rite of passage of staying the course, even though your SPs want you to run away. You have to have courage. You have to allow yourself to go further than you've gone before. Today, we take the leap from spiritual entertainment to spiritual growth. It's a big leap, and I'm proud of you.

So let's do this. Hunker down and be brave.

Interrupting Old Patterns

Go back to the list you created yesterday of stories that hold you back. Re-read them. Then bring your awareness to your body. How are you feeling as you read these stories? And where are you feeling it?

If you've been numb or in your head for most of your life, this won't come naturally to you. So take your time and really try to become aware of your feelings. Another way to access these feelings is to read your limiting stories out loud and then ask yourself out loud, "How do these stories make me feel?" Then notice your response.

The response you have may be the urge to return to limiting behaviors—to relapse, pick up that drink, eat the doughnut, have sex with someone you don't love, cheat on your spouse, get buried in work, or want to use again. These feelings will seem like your emotional home, but this time let's interrupt the pattern. Let's notice how you're feeling and simply bring awareness to that feeling, rather than acting on it.

Your negative feelings are there for a reason. Like pain in the body, they are a call for awareness and healing. *There's nothing wrong with you.* You are not your emotions. But your emotions do come bearing lessons, and you can't learn those lessons until you feel them.

I feel my negative emotions most in my solar plexus and stomach. Some people feel theirs in their legs. You may feel yours in your neck or in your arms. For me, the physical sensation often feels like loneliness, an empty hole, anger, sadness, or terror. The important thing is to be aware of it and to allow yourself to feel your emotions, no matter what they are or how they show up in your body.

Think about all the times your limiting behaviors and stories have held you back. Look at the pain you've caused others. Look at the pain you've caused yourself. Look at how you've kept yourself small, how you've put others first, denied your own worth and intuition. Allow yourself to go there for just *five minutes*. Look back over your whole life and see how you've held yourself back. And then notice how that makes you feel and where you feel these feelings in your body.

After five minutes, come back here . . .

Naming Your Emotions

I know you might be feeling raw right now. But that's okay. You just took a big step on the path toward claiming your power. You could spend a lifetime trying to avoid these feelings, but today you are taking your power back instead.

Now, in your journal, list at least five emotions that you feel as a result of these limiting behaviors and stories, and the area(s) in your body where you feel them.

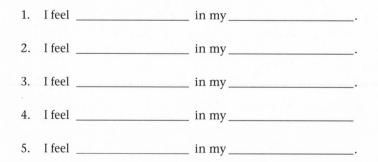

1. I feel _____ in my _____.

2. I feel _____ in my _____.

3. I feel _____ in my _____.

4. I feel _____ in my _____

5. I feel _____ in my _____.

These emotions can manifest in many physical sensations, such as a tightening in the chest, pounding in the head, an upset stomach, a tight jaw, and weakness in your legs, among others. So pay close attention. In fact, you may want to do a mental full-body scan right where you are. Start at the top of your head and work your way down slowly, paying attention to any physical sensations you have while focusing on the emotions.

If it's hard to access your emotions, or if you're getting frustrated that you aren't feeling anything, this is good! You are feeling frustration! Where do you feel it in the body? In your shoulders or your clenched fists? Just because you *don't feel* the emotions you think you should be feeling doesn't mean you *can't feel*. Your job is to go with whatever is present in the here and now.

Common emotions my clients have felt include anger, hate, powerlessness, guilt, shame, sadness, unworthiness, betrayal, regret, depression, stress, self-doubt, a lack of belonging, and resentment. These are difficult things to feel, and you may want to turn back. But don't do that. Stay with it. I know it can feel like these feelings will never pass, but they will. They will fade. These emotions do not control you. In fact, feeling them is the first step toward setting yourself free.

Be kind to yourself today. Take care of yourself. Drink lots of water. Get a massage. Attend a yoga class. Spend time in prayer and meditation. Rest. Make today a day of self-love and self-care. You're right where you need to be.

Today's affirmation: My emotions contain a powerful spiritual lesson for me. I am open to feeling these feelings and learning this lesson.

Today's prayer: Dear Creator, please give me the courage to feel my feelings. Help me stay centered, present, and calm. Allow my emotions to pass over me and help me gain insight as to why I feel this way. Help me love myself today as You do. Help me find solace in Your Love today as I feel my previously buried feelings.

DAY 5:
DISCOVER THE LIMITING BELIEFS THAT KEEP YOU DEAD

"Beliefs have the power to create and the power
to destroy. Human beings have the awesome
ability to take any experience of their lives and
create a meaning that disempowers them or
one that can literally save their lives."

– TONY ROBBINS

Here we are, on Day 5, on the other side of feeling your negative emotions and understanding where they are in your body. It's important to keep in mind that relating to your emotions is a new skill that you are discovering, and learning a new skill takes time. Malcolm Gladwell says it takes at least 10,000 hours to master something, and we've just been at this for less than a week.

So be patient.

I'm proud of you for coming this far. Many people would have turned back yesterday, but not you. You are a committed seeker who is well on your way to claiming your power and discovering your Purpose. And today we will dive into the limiting beliefs that are keeping you dead.

First, we need to make the distinction between a belief, an emotion, a story, and a behavior, since these are terms we'll be using frequently:

- An early trauma or crisis (the OI) produces a belief (the meaning[s] created from past events).

- A belief produces an emotion (a felt sensation in the body).

- An emotion produces a story or thought (how you describe your circumstances).

- And a story produces a behavior (how you repeatedly react to your circumstances).

Tony Robbins has the best definition of a belief that I've found: A belief is "a feeling of absolute certainty about what something means."[2] This one sentence contains a lifetime of wisdom. The three key words are: "what something means."

I'll let psychiatrist and Holocaust survivor Viktor Frankl explain further: "Between stimulus and response there is a space. In that space is our power to choose our response. In our response lies our growth and our freedom."

You see, there's what happens in life, and then there's meaning we assign to what happens in life. When something happens in life, you and only you get to decide what it means. The core difference between people who claim their power and those who don't is this one skill: mastering the art of deciding what the events in your life mean. The meaning you choose can bring you great fortune or cause you much lack. This is a huge, major lesson—so don't rush past it.

An empowering meaning can sometimes be the missing ingredient in your healing crisis. And the purpose of crisis is to reveal the SPs that need to be interrupted in order for you to grow.

Medical intuitive Caroline Myss calls the phenomenon of living your life through disempowering meaning "Woundology," which she describes as "the tendency to insistently hold on to old traumas. You define yourself by your hurts, not by your strengths, and there in those hurts you stay stuck forever."[3] In her *New York Times* best-selling book *Why People Don't Heal and How They Can*, Myss writes:

> We are not meant to stay wounded. We are supposed to move through our tragedies and challenges and to help each other move through the many painful episodes of our lives. By remaining stuck in the power of our wounds, we block our own transformation. We overlook the greater gifts inherent in our wounds—the strength to overcome them and the lessons that we are meant to receive through them. Wounds are the means through which we enter the hearts of other people. They are meant to teach us to become compassionate and wise.[4]

2   Tony Robbins, Tonyrobbins.com, https://www.tonyrobbins.com/stories/from-limitations-to-no-limits-at-all/.
3   "Woundology," http://themeaningseeker.com/tag/caroline-myss/.
4   Caroline Myss, "Woundology and the Healing Fire," *New York Times*, https://www.nytimes.com/books/first/m/myss-heal.html.

One of the reasons you're dead (remember, *dead* means stuck, numb, or devoid of growth) is because dead is safe. You've been through hell. A dark night of the Soul. A Divine Storm. And you don't ever want to go through that again.

You've got to uncover the limiting beliefs that hold you back so you can create a new meaning, step out of Woundology, and fully claim your power. After that, you'll be on the fast track to discovering your life's true Purpose.

It all boils down to meaning. You see, Frankl was in the Holocaust and imprisoned at the Auschwitz concentration camp. His wife, mother, and brother were killed in the Holocaust, and yet in the worst of circumstances he was still able to see that "in our response lies our growth and our freedom."

To find an empowering meaning is not the same as living in denial. Frankl never denied having survived the Holocaust, and he never denied how terrible an experience it was. But he made the choice to find an empowering meaning in the aftermath. Likewise, your future won't be the same as your past unless you bring the past with you. It's your choice.

Letting Go of Victim Consciousness

You can tell by now that this book is not about pretending that something didn't happen and lying to yourself by just thinking happy thoughts. This is a serious discussion about why you're dead and how to get free. To do that, you've got to be real with yourself about what has happened to you and, most important, your part in it.

What? My part in it?! Well let me tell you something . . . I can hear it now.

But before you get defensive or shut down, let me be clear: *it was not your fault that you were victimized*, but you are currently participating in your victimization by staying in victim consciousness. And you will continue to do so until you change the meaning of the past.

It is your Creator's will that you find a meaning that sets you free and allows you to live your Purpose. Not only for your own salvation but for the salvation of all those lives you are meant to touch through your transformation.

When you find an empowering meaning for your deepest hurts and live life from that place, everything will change. To get there we must first investigate the disempowering meanings you have assigned to the darkest moments of your life.

As we get ready to do that, I want to make something very clear. The work we are about to do in no way diminishes the pain you've been through. In no way does it justify what's been done to you by others.

In taking my clients through this process, I've heard of many hurts that are inhumane and downright evil. This process is not about denying what's happened to you, or being a Pollyanna and pretending like everything's all good. On the contrary, this process is about seeing how you have held yourself back and ultimately allowed those who have hurt you to *keep hurting you* long after the first hurt.

The hard truth is that if you are still playing small in your life because someone hurt you, *the person who hurt you is still winning.* The best way to get back at those who have hurt you is to shine. And that is our aim, for you to shine, no matter what has happened to you in the past.

Right now you are brand new. Your decision to go on this journey makes it so. For you to shine, we have to courageously stare at your pain and discover the beliefs that you have either consciously or unconsciously created because of hurtful or scary events in your past. Not everyone reading this book has been through massive trauma, and that's okay. No matter what you've been through, pain is still pain in the brain. It might be something simple like being yelled at by a parent, or it could be some kind of abuse. Don't judge the pain of your past and discount it because it's not the most significant pain any human being has ever felt. Just allow whatever comes to come.

That's all you have to do. Just get out of your own way while we discover the old limiting beliefs that have held you back. Let's begin by flipping back to yesterday's work about emotions.

Uncovering Old Beliefs

Recite the emotions you wrote down. Allow your body to feel these emotions fully once again. Then ask yourself out loud: "What beliefs about myself and my life have created these emotions?"

These beliefs are usually deep-seated. You may need to ask yourself this question a few times to get an answer. Be patient and remember to ask the question out loud.

The Anatomy of Transformation Ladder

5—Behavior

4—Story/Thoughts/Mental Level

3—Emotion

2—Beliefs

1—OI

In my own life, any chronic problem or long-term pain, like addiction and money issues, have come from the victim consciousness. These caused limiting beliefs that said, "I'm a fraud. I'm not enough. If I play big, my needs won't get met. I'm all alone. If I love someone, I'll hurt them. Confrontation will kill me." These are all lies, of course. But they're powerful lies.

Beliefs are deeper than just the stories we tell ourselves, which we talked about on Day 3. Beliefs are more powerful than stories, because beliefs are in many ways the origin of the stories we tell about life, because beliefs are based on the meaning we gave past events in our life. In others words, belief determines how we see or perceive an event (you can think of it as a filter), and a story is the account of what happened or what will happen based on your beliefs.

Limiting beliefs are the deeply held constraints that keep us small. Here are some common limiting beliefs:

- Men can't be trusted.

- Women can't be trusted.

- Life can't be trusted.

- I am worthless.

- I am powerless.

- In order for me to stay safe, I have to play small.

- If I'm vulnerable, I will get hurt again.

- Nothing good ever happens.

- I am alone.

- I am not safe.

- I will never be safe.

- I am not safe when I trust myself.

- I can't rely on anyone.

- I deserve all the bad things that happen to me.

- I can't love and be safe at the same time.

- I am all alone.

- God abandoned me.

- Nobody will ever love me.

- This is what I deserve.

Once more, ask yourself: *What beliefs about myself and my life have created these emotions?* Then list your top five limiting beliefs in your journal:

1. _____

2. _____

3. _____

4. _____

5. _____

You may be surprised at what comes up for you as you do this. Trust yourself as you go through the process and remember not to overthink it. The long-held beliefs that hold you back are trying to come up, so don't block them. Trust what comes "out of nowhere." Even if it seems like you're just making stuff up, trust yourself. Your Soul is speaking to you through your subconscious, so trust it.

Hear me? Trust it!

Today's affirmation: I am listening for the messages from my Soul.

Today's prayer: Dear Creator, please help me forgive myself for holding myself back. Help me see the clarity of Your Purpose in my life. Show me the lessons You wish for me to learn. Help me keep my mind open and new, for today I am curious about Your will in my life. Show me the beliefs You wish for me to have.

DAY 6:
THE ROOT CAUSE

"If you are a card-carrying human being, chances are that you share the same fear as all other humans: the fear of losing love, respect and connection to others. And if you are human, in order to avoid or prevent the pain, trauma and perceived devastation of the loss, you will do anything to avoid your greatest fear from being visited on you."

– IYANLA VANZANT

Divine order does not operate according to human logic. To claim your power, you must be willing to let go of everything you thought was true and begin to see your life through the lens of truth.

Here's the truth: We cannot change what happened to you. However, we can find a deeper Purpose for what happened beyond the constraints of victim consciousness. And that will not be easy.

The Divine works in paradox. What's big is small. What's insignificant is most significant. To heal from your Original Incident (OI), I will teach you how to find meaning and a deeper spiritual Purpose for it.

As you begin to view your OI with a new awareness and spiritual perspective, you experience more clarity on how this event was not just one of victimization but also, and more important, the beginning of you living your Soul's Purpose. Your OI, at its core, is the catalyst that prompted you to seek answers. While it's 99.9999 percent hurtful, the .0001 percent that is meaningful is the doorway to your salvation and transformation.

This means the area of your greatest frustration in life is the doorway to living your Purpose. You will see old wounds with new eyes. Let's go there today.

Naming Your OI

Today, you will need to be honest with yourself, accept yourself, and allow whatever comes to come.

Today will feel a lot like Day 4, when you felt your negative feelings. We are going to go back to a time of hurt, a time you have pushed away for so long, a time that you may even have pretended didn't happen and that you don't want to talk about. It is your moment or moments of trauma, pain, and original hurt.

OIs are moments in our past when something happened and we decided to form a belief about the world and what life meant. They can come from all kinds of places. Yours could be something so simple, like being left behind at school, a kid calling you fat, or the tone in which a parent said something to you as a child. Or your OI could be more extreme, like sexual, emotional, or physical abuse. You likely have several of these early trauma-inducing moments.

You can think of OIs as your blisters. Remember, to find your bliss, we've got to follow your blisters.

What I've found with most of my clients is that majority of OIs start before the age of 10. Because they are never addressed or worked through, the same SP perpetuates itself into adulthood. This is why that part of us stays dead.

One of my OIs happened when I was four years old. My mother had broken her back long before I was born, and the doctors told her not to have a child because it would make her situation worse. Against their advice, she decided to have me. My birth was a little miracle allowed by the courage of my mother to carry me, even though it would make her life more physically painful.

Four years after I was born, she had multiple back operations. We were living in Fredericton, New Brunswick, in Canada, and she was flown to Toronto for a couple of weeks for the surgery. I missed her and worried about her very much. I didn't know it then, but she died on the operating table and had a life-after-death experience where she was given the choice to leave her life or come back. She chose to come back. (Thank you, Mom!)

A few days after her surgery she was airlifted back to Fredericton, and I met her at the airport. When she and my dad got off the plane, she was on a stretcher surrounded by medical professionals. I had no idea she was in pain; I just missed her so much that I jumped on her and gave her a really big hug. This caused her a lot of pain, which she took well. However, everyone else around me reacted with shock and disdain. As I was hugging my mom, I heard people behind me gasp and yell, "Oh my God! Get off!" It was instant disapproval, and while my mom was cool with it, the negative reaction of the other adults around me trumped her validation.

I was in trouble, and I didn't know why. In this moment of receiving disapproval, I decided, at the age of four, that *when I express my love, I hurt people.* That limiting belief stemming from my OI was with me for almost 30 years after that, until I did the work of going deeper.

Because I believed if I loved someone I'd hurt them, that meant no serious romantic relationships. In fact, I had only one girlfriend before I met Jenna. And in my early professional career, I couldn't have taught seminars or do any mentoring in person because I was afraid to hurt people.

In order to change the story, OIs must be seen with new eyes. Today, when I remember that moment, I see a happy kid, with no clue what his mother had been through, making a mistake out of love. But I didn't see it that way for a long time, so I held back my love, from myself and from others. That's an expensive price to pay for a decision I made in a single moment in time when I was only four years old.

It's time to stop paying the price for the limiting beliefs you created to protect yourself long ago, and step instead into a new, more powerful life. To do that, we've got to go deep.

Which One Is the Right One?

If you can't get to your very first OI, don't worry. Personal growth happens in layers. Also, don't worry about finding the "perfect" OI—there's no such thing. And it doesn't matter if you pick one and then remember one that may have happened earlier or that felt more impactful. Go with the first one that comes to mind.

You will have many OIs that you will only find after going through this process a few times. See yourself as an onion with deeper and deeper layers to discover. OIs really never stop happening either. To be human is to be in crisis, and trauma can happen at any moment.

It's very possible that you've done therapy around your OIs already. It's also possible that you've never allowed yourself to go there. Your OIs may be so repressed that you don't even know you have them.

Whatever your situation, decide to meet your OIs today with an open mind and lots of curiosity. If you've been back to your OIs many times before and think you have nothing left to learn from them, decide that today you might learn something brand new. If you've repressed your OIs, don't try to force anything to happen. Allow yourself to be guided and know that what comes up is exactly what needed to come up at this point in time.

Sometimes OIs can be blurry, vague, or seem like a dream. Don't worry about getting it right. Don't worry about every detail. Know that you will be shown exactly what you're meant to be shown.

You don't have to do this perfectly. All you have to do is show up and trust what comes. Remember, keep an open, childlike mind.

Here is a list of common OIs that I've seen:

- Sexual abuse

- Physical abuse

- Emotional abuse

- Violent family members

- Being required to be perfect, rather than yourself

- Being abandoned by one or both parents

- A parent's addiction

- Needing to be the caregiver of your parent(s) as a child

- Other people condemning you

- Being made fun of at school

- Witnessing violence

- The death of a loved one

- Not being recognized by your father

- Not being nurtured by your mother

As you read the list, it's possible that one or more OIs came to mind. If not, no problem. Go back and read your top five limiting beliefs. After you've read them, take a moment to allow the oh-so-familiar emotions to wash over you.

Then, as you are looking at your old limiting beliefs, ask yourself: "What Original Incident happened in my life that made me believe these things?"

Don't rush. Let yourself feel. Let your Soul answer. Don't try to overthink it or come up with the perfect answer.

Again, out loud: "What Original Incident happened in my life that made me believe these things?"

List the top one to five things that come up as your OIs:

1. _____

2. _____

3. _____

4. _____

5. _____

Revisiting these moments can be difficult. It can feel like it's happening all over again. Tell yourself that your trigger is not your trauma. Even though your body may feel the uncomfortable sensations as if you are back in that moment, you are not there. You are here with me now, and you are safe.

The past is gone and today is a new day. Let yourself begin to see your OIs from a new and more empowering perspective.

Today's affirmation: I accept my past with Grace. I view my life with a new perspective.

Today's prayer: Dear Creator, be with me as I revisit the painful experiences of my past. Give me the courage to revisit my greatest pain and help me see it with new eyes. I am Your child, and I know that You send me only what I am ready to go through. Thank You for the freedom that accepting my past brings me. I am Your servant. Help me love myself today as You love me.

DAY 7:
HOW THE ROOT CAUSE HAS STUNTED YOUR GROWTH

"Love opens the doors into everything, as far as
I can see, including and perhaps most of all,
the door into one's own secret, and often
terrible and frightening, real self."

– MAY SARTON

The new model of transformation informs us that we can't just put what we want on a vision board and expect it to come true. We've got to do the hard work. We've got to dive in, as you did yesterday, and really see the limiting beliefs, emotions, stories, and behaviors that hold us back.

We must transform on an emotional level. One of the best ways to get intensely emotional about your transformation is to be real with yourself about how you've been held back.

If you think that focusing on the negative will bring negative results, you're living in an old-model mind-set. We must focus on what we've lost out on to create enough emotional drive to catalyze our growth.

When you focus only on the positive, you create a Spiritual Bypass—which is pretending everything is okay, doing the chanting, the praying, the meditating, but not being honest with yourself about how you're really thinking or what you're really feeling. That's why we have to allow ourselves to go into the dark recesses of our fears. Not to punish ourselves and not to dwell there forever, but so that we can break free.

Today, it would be easy to fall into guilt or shame. It was only yesterday that we visited your OI and saw how this moment in time changed the course of your life. Do your best to keep your head above water and just be here with me. Accept how you are feeling. Don't try to change anything. Don't try to push away what's coming up for you.

Today may produce more sadness, anger, guilt, and negative emotions, and that's okay. Just allow whatever you feel today to be what it is.

We've been together a week now and done a lot of digging. We've come a long way already on our journey. So let's pause for a moment and review what we've discovered so far.

Look back at what you've written about your limiting behaviors, stories, emotions, beliefs, and your OIs. And then let's get real: How have all these factors limited your life?

You might be angry about what you missed out on. Or you might try to take the higher road by saying, "Everything happened for a reason." While that is true, saying it right now is just another way to not feel your feelings. It's a Spiritual Bypass.

Let yourself dive into how your life has been messed up because of the limiting factors that have held you back. What has gone wrong? What has been broken? How have you not lived up to your greatest potential? How have you let yourself down? How have you fallen short of your Creator's vision for your life? What have you lost that you can't get back?

Understanding and *feeling* the answers to these questions is vital for the next phase of our work together. The answers to these questions are not comfortable, but I am not interested in your comfort. I am interested in your growth.

Cultivating Curiosity

You cannot measure your Creator's love for you based on your own level of happiness. Remember, we are dealing with Divine Timing and Divine Lessons, which by their very nature create discomfort. And you've lived long enough in the safe, comfortable place of being dead.

Coming face-to-face with the good that you've missed out on will produce a powerful burst of energy that we can use as rocket fuel for your transformation. Marianne Williamson said it best: "You must go through your crucifixion, but not dwell on it."

There is no shame, no guilt, and no self-hatred needed today. Leave all of that at the door. Be curious about the answers, and let's see what comes up for you.

We are coming to the end of the Separation phase of your journey, which means that in the next couple of days, you will be more than ready to welcome the uncertainty of the future. You will understand that there is more pain for you if you stay the same, and less pain when you venture out into the unknown callings of your Soul.

With that said, let's dive into what you've missed out on as a result of your limiting factors. In your journal, write down something for each category of your life. Be as honest and blunt as possible. Don't hold back. You may find yourself getting emotional as you make your list. Let yourself go there. Remember, today is not about looking good, playing it cool, or pretending like you haven't missed out.

ROMANCE:

FAMILY:

YOUR BODY AND HEALTH:

YOUR JOB/CAREER/VOCATION:

YOUR SPIRITUALITY:

FRIENDS:

FINANCES:

YOUR CREATIVITY:

If, as you filled out the categories above, you found that there's an ugly cry on today's agenda, that's just fine with me. Do yourself the honor of being truthful.

When you are done, answer the following question: *What is there less of in the world because I have been dead up until now?*

Today's affirmation: I am honest with myself, and in doing so, I begin to claim my power.

Today's prayer: Dear Divine Source, help me forgive myself for all that I've missed out on. Help me forgive myself for not living up to the potential that You created for me. Help me forgive myself for hurting those that I loved, and show me how to use my hurt and pain as fuel for living Your will in my life. Show me how I can make progress toward claiming my power from this moment forward.

DAY 8:
YOUR COPING MECHANISMS

"Problems are not the problem;
coping is the problem."

– VIRGINIA SATIR

Uncertainty is a fact of life that all human beings must deal with. What's so ironic is that when you decide to claim your power and live your Purpose, you actually *increase* the amount of uncertainty in your life.

In the areas where you are dead, you are dead because of how you have chosen to cope with uncertainty. Addiction stems from choosing unhealthy coping mechanisms (SPs) for uncertainty, as do any limiting beliefs, emotions, stories, and behaviors. People who claim their power and live their Creator's will on earth have, in one way or another, created a rock-solid relationship with uncertainty. In fact, when you can have faith amid massive uncertainty, you have reached mastery.

The spiritual path is uncertain. If you think that life is not uncertain you are not awake to the true nature of existence. Even if you have built yourself a comfortable existence, where risk is mitigated, if you are reading this book, then that comfort no longer feels all that comfortable to you. You yearn for more, and yet you can't seem to take sustained courageous action.

Why?

Because you think that if you make any move that creates uncertainty, then you will die. That's how the brain is wired. It's wired for comfort and survival. It's cosmically ironic that your Heart and Soul are wired for adventure. The play between your SPs of your brain and the growth mechanisms of your Soul creates the dramatic and epic journey of the spiritual seeker.

All spiritual practices are designed to help you orient yourself with faith in the face of uncertainty. The by-product of meditation, yoga, church, prayer, chanting, journaling, therapy, life coaching, and any other tool used for personal growth is faith, in spite of uncertainty.

Up until now, you have done a wonderful job of coping with uncertainty in a way that has helped you survive. I know what you've been through has not been easy, and at times you weren't sure if you were going to make it. That deserves applause and recognition. But we cannot stop there. We must keep going.

My aim is not just to celebrate how far you've come. My job is to help you break free and get to the next level. To do that we must examine your relationship with uncertainty up until now. As always, this is a time for radical honesty.

What I've found in working with clients is that not all their behaviors are limiting. In fact, you have behaviors that I would consider growth behaviors. However, that is not what we want to look at today. Today we want to look at your behavior when you are scared, uncertain, and feel powerless.

From Powerlessness to Powerful

The root emotion of almost all trauma, hurt, and pain is powerlessness.

Feeling powerless and separate is the cause of addiction, hate, anger, jealousy, sadness, war, violence, and all unloving behavior. The spiritual path of claiming your power will teach you how to feel powerful and certain *within* the feelings of powerlessness and uncertainty. This is the Love of your Creator made real.

Perhaps one of the greatest demonstrations of faith in the face of fear was Jesus in the Garden the night before He was crucified. He was under such stress that He was crying tears of blood and asked God to take away His burden. At the same time, Jesus uttered words that would ring throughout the ages: "Thy will be done."

When you say this prayer, it's a game changer. You see, having faith and living your Creator's will on planet Earth does not guarantee your comfort. It does guarantee you self-respect and a life well lived.

In your Heart of hearts, you do not want a comfortable life. You want a life that makes you come alive. Therefore, you must learn to face uncertainty with the knowledge that no matter what comes, you will be taken care of and you will never walk alone.

But that isn't how it's been for you, not up until now. You and I have a lot of work to do to find our faith in the face of uncertainty.

With that in mind, I'd like you to think about times in your life when you felt scared, triggered, or powerless. This doesn't happen all the time, but there are *those* times that we all experience. How well you navigate those times will begin to shape your destiny.

Examples of times when people feel powerless include the following:

- At night, when cravings for food, alcohol, and promiscuous sex increase

- When you look at your bills

- When you get into a fight with a loved one

- When you find yourself in a situation similar to the trauma of your past

- Right before you are about to make a massive change or transition

- Any time of excess stress

- When you have low blood sugar

- When you aren't getting enough sleep

- When you are getting closer to someone in a romantic relationship

- Right before a major growth spurt in your life

- When unexpected events happen that threaten your survival

- When you are feeling a craving for anything you are addicted to

In the past, when you found yourself in any of the above situations, what did you do to cope with feeling powerless? How did your coping mechanisms have a negative effect on your life? Below list 5 to 10 moments in your life when you have felt powerless and the negative ways in which you dealt with them.

1. _____

2. _____

3. _____

4. _____

5. _____

6.   _____

7.   _____

8.   _____

9.   _____

10.   _____

The coping mechanisms you default to when you feel powerless should be very familiar to you. In fact, they may be behaviors you are trying to work through in a 12-step program, therapy, or spiritual practice. My clients often ask me, "Why do I do this? Why do I sabotage myself by continually engaging in these behaviors?"

I've never met a person on the path to claiming his or her power who wakes up in the morning and says, "Yes! Today is a great day to sabotage my dreams!"

Sabotage is a word we need to banish from our vocabulary because it is filled with only guilt, shame, and negative associations. We must start to understand that our behavior in moments of powerlessness and uncertainty is not self-sabotage at all. It is self-protection—SPs that kick in to make sure you don't die.

All human beings are programmed to survive. It's in our DNA, wired into our nervous system. Our brains are always on alert for possible threats, and our bodies are ready in a moment to defend us from possible risk.

To anyone who's been through something traumatic, the spiritual path can feel like a retriggering of that trauma, simply because the spiritual path is uncertain. But you can let yourself off the hook. It's time to realize that you haven't been sabotaging yourself; you've been trying to protect yourself from death. It's also time to realize that you don't need to protect yourself anymore. Death is not what's coming for you. What's coming is an even greater awareness of who you really are: a powerful and Divine being.

Up until now you've done a wonderful job of surviving, but it's time to step into a greater reality. Yesterday's medicine has become today's poison, and you are ready to let go of what no longer serves you. So look at the most painful coping mechanism you've listed on the previous page or above and ask yourself: *When is the first time I can remember doing this?*

Just trust yourself. Don't let your mind get in the way of an answer that will set you free.

Then ask yourself: *Who could I be if I wasn't trying to protect myself in these destructive ways?*

Today's affirmation: I release the need to protect myself and surrender to my Creator's protection.

Today's prayer: Creator, please show me how to trust life beyond my protective behavior. Show me how to trust You even more, with my whole life. I am Yours to use as You please. Help me feel Your presence with every heartbeat, every breath, and every step. I am ready to embrace a new life filled with Your love. Help me trust You and myself again. I'm ready.

DAY 9:
YOUR APPROVAL MAP

"People's lives are a direct reflection of the expectations
of their peer group. . . . Your life experience will never far
exceed the expectations of your peers, because to stay
connected to them there is an unconscious contract that
says we're going to be within this range of each other."

– TONY ROBBINS

Needing other people's approval to live your dreams is one of the most common SPs that hold people back. I've seen this pattern negatively affect people from all over the world. Breaking free of your family's or peer group's expectations of you is some of the hardest work you can do. To become who you are, you must first break free of the rules of your tribe.

Epigenetics is the study of how trauma is passed down in the genes. Studies have confirmed that these changes can even affect our evolution.[5] That means if something traumatic happened to your grandmother, the trauma may have been passed down to you. In fact, in a recent study of Holocaust survivors, it was found that their descendants had altered stress hormones—a change that occurred during pregnancy—which made it harder for them to heal from a traumatic event.[6]

And it's not just family members who are capable of passing trauma to us. The limiting behaviors, stories, emotions, and beliefs of your significant other, friends, neighbors, co-workers, and others can all get transferred to you. And you do the same to them, as well as to your children—even your pets!

You see, we can be so terrified of change that a part of us will unconsciously surround ourselves with people who will *not approve* of our dreams. Why?

---

5   David S. Moore, *The Developing Genome: An Introduction to Behavioral Epigenetics*, 1st ed. (Oxford, UK: Oxford University Press, 2015).
6   Toni Rodriguez, "Descendants of Holocaust Survivors Have Altered Stress Hormones," *Scientific American*, March 1, 2015, https://www.scientificamerican.com/article/descendants-of-holocaust-survivors-have-altered-stress-hormones/.

You guessed it: It's an SP kicking in yet again. There is a sense of safety in the tribe, safety in numbers, and safety in what other people think and believe.

This is one of the final days of the Separation phase of your journey, and one of the final things you need to separate yourself from is the approval of others. When you're on the path to claim your power, you have to become less interested in what others think and more interested in the whispers of your Soul.

Today could be a challenging day. You will begin to see how you have allowed well-intentioned people, whom you may love dearly, to help prevent you from living your Purpose. That's right—even though you may be upset or frustrated with the people whose approval you needed in the past to survive, at the end of the day, the hard pill to swallow is that it has been *you* who has held yourself back. You may be projecting your frustration onto them, but it is actually *you* that you are frustrated or angry with.

Creating Our Own Realities

One of the great spiritual messages is that we all get to create our own realities.

As you've been reading my words, some people have probably popped into mind. They might be your mother, your father, your child, or your significant other. You might even include God on that list. You may find that you still need approval from someone who has passed on. It doesn't matter if the person is dead or alive; there is still a part of you waiting for them to say, "Go for it!"

The hard truth is that these people may never approve of your dreams. They may never approve of what you *really* want to do with your life.

Let's take a moment to look at the major players in your life from birth until now. These can be family members, friends, co-workers, or anyone else whose approval you've wanted or needed. List them below and on the following pages:

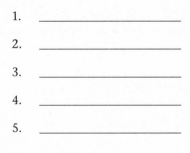

1. _____

2. _____

3. _____

4. _____

5. _____

6. _____

7. _____

8. _____

9. _____

10. _____

Now, thinking about the people you've listed, consider how you've allowed them to hold you back. What have they said that you internalized? What did they do? What went unsaid but was still a rule? What behaviors, stories, emotions, beliefs, and possible OIs have these people demonstrated that were transferred onto you and held you back?

Common examples of limiting phrases and behaviors are numerous. Here are some you might hear:

- "We've always done it this way."

- "Don't trust men."

- "You can't rely on a woman."

- "Life is hard."

- "You'll never amount to anything."

- "You've got to play it safe."

- "You've got to live a normal life."

- "Don't get your hopes up."

- "Life's not fair."

- "Rich people are evil."

And here are some limiting behaviors you may have learned from others' behavior, though they might not have been verbalized:

- Adults needing you to take care of them, even though they were supposed to be the caretakers.

- Always being wounded.

- Always being closed or withdrawn.

- Someone threatening to leave you if you made an empowered choice.

- Guilt trips.

On Day 3, we talked about limiting phrases. But now since you understand how deep these patterns are, and the multiple places they come from, list the limiting phrases and behaviors that you have *internalized from others*:

1. _____

2. _____

3. _____

4. _____

5. _____

How long have other people's opinions and behaviors held you back? How long have you allowed other people's limitations to define what's possible for you?

If you're honest, it's most likely been your whole life.

Now, an important thing to understand today is that we are not about trying to judge or look down on others. The truth is that the people you named are doing the best they can from their perspectives. I've seen many clients, once they've started making progress on their journeys, develop a spiritual ego and start judging their friends and family without meaning to. That is not our aim here.

Our aim is simple awareness. If someone is not as far long as you are on the spiritual path, or if they are not open to this conversation, what they really need is Love, not judgment.

Later in our work together I'll teach you how to set healthy boundaries with people like this. But for now let's simply become aware that one of the reasons you are dead in your life is that you've given your power away and allowed others to decide what's possible for you.

This stops now.

Let's rest in the awareness that the only person who decides what's possible for you is *you*. No matter what you've been told, you are supremely

Loved by your Creator. And in the eyes of your Creator, there is so much more for you to become—starting now.

Today's affirmation: I decide who I am and what's possible for me.

Today's prayer: Please help me forgive myself for allowing others to define my path and lead my astray. I know that I already have Your approval, dear Creator. Give me signs of Your Love and approval. Show me what You want from me. Show me my next steps. Help me take my power back from those I've given it to, and help me find the courage to learn how to trust You. I am Your humble servant and wish nothing more than to live Your will in my life. Show me how.

DAY 10:
THERE'S NO TURNING BACK NOW

"The Fates lead him who will; him who won't, they drag."

– JOSEPH CAMPBELL

We've come to the end of this phase of your journey. By now you are starting to understand all that holds you back, your SPs, and why you are dead in your life. But there is much of the journey still ahead for you.

We have done work to illuminate the patterns that keep us bound in fear. What comes next is actually changing and transforming these patterns. That is the work truly worth doing and the work that will terrify you the most.

Today is your day of courage. Today, we vow together to no longer just talk about self-help concepts like love, forgiveness, compassion, empathy, joy, Purpose, highest potential, and so on. Today, we begin the truly heroic process of embodying these spiritual concepts we say we believe in. To claim your power, the rhetoric, the talk, and the concepts must transform into action.

Leaving a Legacy

Look at what you've already discovered about yourself. Look at the old behaviors, stories, emotions, beliefs, and OIs. Then ask yourself: *Is this the life I truly want? Is this the life I will have been proud to have lived when I arrive on my deathbed? Is this what I want my legacy to be?*

I think not.

Personally, I would love to leave a legacy of being able to help people resolve conflict within themselves and elevate the level of compassion we have for all, regardless of trauma or background. I bet you have a beautifully powerful legacy you'd like to leave as well.

So we must change. We must commit to courageously embodying the concepts we've come to know.

To do this, I want you to think about what life would be like over the next 10 years if you didn't change. Imagine that you turned back now and said, "Screw it!" Imagine if this book was simply spiritual entertainment for you and you went back to your old behaviors, stories, emotions, beliefs, and OIs. What would life be like in 10 years if that was what you did?

Really let yourself go there. Let yourself step into the unfulfilled, sick, tired, wasted, regret-filled life that awaits you if you do not change now. How does this thought make you feel? Sad? Anxious? Terrified?

You have come to a point in your life where your Creator has given you an opening to transformation. Maybe you were at rock bottom when you picked up this book, or maybe this book landed in your possession for reasons you do not yet understand. Either way, when you are presented with an opening, you should understand that it has taken a lot for that to happen.

So grab it. Don't go back now. You can choose to courageously step through now, or you can be dragged through later.

Once again, think about your future and how awful and lackluster it will be *if you don't change*. In your journal, describe what that future looks like in the worst-case scenario in each area of your life if you change nothing:

FINANCES:

JOB/VOCATION:

HEALTH/WELLNESS/BODY:

FAMILY:

ROMANCE:

SPIRITUAL LIFE:

YOUR PURPOSE:

YOUR LEGACY:

REGRETS:

When you envision this uninspiring life of the future, you have to ask yourself: *Is this the life I truly want?*

If you are still reading this, then I know the answer is no.

One of the best pieces of advice a coach ever gave me was about my weight. I had gained more than 50 pounds while writing my first book, which was a memoir. That required me to relive my addiction stories, and that triggered one of my patterns that was (and still is) overeating.

When I started working toward losing the weight, my coach said, "You have to get serious about this. You can end up either losing 50 pounds or gaining 50 more."

That advice shocked me and got me to shape up. It was a sobering reality check that life can indeed get worse. It was enough to motivate me to do the courageous work of personal transformation, because I didn't want to create potential health concerns for myself due to extra weight. I wanted to be healthy and happy.

What's Your Why?

Today, we acknowledge and create your new *why*. Again, let me quote Friedrich Nietzsche: "He who has a why to live for can bear with almost any how."

You will find your *how* as you move forward in this process. Right now it's time to declare *why* you are setting yourself up for transformation. Is it just for you? Is it for a cause? For loved ones? Why are you moving forward to Claim Your Power? In your journal, declare your *why* for moving forward.

My Why Is:

Beautiful. We have now crossed over from the familiar world of your past and are moving forward into the unknown.

Your life will be turned upside down. Your survival instincts will be triggered. And yet you are about to find out just how powerful you truly are.

Today's affirmation: I am ready for transformation, knowing that what's ahead is only for my benefit.

Today's prayer: Dear Creator, please give me the strength and courage to keep going. I wish nothing more than to live Your will in my life. Show me how to find joy. Show me how to find love. Show me how to love myself as You love me. Give me courage when I want to stop and faith when the going gets tough. I commit my whole life to You. Help me cross over into Your loving guidance, and nudge me toward growth.

Part II

INITIATION

"Not all who hesitate are lost. The psyche has many secrets in reserve."

– JOSEPH CAMPBELL

You have crossed the threshold of your fear and begun the next phase of your journey to claim your power. This phase of your journey is called *Initiation* because we will be initiating or introducing you to a whole new way of thinking and being.

In Part II we talk about Purpose, finding the courage to change, discovering our relational hierarchies, committing to both yourself and your Creator, and setting boundaries.

From now on, you are in a strange new land. People who venture this far find out many things about themselves. The weak find out they are strong. The confident find out they are insecure. The happy discover they are deeply sad. Whatever your outward face to the world has been, we will find that the opposite is also true. We also begin to find out that on the journey of arriving at your Purpose, you are so much more than you've been told.

You've been suppressing your negative emotions, and as a result, you've been suppressing God. This is why on your search for your Purpose, you must meet the negative and avoided areas first. Then and only then can you make the leap to the bliss of feeling alive as your true Self.

During the first phase of this journey, we discovered that all the limiting beliefs you bought into turned out to be convincing lies you told yourself. The irony, dear one, is that the opposite of what you've believed about yourself is what's true. Our Creator orchestrates each and every experience for our benefit, but we have missed the gift until now.

Finding Fulfillment

We have done a wonderful job of surviving life up until now, but we must realize that life is about more than simple survival. Life is about thriving. Life is about fulfillment.

We have been confused about what fulfillment is. We started looking for it outside of ourselves.

We thought if we could just lose the weight or find the perfect person, then all would be well. We picked up yoga. We decided to eat better foods. We meditated. We prayed. We searched the Internet, trying to find what was missing from our lives. We signed up for newsletters. We followed people on social media. We read book after book, running through highlighters at a record pace. We wondered if we were the only ones who ever felt this way. We imagined that other people had it figured out and that something must be wrong with us.

We decided that we had tried everything, and in one moment of despair, we gave up and decided to settle. We decided that we should be grateful for what we had and that getting our hopes up was something only for the naive or young.

After that our lives simply went along with no real Purpose or aim. We got by on autopilot. And yet there was a stirring in our Hearts and Souls. That yearning still existed even though it had become small and faint. Then, by some miracle, an opening came.

Perhaps it came through tragedy. Perhaps it came as a result of an unexpected event. Something stirred us and gave us a renewed sense of hope that life can indeed change.

But do we risk being hurt? Or let down?

"Yes," the Heart says.

"Hell no," the mind says.

We went on a search for something that has been within us, waiting for us to discover it. Like Dorothy in *The Wizard of Oz*, we seek to come home, and we need to go on our own journey to remember that we've always had it within us.

Welcome to the Initiation phase of your journey home. It begins with finding your Purpose and then bringing it to life. Let's start right now.

DAY 11:
WHAT IS PURPOSE, ANYWAY?

*"I've come to believe that each of us has a personal
calling that's as unique as a fingerprint—and that the
best way to succeed is to discover what you love
and then find a way to offer it to others in the form
of service, working hard, and also allowing
the energy of the universe to lead you."*

– OPRAH WINFREY

When you wander through life without knowing your Purpose, you feel dull inside. When this feeling is as its worst, you may even want to end your life.

Yet when you discover your Purpose, everything can change. You find your true north. Your Heart is validated, not by some outward board of advisors but by the simple knowing inside yourself that you do have a Purpose and it is real.

The hard truth is that what we have been looking for is the part of us that has been doing the looking. In discovering and living your Purpose, you will find that what was important is meaningless, and what was meaningless is now important. All that you have put your faith in may come crumbling down—not as punishment but as a wake-up call. Unforeseen setbacks, even a crisis, are not-so-subtle ways that your Purpose tries to get your attention.

It doesn't matter how outwardly successful you are. There are plenty of rich people who are not living their Purpose, and plenty who live with a rich sense of Purpose each day. Living your Purpose doesn't mean you can't have a lot of money. I have no rules or judgment about money. Money is just energy. It's how you use it that counts. However, if you worship money more than your Creator or your Purpose, then you will never—and I mean never—find true fulfillment.

What Purpose Isn't

Many people make the mistake of thinking that their Purpose is something they do.

It's not.

Your Purpose is not your job, your children, your business, your house, your wife, your husband, your mother, your father, your bank account, your yoga practice, your nonprofit work, your religion, or anything else "out there."

Many of my clients have thought that their Purpose was to "be" something, to embody a title:

- A mother

- A business owner

- A caretaker

- An entrepreneur

- A hard worker

- A girlfriend or wife

- A husband or father

Purpose is not about these things. It's about something far deeper.

When you believe that your Purpose is outside you and that it depends on others, then you set yourself up for massive heartbreak. Why? Because loss is a part of life. You will lose people and things you care about. While I would never wish this kind of loss on you, the truth is it will happen. The good news is just because you've lost someone or something you care about doesn't mean you've lost your Purpose.

Losing someone is sad, but if you believe that your Purpose is somehow attached to the person you've lost, then that loss can be life ending. When the belief that we have no Purpose starts to take over, boy oh boy, are you setting yourself up for a whole lot of pain.

Purpose is not something you do, nor is it attached to something outside you. When you start to understand that in every moment of your life you have control over whether or not you are going to live your Purpose, then you start to take your power back. Even if you decide not to live your Purpose, you have exercised your power to make that decision.

After working with thousands of people, I've come to find that no matter what has happened to us over the course of our lives, our Creator has given us all the awesome ability to choose how we want to respond. When tragedy strikes, if we are not aware of our Purpose, we can easily become victims of circumstance. However, anyone you have ever admired was either consciously or unconsciously living on Purpose. They had a reason beyond their circumstances to continue, despite the worst of the worst. They were connected to their inner power, strength, love, and compassion, which helped them endure hardships.

When you start to understand what your Purpose is, you begin to manifest the incredible Love of the Creator on earth. Oftentimes well-intentioned people will try to save the world when they're the people who truly need saving. In reality, the world will be saved by people who have woken up to their Purpose and who then become teachers through their examples.

Nothing inspires more change than your positive example. Hypocritical preaching doesn't work. "Do as I say, not as I do" doesn't work. What works is you coming alive to your life's Purpose, and then living it awesomely in the world with no apologies.

What exactly is Purpose, then?

What Purpose Is

You were born to connect back to your Creator's love and make it real on earth.

Each day, each moment of each day, is an opportunity to start again. The past is gone and cannot touch you. The future is unwritten, and the only thing you can accurately say about it is *perhaps*. All you and I have is this moment, right here, right now.

What's so awesome about this moment is that you can decide to make a brand-new choice. You can decide that no matter what has happened to you, nothing is so powerful that it can take away your ability to step into the awesome realm of living your Purpose.

How do you begin to embody the Love of your Creator and make it real on earth? Well, that comes from self-knowledge. We were made in our Creator's image, which means that when we begin to pay attention to our hopes, dreams, and, most important, emotions, we begin to understand both our Creator's will for our lives and our Purpose, which are ultimately one and the same.

Later in this book, you learn how to follow your Heart because in doing so, your Heart will create the proper beliefs for living your Purpose. For now, all you need to understand is what Purpose ultimately is: *An emotion you cultivate within yourself and give away to the world in the form of service to others.*

Life is emotion. When there is no emotion, there is no life. It doesn't matter whether you are in a romantic relationship, corporate job, or on a spiritual quest—emotions are driving you forward or keeping you dead.

In fact, we set goals to produce feelings. That means you don't set a goal to get wealthy, for example, just for the money—you want the feeling of freedom, certainty, or power that money brings you. You don't set a goal to lose weight just to lose fat on your body—you want to feel alive, attractive, and energized.

When you can tap into and understand the emotions you want to feel, how to produce them in yourself each and every day, and then how to give those emotions away to the world, that's when you take a massive leap toward living your Purpose.

The rest of this book teaches you how to discover the emotions that bring you the most joy or, as Joseph Campbell would say, bliss.

I am not going to give you a list of the top 100 emotions my clients have felt and ask you to just randomly pick some. Instead I will take you through a guided process to help you uncover the emotions that will drive your Purpose, which are personal and just for you. After we go through this process, I am going to teach you how to live your Purpose in the world, what will trip you up, and how to listen to your Heart so that you are giving life new meaning in each moment.

Ready? Let's do this.

Reflection Questions

Take a few moments to reflect on what Purpose has meant to you thus far by answering the following questions:

In the past, what external things did I identify as my Purpose (romance, family, business, etc.)?

Have I lost any of the above things in my life and decided that I had no Purpose?

What has this belief—that I've lost my Purpose—cost me?

What would be possible in my life if my Purpose still existed, even though I've lost out in the past?

Today's affirmation: I am open to discovering why I was born.

Today's prayer: Dear Creator, help me mend the hurt of the past. Help me accept my disappointments and all that I have lost. Aid me in seeing that each moment of loss has led me to this moment of expansion and growth. Help me see Your will in my life. Show me why You made me. I am ready for a new chapter.

DAY 12:
DISCOVER YOUR PURPOSE

"Don't ask what the world needs. Ask what makes
you come alive, and go do it. Because what the
world needs is people who have come alive."

– HOWARD THURMAN

You can think of the process of discovering your life's Purpose as intentionally living in mystery. As Campbell wisely notes, simply because you are hesitating does not mean you are lost. Your psyche, your emotional body, and your Purpose have secrets that are yet to be revealed to you.

The spiritual path will always lead you back to yourself. You can search far and wide for answers, but it will not be until you've come home to yourself that you will discover the truth. This can be confusing. Up until now you have looked to the world to tell you what your Purpose is. You thought that it was in a relationship, or a child, or a job. You went on an outward search for something that can be found only within, which is why the search took so long. It's why you came up empty-handed again and again.

Hopefully, as you did the work of *separating* in the first part of this book, you began to see that just because life was the way that it was doesn't mean that it has to be that way moving forward.

As you move forward today to discover your Purpose, keep in mind that your old behaviors, stories, emotions, and beliefs can creep back into the mix. Why? Because as we begin to discover your Purpose, our old way of thinking will be challenged, which can be scary. And when you're scared, you may find it easy to fall back on the old SPs you put in place to keep you safe. The best things you can do about this is to be aware and try to catch yourself when it happens.

As I explained yesterday, your Purpose, in its simplest form, is emotion. Emotion is what creates life. The emotion of Love is the evolutionary impulse of your Soul. When you tap into, understand, and own the emotions you want to feel, life opens up. You find yourself on a path of synchronicity, and what seem like miracles start to happen—not because this is magic, but because when your life matches the beat of your Soul, and hence the beat of The Universe, so much more is possible. And because your Purpose is ultimately *an emotion that you generate within yourself and give away to the world*, your transformation has to happen in a somatic, emotional way.

What I've found with my clients is that even though the peak experiences of their lives vary as they get older, the emotions underlying each experience tend to remain the same. What do I mean? A peak experience for a child may be going to Disneyland or playing with friends in the backyard. A peak experience for someone in their 20s may be starting a career or falling in love. These are different experiences, but the *emotional content* is the same. The emotions the person wishes to feel, whether in childhood or as an adult, tend to remain the same.

I've found that based on our upbringing, belief system, and specific needs, each of us has a unique type of emotion we wish to feel. Getting the emotion right is important, but don't worry too much about this. All emotions have value if you are open to the messages they bring.

Experiencing positive emotion means that you are aligned with your Soul.

Experiencing negative emotion is a call to change a limiting belief and associated behavior.

As we step forward today, I'm asking you to let go of the need to get it perfect and do your best to avoid falling back into the old patterns that we've already brought to light.

Understanding what creates the peak experiences of your life, which happen when you are aligned with your Purpose, is rather simple. But, as I've said before, please do not confuse simple with easy. Living your Purpose is difficult because it will, at first, turn your world upside down.

Small Things Matter Most

To discover your Purpose, all you have to do is look back on your life and remember the moments that made you feel like you had come alive. Here's what's true: after taking thousands of people through this process, I've found most people's happiest memories aren't about significant moments like a big pay day, getting an award, or being named best in class. Usually they are gentle memories where the small things mattered most, such as a loving embrace by their mother at a picnic. Driving and laughing with parents. Playing in the pool with friends. The way he or she looked at you for the first time in a relationship. It's the small stuff that adds up over time to create the big stuff.

You've been given clues your whole life as to what your Purpose is. The problem is that without any education on the matter, you may not have realized how important those small moments were. You may have thought of them as nothing more than happy memories from the "good ol' days," rather than clues to what your life was really meant to be.

Some of my happiest memories involve being picked up by my parents from kindergarten and realizing the car was packed and ready to go. They'd surprised me with a road trip to my grandparents' house. I had a sense of positive expectation. I felt loved and connected because we were a family unit.

Another happy memory is my first date with Jenna up on the Observatory in Los Angeles overlooking the city. I felt a sense of peace and connection, finding someone I loved from the moment I met her.

Or being in Bali, immersed in the sacred water of the Holy Water Temple. As soon as I descended into the water, this sense of peace and belonging came over me. There was no pomp and circumstance. It was just a moment, a moment that meant so much to me.

When I look back at my memories, it's all about belonging and feeling connected to a power greater than me. That's what I want you to focus on when reviewing your memories too.

I know that the idea of discovering your Purpose can feel larger than life. It can feel like something so big it's impossible. Today we are taking just one small step in that direction.

This day's exercises are a little more complex than the others because Purpose is a multilayered topic. It's easy to get overwhelmed, so if you start feeling this way, simply notice it and let it go. Then remind yourself that all you have to do today is go back through your life and remember your happiest moments. That doesn't sound so hard, does it?

They don't have to be perfect memories. It might even seem as if you are making some of them up. It doesn't matter. Your job is to get out of your own way and trust the process.

Also know that they don't have to be the earliest memories you're able to dig up. As you're working through this, you may remember things you've forgotten for decades. But that doesn't mean you have to go back through this process and start over.

Repeat after me: "I trust the process and will get out of my own way!"

One more time: "I trust the process and will get out of my own way!"

Okay, great. Now let's dive in.

Step 1: Breathe

The first thing I'd like you to do is connect with your Heart Breath. You are going to want to do this in a sacred or private place.

Start by placing your hand over your Heart and closing your eyes. Then just breathe.

As you breathe, bring your attention to your chest and to your Heart. Continue this way for 10 minutes. If your mind wanders, simply bring it back to your Heart.

Step 2: Remember

When 10 minutes are up, open your eyes and take a moment to check in with yourself. How are you feeling? Do not judge or worry about how you are feeling. Just notice and allow.

Now close your eyes again and ask yourself, "What is the earliest, happiest memory I can remember?" Accept the first memory that comes to mind.

Just ask yourself the question and listen for the answer.

Step 3: Write It Down

Whatever memory comes to mind, write it down in your journal. Then answer the questions that follow.

My earliest, happy memory is:

Who was in this memory?

What did I believe about life in that moment?

Take a moment to sit with this memory and think about how it makes you feel to recall it.

Step 4: Repeat

Close your eyes and ask yourself, "What is my next happiest memory?"

You may want to ask yourself the question more than once, and then listen for the answer. Again, go with whatever memory comes to mind. It could be anything—a thought, a feeling, an image . . . anything. It also doesn't necessarily have to be in chronological order from what you listed as your earliest happy memory. When you have something in mind that feels good, write it down.

My second happy memory is:

Who was in this memory?

What did I believe about life in that moment?

Now notice how you feel after going back to just these two happy memories. Let the memories flood your body with emotion—happy, sad, nostalgic, and so on. Give yourself full permission to feel whatever comes. Don't hold back; bring the emotion forward.

Step 5: Repeat

Close your eyes and ask yourself again, "What is my next happiest memory?"

Go through the same process as before. When you have something in mind, write it down.

My third happy memory is:

Who was in this memory?

What did I believe about life in this moment?

Now, with your first, second, and third memories in mind, take a moment to comprehend the fact that life has not been all bad. We tend to focus on the negative, which is an SP that keeps us dead, but there has been good in your life too. There has been joy.

Allow yourself to feel, throughout your whole body, the feelings these memories bring up for you.

We are almost there. Just two more memories to uncover.

Step 6: Repeat

Close your eyes and ask yourself again, "What's my next happy memory?"

Really allow yourself to trust what comes, and do your best to *feel* the answer rather than to think it. After you've thought of your fourth memory, fill in the blanks.

My fourth happy memory is:

Who was in this memory?

What did I believe about life in this moment?

Allow yourself to consider all four memories that you've had up until now. Bring your first memory to mind, pause for a moment, and allow yourself to feel it. Bring your second memory to mind and allow yourself to feel it. Do the same with your third and your fourth. Really try to see all the people, places, and experiences, and consider the feelings inherent in these memories.

You have been blessed, and there are more blessings to come. We are going to use these memories to uncover the emotions that bring you your greatest joy. Then we are going to design a life in which the emotions that these memories bring up become your new normal.

The love and joy you feel when you remember fond memories is what it is like to be connected with your Soul. Connecting to the emotions of your Soul is what creates Heaven on earth.

Don't worry if that seems impossible right now. Just go with the process. We have one more memory to uncover.

Step 7: One More Time

I'd like you to think about your most recent happy memory. Remember, the memory can be something quite simple.

Close your eyes and ask yourself, "What is my most recent happy memory?" Then listen for the answer. When it comes, fill in the blanks.

My most recent happy memory is:

Who was in this memory?

What did I believe about life in this moment?

After you've written down your most recent happy memory, close your eyes and take five minutes to think about all the memories we just discovered and feel what comes up for you. Allow all the memories, and the emotions that go with them, to flood your body and mind. Take time to focus on the joy from the past, and let this joy be amplified throughout your whole body.

Don't think about any other memories from the past. Don't think about the future. Let your stress go. Just focus on these five awesome memories for five minutes and review the blessings in them. Give yourself the gift of emotionally connecting with your Soul, perhaps for the first time in a long while.

Your Emotional Blueprint

The next thing we're going to do today is to discover your emotional blueprint. In connecting with the emotions of your Soul, you can take your power back. In order to truly claim your power, you have to understand what I call your "emotional blueprint." That is to say, let's find out what emotions really light you up and make you want to jump out of bed every morning.

As I said before, over the course of your life, the emotions you seek tend to remain the same. When you look back over the five memories we just discovered together, you will notice that each memory is different. As you got older, your life changed and the external circumstances that made you happy also changed. But the emotions you desire have remained the same over the course of your life.

Why? Because you have an emotional blueprint that is running the show.

When my clients first find out they have an emotional blueprint, they are often confused. If you feel the same way, don't worry. Just stick with me, and you will find clarity in no time.

Discovering your emotional blueprint will simplify your life and bring it into laser focus. When we're done, your emotional blueprint will be the lens through which you look at the world, and the foundation that informs all your choices.

At first it will also scare you. That's okay. New ideas can be scary, but trust me—what's waiting for you on the other side is worth the courage you will need to get there.

To begin to understand your emotional blueprint, let's start by listing your five memories again here (this time in chronological order).

Memory #1:

Memory #2:

Memory #3:

Memory #4:

Most recent happy memory:

The aim now is to discover the emotions behind each memory. So think about Memory #1 and then ask yourself, "What was I feeling during this moment?" Ask yourself that question over and over again, and then note every feeling that comes to mind. Don't hold back. Write them down in your journal, and then do the same for your other four memories.

Emotions from Memory #1:

Emotions from Memory #2:

Emotions from Memory #3:

Emotions from Memory #4:

Emotions from most recent happy memory:

When you look at the five lists you made, you will see that there are many similar emotions contained within each memory. We are getting closer to discovering what makes you tick and the core essence of why you were born.

The next thing we have to do is pull them together into a master list. In your journal, please write out all the different emotions from all your memories in a numbered list under the header: Master List of Emotions.

Primary Emotions

After working with thousands of folks from all over the world, I've found that there are two primary emotions that, when felt or experienced, make all other emotions possible. Without these primary emotions, the rest will not emerge. You can think about them as the foundation on which your life is built.

If you don't believe in or can't imagine ever feeling these emotions again, then you will have a bleak view of life. If you believe that something or someone else has to give you these emotions, instead of creating them for yourself each and every day, then you cannot fully live your Purpose.

Let's discover your primary emotions. Look back at your Master List of Emotions and ask yourself which emotion you would rather feel, #1 or #2? For example, here's my list from the first time I did this exercise:

1. Love

2. Belonging

3. Connection

4. Joy

5. Excitement

6. Passion

7. Positive anticipation

8. Togetherness

I start at the top and ask myself, "Which would I rather feel, love or belonging?" My answer is belonging.

Then I ask myself, "Which would I rather feel, belonging or connection?" My answer is connection.

Then I ask myself, "Which would I rather feel, connection or joy?" My answer is connection.

After that, I keep going down the list, and "connection" wins each time, so my first primary emotion is connection.

I go through the process again to find my second primary emotion, which happens to be belonging. So my two primary emotions are belonging and connection.

Now it's time to find yours. Once you've done this, write them here:

Primary Emotion #1:

Primary Emotion #2:

Your primary emotions can change over time. Better to say that they can be refined over time. My first primary emotion used to be connection, but after a few years I had a breakthrough and it changed to wanting to feel as if I matter. I realized that I didn't feel that way, and the only way for me to "feel like I mattered" was to matter to myself. I realized that the choices I make matter, the decisions I make matter, and the impact I can have on others after this realization matters very much. Of course, connection is still on my Master List of Emotions, but it's no longer one of the two primary ones.

It's also important to note that your initial primary emotion might be the exact opposite from your SP. If your initial primary emotion is freedom, your SP could be perfectionism, which is a cage. These are polar opposites. So whatever your pattern is, most likely your top emotion will be the opposite of that, which is why you'll feel as though you're turning your life right side up (not upside down). And that's why it is a lot of work. And that's why you need consistent reminding.

My initial top emotion was connection, and that wasn't a common experience for me—I had the opposite experience. To feel a connection, I had to come face-to-face with self-worth issues. This included spending money and time on myself and setting boundaries for what I need, including asking for what I need.

That said, don't worry about getting this exercise perfect. We are creating a living, breathing document that can change over time.

Your Purpose Statement

We're almost done! Now we get to create your Purpose Statement. When you figure out your Purpose Statement, it should feel as if you are coming home or like a huge hug, and somewhere inside yourself you will know that this is what you've been looking for all along.

You may find yourself reading your Purpose Statement, feeling excited, and then immediately wondering, *Okay, but how will I get there?* Don't worry. The rest of this book shows you how. For now just enjoy the moment.

Here is a basic template for your Purpose Statement:

I was born to _____ myself and my Higher Power, and feel the _____ that results while inspiring others do feel the same.

Everyone's Purpose Statement has the same structure. What's unique are the emotions that go in the blank spaces. All you have to do is write your first primary emotion in the first blank space and your second primary emotion in the second blank space.

Yup, it's that simple. (Remember: *simple but not easy.*) As an example, here's my Purpose Statement:

The Purpose of my life is to <u>matter</u> to myself and to my Higher Power, and feel the <u>connection</u> that results while inspiring others to do the same.

When I read my Purpose Statement, I can feel the *yes* inside my body. My Soul knows that this is the truth. Now it's your turn.

Write Out Your Purpose Statement:

The Purpose of my life is to _____ myself and my Higher Power, and feel the _____ that results while inspiring others do feel the same.

Congratulations! You have taken a huge step toward claiming your power! In the following chapters, I'll show you how to bring your Purpose to life. Before I do, I want to get real about why you haven't until now.

The next few chapters are going to turn your life upside down, and that's okay. And the next few steps are going to be massive leaps toward understanding why your life was dead and how to make it come alive again.

Stay with me; it's just starting to get interesting! Let's move forward with faith.

Today's affirmation: I choose to embody my Purpose from now on.

Today's prayer: Dear Creator, thank You for reminding me of what I already knew. Thank You for showing me the way home to You and to why I was born. Please help me live Your Purpose in my life, help me remove the blocks to my Purpose, and give me eyes to see that my work ahead is Your work. I surrender all to You. And today I am grateful for Your Love.

DAY 13:
WHY YOUR PURPOSE HAS EVADED YOU

"'I shall no longer be instructed by the Yoga Veda
or the Aharva Veda, or the ascetics, or any other
doctrine whatsoever. I shall learn from myself,
be a pupil of myself; I shall get to know myself,
the mystery of Siddhartha.' He looked around as
if he were seeing the world for the first time."

– HERMANN HESSE

Before we can bring your Purpose to life, we've got to get honest and ask: *Why have you not lived your Purpose until now?*

This is not a shaming session. This is not a beat-up-on-yourself moment. It's a reality check.

You see, we've all been hurt. We've all had our traumas and OIs. Why then, as Tony Robbins teaches, do some people experience post-traumatic stress and others post-traumatic growth? Why can some people go through the darkest experiences that life has to offer and come out fully realized, while others who have been given every advantage wither?

Life is not about the external. Hear me when I say this: *Your external world is a reflection of your internal world.* And the external world around us is a reflection of our collective internal worlds.

When you start to realize that your Soul chose this life and its traumas before your birth, you can begin to find meaning in the hurt. That is a bold statement. The idea that you chose this life before you got here pisses a lot of people off. But remember, you've got to start looking at life with new eyes, from a new perspective, in order to grow.

The good news is that you are more powerful than you realize. Life is malleable. Circumstances can change. You can change. Circumstances do not define you; they show you what you believe.

Much of this book is designed to help you become aware of and transform your beliefs. The reason why this is so hard is twofold:

1. We are scared to feel our feelings.

2. We are scared to change our beliefs.

I've worked with all kinds of people. Veterans. Single moms. Hollywood producers. Actors. Therapists. Psychiatrists. Athletes. Coaches. Entrepreneurs. All sorts of everyday people looking to unlock their dormant potential. As far as I can tell, no matter who a person is or what they have done, we are all afraid of change.

We've all had our traumas. We are designed to survive. As a result, until we are taught otherwise, we allow our survival impulses to run our lives. The problem is the part of us that is wired for survival is horrible at creating beliefs that help us grow.

It's like allowing the tail to wag the dog, or the child to be the parent. We've got to take control of our meanings and learn the lessons from our negative emotions. We must celebrate the fact that we've survived until now, pat ourselves on the back for coping with our lot in life, and then focus on gaining forward momentum, in spite of our fears.

Change is uncertain, and our brains are designed to create certainty as a survival skill. When it comes to feeling your feelings and changing your beliefs, you're going to get a ton of resistance from your survival responses.

It will sound like this: "Yeah, but," "You've always," "Last time," "Dad says," "Mom says," "The reason why this won't work is," and so on.

As we continue through this process, notice when those kinds of stories come up. They are just trying to keep you safe, but that is not our aim.

When you begin to create a new life, you consciously invoke uncertainty into your life. This makes the Soul happy and the brain scared. The survival part of you is going to want to defend your old limiting beliefs and not feel your negative emotions. And yet that is our work.

In Search of a Soul Connection

Why haven't you lived your Purpose until now? It's simple: you have been scared to change because change feels like death. So instead you went out in search of an external something or someone to fill the void.

The problem is that the external world will never satisfy you. What you're really looking for is a connection to your Soul. What you are looking for is a profound, deep, and intimate relationship with yourself and your Creator. When you find this, you will show up in the world in a new way.

Let's find out where you've looked externally for what can be found only internally. Begin by going back to your Purpose Statement. You will notice that your Purpose Statement has three parts to it. The first part is you. The second part is your Higher Power. And the third part is others. We'll dive deeply into each of these in the coming chapters, but for now just notice these three parts. Then say your Purpose Statement out loud *four times*. As you do so, think about truly loving yourself, truly loving your Creator, and truly loving others.

Now let's explore the areas of your life that aren't working. This is another time for radical honesty. Don't BS yourself. Don't BS me. Total truth, okay?

Following is a list of different areas of your life. I want you to give each one a ranking, 1 through 10, based on how well you feel each area of your life is working right now. The number 1 is rock bottom and 10 is out-of-your-mind joyful:

Physical Health and Wellness

Romantic Life

Career/Vocation

Spirituality

Family and Friends

Self-care

Time

Emotions

Beliefs

For any area of your life that you've ranked below an 8, please grab your journal and write down the stories you've told yourself about why this area of your life isn't at a higher level. Also write any behaviors you would like to change in this area of your life.

Physical Health and Wellness

Romantic Life

Career/Vocation

Spirituality

Family and Friends

Self-care

Time

Emotions

Beliefs

Now, look back at your two primary emotions and list them again here.

Primary Emotion #1:

Primary Emotion #2:

Make a list of the external sources you've expected to fulfill these emotions in each area of your life.

So, if your first primary emotion is love, who or what did you look to outside yourself to provide you with love in each of these areas?

Physical Health and Wellness

Romantic Life

Career/Vocation

Spirituality

Family and Friends

Self-care

Time

Emotions

Beliefs

How did you give your power to love yourself away?

If your second primary emotion is connection, who or what did you expect to provide you with a sense of connection in each of these areas?

Remember, *your Purpose is an emotion that you generate and give away to the world*. If you are not at an 8 or higher, then you are not living your Purpose (i.e., generating emotions) in that area of your life. You have given away your power to a person or a thing that you think will bring you that emotion, but that will always come up short. As a result, you live your life in emotional debt and blame others for your plight.

Most people understand what it feels like to be in debt, to feel powerless, and to experience the weight and stress of that. Imagine being in financial debt and being powerless to change it. The bank can decide whether you're happy or not. Emotions work the same way. Being in emotional debt means you think something (or someone) else, somewhere outside you, is in control of how you feel. It could be the government, your parents, your child, money, or your circumstances.

We want to live an emotionally rich life. We want to be generative in the creation of the emotions we want. Being emotionally wealthy is the bedrock of a happy life.

So all those years we've spent in emotional debt—that stops now. Again, it's honesty time.

Where in your life have you been trying to take or consume emotions from the world, rather than creating them yourself? Fill in the blanks in your journal for any areas that totaled 7 or below.

Area:

Old limiting story:

Old limiting behavior:

I was consuming emotions from:

Area:

Old limiting story:

Old limiting behavior:

I was consuming emotions from:

Area:

Old limiting story:

Old limiting behavior:

I was consuming emotions from:

Area:

Old limiting story:

Old limiting behavior:

I was consuming emotions from:

Area:

Old limiting story:

Old limiting behavior:

I was consuming emotions from:

For now, we are focused on becoming aware of the old stories, old behaviors, and the fact that you've been consuming rather than generating the emotions you want. In the coming days, we will start to chip away at the validity of the limiting stories and behaviors in the areas that need the most work.

Walking through the Doorway of Purpose

You know what's fascinating? I've found the areas that bring you closer to your Purpose are those where you tend to find the most resistance and dissatisfaction. So if you have certain areas of your life that need a lot of work, rejoice! Those tend to be where your greatest growth potential dwells.

In other words: *The area of your greatest frustration is the doorway to your Purpose.*

It's common at this point in your journey to want to beat yourself up for making mistakes and having areas of your life that you're so dissatisfied with. That's a normal and natural response, but here's the thing: when you beat yourself up, when you're hard on yourself, that is more defensive behavior that keeps you dead. Beating yourself up is another SP that must stop. When you are kind to yourself, you open the doorway to transformation.

Let's create a new paradigm. Let's celebrate the fact that you're learning all this new stuff about yourself. With this new awareness comes incredible power. You are taking your power back from the world and gaining the ability to radically, massively, and powerfully change your life . . . forever.

That deserves celebration!

The process you're going through right now is one that many people avoid, which is why they remain dead. But that's not you. You are a committed seeker. You are one of the few who will stay with this process, even when it gets hard, because you know in your Soul that now is the time. You know that if you don't do it now, you'll have to do it later, so you might as well keep up the good work.

Tomorrow we have some real talk about courage and breaking your Purpose wide-open. But for today, just celebrate how far you've already come.

Today's affirmation: I choose to celebrate all the new awareness in my life.

Today's prayer: Dear Creator, thank You for helping me come this far. I know that You have led me to this moment, to this awareness, and to this day where I can begin to see why and where I've been dead in my life. Help me forgive myself. Help me love myself as You Love me. Show me Your Grace in all my mistakes and help me understand that all I've been through has been a perfect part of Your Divine plan for me. I surrender the outcome of tomorrow to You and trust the unfolding of Your wisdom in my life.

DAY 14:
FINDING THE COURAGE TO CHANGE—NOW

"God, grant me the serenity to accept the things
I cannot change, courage to change the things I can,
and wisdom to know the difference."

– REINHOLD NIEBUHR

The prayer that starts this chapter is well known. It has been said countless times, possibly by you. The thing is, when something is so well known, it can begin to lose its meaning. Even so, this prayer is perhaps one of the most powerful that has ever been said. It's full of wisdom and can literally take a lifetime to embody.

If you read quickly through it, I'd like to encourage you to go back and read it again. This time read the words slowly and really try to absorb the wisdom in them.

Courage is a virtue. It's one of Plato's four cardinal virtues, which are qualities one needs to live a Purpose-driven life—a life where you know your power and live inside it.

I would go a step further and say that courage is *the* cardinal virtue of all virtues. Without courage, living a Purpose-driven life is impossible. Courage is the virtue that makes all other virtues possible. Without courage you can't embody Plato's three other virtues, which are wisdom, temperance, and justice—and you certainly won't be able to live your Purpose.

The quality of our lives is directly related to how well we confront fear, manage uncertainty, and have faith when all seems lost. To be human means acknowledging that we are limited in our understanding of this life and that most of life is filled with massive uncertainty. Living with, embracing, and coming to terms with uncertainty will bring you tremendous peace. It will also be the cornerstone of claiming your power.

Put your faith in the hands of God and then let go of the outcome.

Embracing Surrender

The areas of your life where you are the most dead are also the areas of your life where you have the least courage and the least faith in God.

You may trust your Creator in other areas of your life, but not when it comes to the big stuff, not the stuff that matters most. You like to stay in control there, don't you? It's okay; we all do this at one time or another. But it's when we make the courageous leap to let our Souls drive the ship that we experience the ultimate control. That is when we allow the spark of God within us to lead us toward our destiny.

You can surrender your parking spot, your gas bill, or your space in yoga class to your Creator, but what about the big stuff?

Your romantic life. Can you surrender it?

Your financial life. Can you surrender it?

The need to control those you love. Can you surrender it?

The need for others' approval. Can you surrender it?

Your new business idea. Can you surrender it?

The need to share your pain, trauma, and experiences with the world. Can you surrender it?

The outcome of an illness. Can you surrender it?

Remember, surrendering doesn't mean giving up. It means *giving in* to a Higher Power. You can tell when you have truly surrendered in a certain area of your life because, even though you might be scared, you also feel a certain level of peace. Your beliefs change from "This will take 10 years to happen" to "With God anything is possible—I am open and available for an immediate answer to my prayer."

The scary but real truth about life is that you can't control most of it. All you can control is the meaning you give to the events. Everything else is out of your hands. No one you admire has total control of their existence. Those who have found their Purposes have found the sweet spot between outward attempts to make things happen and the Divine surrender of the outcome to God.

When you live on Purpose, you pay attention to the inner nudges that say, "Let go," or "Try again," or "You can do this." This puts you in a flow with your Creator, rather than in the flow of your fears.

To live your Purpose is to intentionally live out your Creator's will in your life. When things go wrong or don't happen as quickly as you would like them to, it's not punishment. It's a growth process. All dreams need a gestation period. One of the best interpretations I've ever heard about why things can take so long came from Reverend Michael Beckwith, who said, "A delay is not a denial."[7]

That is a great meaning to choose today.

It doesn't matter if you feel as though you've heard some of what you are reading before. It doesn't matter if you've tried to live your Purpose a million times before and it hasn't worked out. It doesn't matter if you think it will never happen.

Why? *Because your Creator has even greater things in store for you than you can imagine.*

Years ago, when I was still deep in the music business, I asked a girl for her number at a conference. Instead, she gave me a CD set called *Energy Anatomy* by Caroline Myss. I kept it in my backseat for a while. It wasn't until I had about 20 hours of drive time over four days, driving to and from shows, that I remembered the CD set.

I can recall feeling blame around how my jobs in the music industry had ended. I felt abandoned and rejected and angry. And I had this big chip on my shoulder. Caroline's message was tough love, and I needed that. She talked about how the most important power we have is the idea of choice. And if I wanted to harness the power of my soul, I needed to learn how to love myself and develop self-esteem. It was such a simple idea, but one I'd never thought about because I was always focused on other people.

While I wasn't doing drugs anymore, I was still drinking heavily and I'd had so much the night before at a Nine Inch Nails concert that I was still hungover. I felt bloated, dehydrated, and awful. I knew I had to stop.

When I got home, I got a napkin and I wrote a letter. I told myself how I deserved more and I was worth more than this, and I signed it "Love, Yourself." It was the first real step I took in acknowledging that I had to take better care of myself. It was the first awareness that I mattered, and it felt right. It was progress, and it was introduced to me in an unlikely and unexpected way.

Progress has never been limited to the constraints or timelines of the human mind or human logic. Progress is made by those who keep trying, who keep going. Breakthrough happens just after you want to give up. But giving up is not going to happen this time.

You are on a path to living and expressing your true Purpose in the world. What's so great is that this is not a selfish act. We must begin to see this process as about more than just you. Yes, you are on this journey

---

7   Michael Bernard Beckwith, *The Answer Is You: Waking up to Your True Potential*, Audiobook, Sounds True, Incorporated (December 28, 2010).

to change your life, but once you've changed your life, then what? Then you must begin to link your Purpose with others. I will talk more about how to do this in the next chapter, but you can start asking yourself now: Who or what else will you live your Purpose for?

When you step bravely and courageously into your Purpose, you will positively change the lives of others. Yes, *you* can change the lives of others. You have that potential, and if you are reading this book, it is inevitable.

Who Else Are You Doing This For?

Who else are you doing this for from now on? Your family? Your children? Your employees? Your Creator? People you haven't even met yet? Are you doing it for the less fortunate? Are you doing it for all those who still suffer?

I'm constantly trying to be a better man for Jenna. I also think about my clients. Any time I want to stop, I think about any woman whose been sexually traumatized and I know that if I stop doing my work, perhaps she won't get the help she needs. I want to be the best I can be so I can give my best to others.

Yes, you are changing your life so you can respect yourself again and love yourself again, in order to step into the highest and best version of you. But once you do that, you will be able to serve others in a greater capacity.

Let's identify who or what you want to serve with your Purpose. Think about whose life you are going to change because you are changing, and write down the answer to the following question in your journal:

Beyond myself, who am I going to serve?

Awesome. Now, one last item to cover today.

Courage counts most when your butt is on the line. Courage is about taking action even though you are afraid. You need courage the most when the pressure is on.

To help you find and keep courage when you need it most, in your journal, list three times in the past when you've chickened out—when you let fear stop you. When you were so close to the finish line and yet you gave up.

The good news is that you are now finding your courage. The not-so-good news is that some version of what you previously listed will happen again. And when it does, you will be able to catch yourself in the act of Purpose sabotage.

Why do you sabotage? Because you want to stay safe. But you know better now. Safety is not what matters most. What matters most is obedience to your Purpose.

So the next time you're too scared to keep going, remember that fear is a good sign, a sign that you are living your Purpose. It's a sign to keep going. And pretty soon you won't know what you were so scared of.

Today's affirmation: I choose courage today. I am ready for growth!

Today's prayer: Dear Creator, comfort me when I am scared. Help me see Your hand in all the challenges and uncertainty of my life. Guide my choices. Guide my words. Guide my thoughts. Guide my actions. Guide my outcomes. I surrender the whole of my life to You. All finances. All relationships. All desires. All hopes. All dreams. All drama. All my affairs. They are Yours to handle from now on. Help me change what I can and accept what I cannot. Show me how to change my thoughts about what's happening when I can no longer change my circumstances. I am Your obedient servant. Fill my life with Your presence.

DAY 15:
YOUR POWER HIERARCHY

"I used to spend so much time reacting and responding to everyone else that my life had no direction. Other people's lives, problems, and wants set the course for my life. Once I realized it was okay for me to think about and identify what I wanted, remarkable things began to take place in my life."

– UNKNOWN

Today, we take a big step. We are going to dive into how you have let the world take away your power.

Let's start by getting clear about some things. Repeat after me:

Choosing to be happy, healthy, and free is not selfish.
Loving myself is not selfish.
Setting boundaries is not selfish.
It's not my job to be the fixer of everyone in my life.

You see, you've unconsciously put your dreams on hold by trying to take care of everyone else. Don't beat yourself up. We've all done it.

We love who we love. And it's much easier for us to try to save the people we love than it is to claim our own power. Taking care of everyone else has been a safer path than stepping into the uncertainty of being ourselves. But it's time to start thinking differently. So, once again, repeat after me:

I am allowed to be who I really am.
I am allowed to play big.
I am allowed to live big.
I am allowed to love big.

This new hierarchy is going to trigger your old trauma and SPs, so watch out for that. Don't make the trauma bigger. Make it smaller. Speak forward in what you want and let go. There's also a pattern that says, "I already did the work, so I shouldn't have to do *more* work." But life is work, isn't it?

In case you forgot, my friend, you are meant to live a big life. You are meant to rise above your SPs and step into a richer, deeper, and much more peaceful version of life. You are here to wake up, to crack open, and to fill yourself up with love—so much love that you are overflowing with it and can easily give it away to others.

But that's not how things have been. You've spent so much time helping others that you are empty. You are not sure who to trust. You feel depleted, and perhaps you don't really trust life to take care of the new person you are becoming. You've only gotten your needs met by putting yourself last. You're not entirely sure that you can get your needs met with self-love and self-care.

You don't yet trust life to support a more powerful version of you.

Your needs will be met. Abundantly met, in fact. Your Soul is meant to live a bigger life than you've been living, and your Creator is ready, willing, and able to support you in any size dream that you have.

But you have to be willing to do the work. You have to find the courage to claim your power and then dedicate yourself to a new way of being. It's your job to step out in faith and allow the miracles to show up. The miracles won't show up if you are playing small. You have no idea the wonder that awaits you on the other side of believing in yourself.

A Healthy Balance

There are many misconceptions in the spiritual and religious worlds about where you, our Creator, and others fit. Most of us have been raised to put God first. This is a widely accepted notion. We've also been taught that it is a good and highly spiritual thing to put others first, to serve others.

The problem is, I've meet countless people who have put their Creator and others first but lost themselves. We need to take another look at what is healthy and actually in alignment with God's will.

Our Creator's will is for us to be fulfilled. We don't get any special spiritual brownie points for suffering more than necessary. Fulfillment comes as a result of taking risk, of being vulnerable, and of braving the storm. You cannot stay the same and feel fulfilled. You must take courageous action outside your comfort zone and let the chips fall where they may.

If you're waiting around for the courage to come so that you can take the leap, you'll be waiting the rest of your life. Create the courage yourself, now, by taking the leap, even though you don't feel fully prepared.

But how?

For the answer, we don't have to look any further than two of our greatest spiritual teachers, who set perfect examples for us to live by.

The Obedience of Jesus Christ

My personal role model is Jesus Christ. His life was lived powerfully, and He shows us how we can live our life by His example.

In my last book, *Daily Love: Growing into Grace*, I wrote about one of my favorite scenes in the Bible. Some call it the "Agony in the Garden" moment. It's the night before Jesus is to be crucified, and He is in the Garden of Gethsemane. He is praying to the Creator to save Him from crucifixion. Jesus knows what's about to happen—imminent painful death.

All Jesus's disciples fall asleep, and only Jesus is left to carry the heavy burden and fear of His own death. In that moment, Jesus is not concerned with what others think. He isn't asking John, Matthew, Luke, or the others what He should do and then going with the group consensus. Jesus has tapped into God's Higher Wisdom and power, and He doesn't need the group's consent to live His Purpose. It comes from within.

Jesus followed the wisdom placed in His own Heart above the thoughts and opinions of the world, even His closest disciples. Christ was obedient, and in being so, He changed the world forever.

You have that power too.

Jesus's courage is widely known. What's not often talked about is what Jesus did to claim His power and thus fulfill His Purpose. Here's what happened—pay attention:

> Then Jesus went with them to a place called Gethsemane, and he said to his disciples, "Sit here, while I go over there and pray." And taking with him Peter and the two sons of Zebedee, he began to be sorrowful and troubled. Then he said to them, "My soul is very sorrowful, even to death; remain here, and watch with me." And going a little farther he fell on his face and prayed, saying, "My Father, if it be possible, let this cup pass from me; nevertheless, not as I will, but as you will." (Matthew 26:36–39)

Notice that in His powerful prayer, Jesus said, "Not as I will, but as You will."

This is the example we must follow, but it's not the example that we've been sold by modern Christianity. Yes, it is vital to align with the will of our Creator. However, there is one important distinction that I want to bring to your awareness, and I'll do it with a question.

Following the will of a spiritual teacher is not following God's will. God, the Holy Spirit, your Soul speaks to you through your own Heart. So did God make Jesus surrender, or did Jesus *choose to turn His will over to His Creator's will*?

In the face of supreme sorrow, in the face of death, Jesus made a courageous choice to allow the will of the Creator to be His action.

Jesus claimed His power. He *chose* to surrender His will to the will of the Creator. Jesus showed us that the only power we can truly claim is our power to follow God's will, and that without that, we have no power of our own. Jesus signed up for pain, knowing it was the greater choice to make.

Jesus's example shows us the way. Your power is not simply in your Creator. Your power is certainly not in others. Your power is in your ability to make conscious choices. You, my friend, get to choose.

The most powerful choice you can make, in every moment, is to line up with your Creator's will, with your Purpose, with why you were born.

By His example, Jesus shows us the Hierarchy of Power.

1. Self

2. Creator

3. Others

You might be surprised to see "Self" listed above "Creator," but as you'll see, this hierarchy is evident in even biblical examples and other religious texts. I'll come back to this hierarchy in a moment, but first let me give you another example.

The Obedience of the Buddha

Buddha became enlightened under the Bodhi tree. Our Creator did not force him there. Buddha's followers did not suggest that he meditate there. This powerful action came from a deep knowing within.

Gautama the sage chose to sit under the Bodhi tree for 49 days. His companions left, but Gautama stayed. When Gautama awakened, he awakened as the Buddha.

The story of Buddha, like the "Agony in the Garden" story, shows us that there is tremendous power in our choice. Buddha made a conscious choice to remain under the Bodhi tree, to be obedient to a deeper knowing that that is where he should be, and that is what led to his enlightenment.

Modern Examples of the Power of Choice

Here's an example from modern times. Every 12-step program covers the same territory, and this same wisdom is found in Step 1: *To admit that you are powerless over your addiction.* Again, we see that it is *our choice to admit anything.*

Let's also look at quantum physics. Arthur Holly Compton, a Nobel Prize–winning physicist, has concluded the following about choice and free will:

> A set of known physical conditions is not adequate to specify precisely what a forthcoming event will be. These conditions, insofar as they can be known, define instead a range of possible events from among which some particular event will occur. When one exercises freedom, by his act of choice he is himself adding a factor not supplied by the physical conditions and is thus himself determining what will occur. That he does so is known only to the person himself. From the outside one can see in his act only the working of physical law. It is the inner knowledge that he is in fact doing what he intends to do that tells the actor himself that he is free.[8]

What do Jesus, Buddha, a 12-step program, and quantum physics have in common? They all demonstrate that we have far more power in our choices than we have previously given ourselves credit for.

Choice is the fundamental power of your life. When you wake up to the choices that you are making, you begin to claim your power.

---

8 "Arthur Holly Compton," *The Information Philosopher,* http://www.informationphilosopher.com/solutions/scientists/compton/.

You lost your power with a choice.

You claim your power with a choice.

This means that we must also wake up to the Hierarchy of Power. My hope is that you clearly understand by now that the power always has been and always will be with you. Your Creator will provide, bring miracles, and assist you. However, your Creator will never do for you what is meant for you to do. Other people are important to serve. However, if we serve them without any regard for ourselves, we will become lost, resentful, and bitter.

Here, now, we take our power back. Your healthy Hierarchy of Power is the following:

1. Self

2. Creator

3. Others

I can say with almost 100 percent certainty that this has not been your hierarchy. Most people choose to live according to an *unhealthy* Hierarchy of Power. Here are four of the most common hierarchies I've seen.

A.

1. Creator

2. Others

3. Self

B.

1. Others

2. Creator

3. Self

C.

1. Self

2. Self

3. Self

D.

    1.   Others

    2.   Others

    3.   Others

Let me show you what these look like in real life.

Hierarchy A

    1.   Creator

    2.   Others

    3.   Self

People living according to this hierarchy believe that their Creator is outside them. They have given their power away, usually to an institution or religion, which makes choices for them. They believe they are separate from their Creator's Grace and Love and must earn it back. These people tend to believe in original sin.

People with this consciousness wait around for their Creator to do things for them. When good things happen, their Creator is blessing them. When bad things happen, their Creator is punishing them. When the things they want don't happen for them, they say out of fear, "It wasn't meant to be," or "It's not God's will."

These people generally look to an authority figure who represents their Creator to give them approval to live their lives. When these people hear that their Creator resides within them, it scares them because this truth forces them to take responsibility for their choices.

Dogma and superstition rule this group. Rules rule this group.

Hierarchy B

    1.   Others

    2.   Creator

    3.   Self

This group is close to my heart. Before I started doing my own work to claim my power, I was in this group.

This group assigns Divine power to other people, thereby making them their Higher Power. This group is prone to guru worship and is full of love addicts. People who assign magical qualities to their romantic partners and expect them to save them and to always be perfect are in this group. They make their lovers into their Creator and always get let down when that illusion bursts.

Instead of waiting around for their Creator to tell them what to do through superstitious projections, this group lets other people make their choices for them. They bend to get the approval of others. This almost always ends with the person being filled with resentment and anger.

Hierarchy C

1. Self

2. Self

3. Self

Members of this group are called narcissists. The only thing that matters is them. They are the center of The Universe. They talk only about themselves and cannot perceive the experiences of others.

In relationships, these people consume 100 percent of the love, affection, and attention. They tend to get involved with people in group D.

Hierarchy D

1. Others

2. Others

3. Others

These people are also close to my heart. They are the codependents. They bend themselves. They save. They focus only on others. These people love people in group C.

Why? When life is all about the narcissists, codependents don't have to face their own pain. They are so busy saving others that they conveniently ignore themselves.

This is a safe way to live for a while. However, these people build up resentment and anger, which often turns into the opposite of the kindhearted presentation they started out with at the beginning of their relationship.

Gaining Clarity about Your Old Hierarchy

We all tend to assume one of these four hierarchies early in life. Why? Safety and survival.

The journey to claim your power is as simple (but not easy) as changing your hierarchy, rejecting whichever one of these it has been until now and choosing the healthy hierarchy instead.

The only problem is that this journey turns your life upside down. What was small is now huge. What was powerful is now insignificant. What was safe is now threatening. What was a threat is now the path that you must take.

Embodying a different hierarchy takes consistent work over time. So let our work begin. Please answer these questions.

1. What has your hierarchy been up until now?

2. What has this old hierarchy cost you (lost time, pain, opportunities, etc.)?

3. Where do you think you learned this old hierarchy?

4. What will your life look like 10 years from now if you keep this old hierarchy?

Take your time as you answer these questions. Today, all we do is step into a new awareness. Tomorrow we will dive deep into your old hierarchy and break it apart.

Today's affirmation: Today, I take back my power.

Today's prayer: Dear Creator, please show me healthy ways to claim my power. Aid me in my endeavor to love myself, follow Your will, and then serve others. Help me become aware of the old Survival Patterns™ that have kept me safe, stuck, and dead. Show me the grandness of Your will in my life. Help me learn that I am safe as I choose myself. Show me how to best direct my willpower and my choices so that I can come home to Your Grace. Show me right here, right now, that I am not alone. Show me how to claim my power, and then use me as You will. I am Your humble servant. Fill me with your Grace and power and allow me to be a guidepost for others.

DAY 16:
DECONSTRUCTING YOUR OLD HIERARCHY

"Your pain is the breaking of the shell that
encloses your understanding."

– KAHLIL GIBRAN

Simply put, the thing that has caused you pain and made you feel like you were dead is your old hierarchy. At its core, your old hierarchy represents all the ways in which you have given your power away.

To claim your power, we must first understand how you gave it away.

You cannot find your Soul "out there," so today we are going to explore your old hierarchy to create a new awareness and the space to welcome in a new hierarchy. Building on the work from Day 15, begin by answering the following questions in your journal:

1. List all the people, places, and things that you gave your power away to in your old hierarchy:

2. Why did you do this?

3. While you were giving your power away, what greater truth, dream, or outcome of your own were you hiding from?

4. What was your greatest fear about this truth, dream, or outcome?

We don't wake up each day and consciously say, "Today I'm going to give away my power." That's not how it works. We weren't trying to give away our power; we were trying to get Love. My friend and mentor Tony Robbins says, "Love is the oxygen of the Soul." We need Love, affection, and connection to survive, so as children, we learned how to adapt and change ourselves to fit our environment and have a better chance of getting Love from others. That is why your old hierarchy feels so familiar. It's how you fed your need for Love and connection up until now. The truth is that there is still a terrified child who's afraid he or she won't be loved, and this child is running the part of your life that you want to change most.

The way in which you've been doing things needs to change, so it's time for your hierarchy to change. Our job is to bring in the wiser part of you, the part that is now aware, forward and allow it to choose your reality.

Diving into Your Past

The first step is to delve even deeper into your past. Do your best to answer the following three questions in your journal, and we will begin to discover how you got your needs met in the past.

1. In the past, before the age of 10, whose love did you crave most—your mother's or your father's? (Not who was more important. We're not trying to pit Mom against Dad. We just want to do some digging. Trust your first hunch.)

2. In order to get love from this parent, who did you have to be? What did you have to do to get this love?

3. Who could you never be with this parent and still get this love? What behavior would the parent disapprove of or shun?

I've asked hundreds of clients this last question. Typically the answers I get sound something like this: I had to be perfect. I had to be seen and not heard. I had to get good grades. I had to do what I was told. I had to fit in and mold myself to how this parent wanted me to be.

In the most extreme cases—in cases of abuse—it wouldn't matter what the child did. He or she could never get it quite right.

In many single-parent homes, I've found that often a child who should have been nurtured by the parent instead had to become the parent.

I craved my mother's love most. She was bedridden and in pain my entire childhood because of a broken back and her addiction to pain medicine. We didn't find out until I was 30 years old that her pain was mostly caused and perpetuated by painkillers.

As a child, I didn't know this; I just knew my mom was always hurting. So I did whatever I could to make sure she was okay. I became very aware of what would cause her pain and what would help her come out of it. She was the main focus of both my and my father's attention. We couldn't speak up, be too loud, or show much emotion because that could cause my mom more pain. So I learned to stifle my emotions and make hers more important. I found "love" in food.

I freely admit that I would not be the man I am today without my amazing parents. Although they were not perfect, they played the perfect part in my life for me to become who I am. And knowing this hierarchy map, which I first learned from Tony Robbins, helped me gain immense understanding into my blueprint of the world. Knowing my blueprint allowed me to Claim My Power and paved the way for me to help you claim yours.

This isn't parent-bashing day; rather, it's a way to gain insight into who we molded ourselves to be as children, so that we can better understand our old hierarchies. Once you see where your old hierarchy came from, you will begin to understand why you are dead in certain areas of your life.

Persistent Patterns

Write down how these old patterns have shown up in the following areas of your life. Go back to your top two emotions and think about how you consumed these emotions from external sources in your life, rather than generated them from within.

Primary Emotion #1:

Primary Emotion #2:

Here are the areas to focus on:

1. Romantic Love

2. Health, Wellness, and Fitness

3. Business/Vocation/Job

4. Spirituality

5. Fun/Hobbies

6. Relationship to Money

Your parents are not necessarily bad people. Getting good grades was not a bad thing to want from you. What holds you back is thinking that you are defined by what you do instead of who you are. Who you are is far deeper and far greater than what you do or the grades you get.

Who you are is enough. You do not need to consume emotions from the world. You do not need to prove yourself to anyone. Rather, you get the awesome opportunity to turn your life around and be an example of a healthy person.

This day can be a heavy day. You may want to beat yourself up. You may feel like an idiot. But this is a day to celebrate. This is a day to know that you are growing and that you are getting on with your life.

This is a great day, even if it feels like a punch in the gut.

Be kind to yourself. As you contemplate the questions and answers on the previous pages, take it slow and know that tomorrow we are going to create your new hierarchy.

Tonight, reflect on your life and consider how this old hierarchy also served you. It kept you alive. You survived because of it. Well done! Now, we must let go of what no longer serves us and welcome in a new paradigm of being.

Today's affirmation: I celebrate all I've done, for it has made me who I am.

Today's prayer: Dear Creator, please help me be kind to myself. Help me see that everything happens in Divine time and that I do not need to rush this process. Allow me to understand Your timing, Your Grace, and Your will in my life. I surrender to what comes next, knowing that You walk with me at every step. Thank You for this new awareness. Thank You for this new understanding. I am ready to heal; I am ready to grow; I am ready to expand—lead the way.

DAY 17:
YOUR NEW HIERARCHY

"This new day is too dear, with its hopes and
invitations, to waste a moment on the yesterdays."

– RALPH WALDO EMERSON

Today is a new beginning that will create a subtle yet powerful shift in the direction of your life. Today we create the blueprint for you to find your Soul again.

Today is when many of your old behaviors, stories, emotions, and beliefs will raise their hands and try to convince you to stop. Don't listen to them. Thank them for sharing and move along.

Here's your new hierarchy.

1. Self

2. Creator

3. Others

Over the next few days, as we wrap up the Initiation phase of your journey, we will spend a day on each of the parts of this hierarchy. But before we do that, let's commit to this new hierarchy as a whole. Remember that your primary concern moving forward will be self-care. Self-care is not to be confused with narcissism or being selfish. What we're talking about here is taking care of you. And all that resentment, anger, and guilt from previous relationships or situations that didn't work out—yeah—we need to address that too in order to take your power back.

Remember, you have the power, and yet up until now you've made yourself unimportant. You've devalued yourself and your time, and it is you who must decide that you are ready to stop doing that. You must decide that you, not others, are worth more than you previously realized. This means setting boundaries. And this means committing to turning your life around and sticking with it for *at least six months*—not two weeks, not three months—to truly see the benefits.

We are also going to start creating or re-creating your relationship with your Creator. This does not necessarily mean going to church. Your spiritual practice is your own, but you must make a daily effort to cultivate a spiritual practice of some kind. I will make recommendations, but for now I want you to think about when you've felt most connected to your Creator. What has life been like? To feel connected to your Creator, to begin to develop a relationship with your Creator, that is a vital part of claiming your power.

Many New Age gurus say that you are the Divine. That you are God. That is true-*ish*. It is true that you are a drop of the Divine, a small piece of the larger whole. You came from and will return to your Creator.

You are like a drop of water. Without a relationship with your Creator, you are on your own and will dry up. But when you are connected to your Creator, like a drop of water connected to an ocean, you gain massive power.

You will no longer have to fight your way through but instead will be pulled by your Creator. You will no longer have to go it alone, even during the darkest moments of your life. If you look back with new eyes, you will see that you were never really alone anyway. Even when you felt that way, your Creator was with you, and you were guided.

Finally, after we learn to put you first, after we deepen your relationship with your Creator, then we will work on how to interact with other people. Up until now other people may have been the primary focus in your life. You've tried to save them. You've bent over backward for them.

We are going to shift all that and help you get to a place where you can trust and respect yourself. After that happens you will automatically start making better choices about other people.

If you don't trust other people, the deeper truth is that you haven't learned to fully trust yourself. As you learn to trust yourself, you will learn how and when to trust others.

Building Excitement

Today is a prep day. We begin the hard work tomorrow, but for now I want you to think about why you're excited to do the following:

1. Develop a deeper relationship with yourself and to finally value yourself.

2. Cultivate a deeper relationship with your Creator and allow for that relationship to be your primary source of inspiration.

3. Develop healthy relationships with others from a place of overflow, rather than a place of burnout and resentment.

Go ahead—in your journal, list all the reasons why this new hierarchy excites you:

And, finally, list any SPs you notice coming up around shifting into this new hierarchy:

Today's affirmation: I am ready to value myself. I am a Divine creation.

Today's prayer: Dear Creator, show me how to love myself as You love me. Show me how to value myself as You value me. Show me how to create a relationship with You so that I may feel Your presence in every moment of my life. I'm ready to transform. Show me the way.

DAY 18:
IT'S TIME TO COMMIT TO YOU!

"I think the most important thing in life is self-love, because if you don't have self-love, and respect for everything about your own body, your own soul, your own capsule, then how can you have an authentic relationship with anyone else?"

– SHAILENE WOODLEY

I hope by now that you understand that to claim your power, putting yourself first has to become your new nonnegotiable. You've not really done this before, not in the way that we are going to get clear on today.

Remember, putting yourself first does not mean that you are selfish, but rather that you are full of your Self, or full of your Soul. That's Self with a capital *S*. Your Self is the greater part of you that yearns for connection, for recognition, and to be trusted. It's the part of you that's always known the way—your Soul Self.

It's highly likely that you have not trusted this part of yourself before. You've let your SPs run the show. And you've survived. But now we are taking things to a whole new level. A level of being truly fulfilled.

The thing that you've been searching for in the world is your inner essence. That connection to who you are. When you stop the external search for that sense of connection and instead come home to yourself, you connect to that "thing" that's been missing until now.

That's right, what's been missing in your life is *you*.

Who you are within is far more powerful than the circumstances of your life. Far more powerful than your past. Far more powerful than your family. Far more powerful than the opinions of other people.

Your Soul, your Heart, your essence is connected to all that is—to your Creator. Your Creator speaks to you within you, through the subtle whispers of your Heart.

On Day 31, I'll introduce you to your Heart with my Kipp Heart Therapy, which is one of the most powerful parts of the retreats and seminars

I lead. Since 2012 I've worked with thousands of people to help them connect to their higher selves and their intuition, and I'm excited to share it with you.

But for this part of your journey, you must declare to yourself, to your Creator, and to one other person (someone you trust who will support you in this process) that you are worthy, that you are lovable, and that you (yes, you) have a direct connection to your Creator within you.

If in the past you felt that you followed your Heart or Soul and got burned, chances are that's not what you were doing at all. When people claim they followed their Hearts and massive pain followed, in most cases what they really did was search externally to fill themselves up with the quest for material things. They didn't set high standards. They set aside their inner wisdom. They bent themselves over backward to make other people happy and were codependent.

That is not following your Heart. That is not claiming your value. To do this, we must radically change your understanding of your self-worth.

What part of yourself should you put first? Your fear? Your worry? Your doubt? Your ambitions? Your competitive nature?

Your Soul comes first. Your Heart comes first.

Your Soul or Heart is that place within you that you *feel* when you are calm, centered, and relaxed. It's that part of you that is powerful. It wants to raise your standards. It knows that you are worth more than your current circumstances and troubles.

The Power in Saying No

Today we make it our intention to tap into that wiser part of ourselves and begin to lead from that place. That wiser part of you already knows change is coming, and it's coming now. That wiser part of you already knows that there are certain boundaries you need to set in your life. That wiser part of you already knows that even though it might be painful, it's okay to let family, friends, and other people down so you can stop abandoning yourself.

Nowhere is it written that you get spiritual brownie points for being a martyr or playing small. In the long run, there is no benefit to setting yourself aside so that others can be happy. What will really make other people happy is a happy *you*. A happy you brings life forward. A happy you gives better. A happy you loves better.

To get to a happy you, we have to start with courage. And one of my favorite words: *no*. Which, by the way, is a complete sentence.

Besides saying no to cocaine, I learned to say no to income that challenged my integrity. I was offered a $10,000 check once, but I turned it down because I didn't want to promote the product. Another time I was in negotiations with an investor and they offered me a half a million dollars to invest in my company, but I said no because it didn't feel like the right choice. I said no to my soul-sucking job and couch surfed for two years. I said no to my mother when she asked if I was going to get a "real job," while pursuing my early blogging career. I've said no to too much socializing because it gets in the way of my work, and no to people who don't bring positive energy to my life. Every time I've said no to each of these things, it was the right decision and it led to something better.

Saying no is a way to create more space in your life for you. It does take courage. But the bigger the no on the outside, the bigger the yes on the inside.

In fact, my mantra when it comes to this is: Fuck it. My clients know the "Fuck it" mantra. It means feel the resistance and do it anyway. Just say, "Fuck it."

It can be so scary to set boundaries, to clear our schedules, to say no. Many of my clients have packed their schedules full of other people's priorities as a way of avoiding their own feelings of resentment, fear, and being dead.

It's also common to believe that your needs will not be met if you put yourself first. But know this: your Creator has been trying to get your attention for a long time. When you choose that wiser part of yourself and put it first, you are starting to also bring your Creator into your life in a deeper way. Your Creator will support you in your Purpose, because that is why you were made—to live your Purpose in the world.

Setting boundaries and putting yourself first will challenge your SPs. And yet, at the same time, you will begin to feel better right away when you do this. So, for today, we want to get clear on two things:

1. Who are you going to begin saying no to, starting today?

2. How are you going to begin saying yes to yourself today?

Let's start by making a list in your journal of all the people who you need to set boundaries with.

Name:

Boundary:

Why are you setting this boundary right now?

Action steps you need to take to set this boundary:

Now let's create another list of how you are going to put yourself first today.

Name five things your wiser self knows you should be doing for yourself:

Why are you going to start doing this for yourself today?

Action steps you need to take to make this happen:

Who can you get to support this new behavior?

It's time to get excited about the boundaries you are setting. Setting healthy boundaries is one of the most important steps in claiming your power. Without proper boundaries and space for your wiser self to emerge, you will remain small.

It's also time to get excited about all that you are going to begin doing for yourself. You've been craving these things for such a long time. It's your time; no more waiting!

Today's affirmation: I celebrate setting boundaries, and as I do, all my needs are abundantly met.

Today's prayer: Dear Creator, please give me the courage to set healthy boundaries in my life. Allow me to do so in the healthiest and most loving way possible. Give me strength to keep these boundaries firm when I'm weak or scared, and show me Your Love and support as I choose the wiser part of myself that is connected to Your wisdom. I am grateful for this opportunity to feel Your Love and presence even more.

DAY 19:
COMMIT TO YOUR CREATOR

"Father, if You are willing, remove this cup from
Me; yet not My will, but Yours be done."

– JESUS (LUKE 22:42)

As we've learned, the above prayer is perhaps the most powerful prayer ever said, even more so than the Serenity Prayer. The moment you consciously choose to turn your will over to God is one of the greatest, most powerful moments of your life.

It is also how we must choose to live in each moment going forward. In this way, every moment can be the greatest moment of your life.

We must be willing to become aware of what we can and cannot control. We must be willing to see the bigger picture, and, as we begin to embark upon our spiritual journey, we must choose to see with new eyes and think new thoughts.

Your best thinking got you here. Your beliefs held you back. That's why we are creating new beliefs, one of which is *I am always supported as I surrender my will to the will of my Creator.*

This idea can be confusing. But I believe Caroline Myss summed it up best in this excerpt from her book *Anatomy of the Spirit*:

> It may help you to arrive at the point of surrendering if you can use symbolic sight to view your life as only a spiritual journey. We have all known people who have recovered from dire circumstances—and credited the fact that they let the Divine takeover. And every one of these people shared the experience of saying to the Divine "Not my will but Yours." If that one prayer is all that is required, why are we so afraid of it?
>
> We remain terrified that by acknowledging Divine will— by surrendering our will to a greater will—we will become separated from all that brings us physical comfort. So we struggle with our will against Divine guidance: we invite it in, yet strive

to block it completely. Again and again I observed people in my workshops who are in this dilemma; they seek intuitive guidance, yet fear what that voice will say to them.

Remember that your physical life and your spiritual path are one and the same. Taking pleasure in your physical life is as much a spiritual goal as achieving a healthy physical body. Both are the consequences of following Divine guidance in making choices of how to live and of acting out of faith and trust. Surrender to Divine authority means liberation from physical illusions, not from the delights and comfort of physical life.[9]

Today is the day when you and I step out in faith, knowing that we will be provided for. When surrendering to the will of your Creator, here are some of the basics to keep in mind:

1. God knows the solution to all your problems *before* they happen. Your job is to get still and listen.

2. Surrendering to the will of your Creator does not mean that you must suffer, but rather that you must step into who you really are. The by-product of this is bliss.

3. From now on you must interpret everything that is happening for and to you through new lenses. Instead of asking, "Why is this happening to me?" ask, "What is the Divine gift of this moment, and what am I meant to learn?"

4. Surrendering what you can't control is most important when you are the most freaked out. Faith is not faith when you are happy and all is well because there is no test of your Soul.

5. When you surrender to the will of your Creator, you begin to use Divine Wisdom rather than human logic. Instead of using logic, let intuition guide you in each circumstance.

6. Interpret moments of crisis as a way to see a larger yes from your Creator.

7. This is not about being in denial or falsely positive. This new outlook on life allows you to walk with power through the best

---

9   Caroline Myss, *Anatomy of the Spirit: The Seven Stages of Power and Healing* (New York: Harmony Books, 1996), 225.

and the scariest moments of your life, and live from your Soul rather than from your fears.

This will be scary at first. When I first started surrendering my will to my Creator's will during my couch-surfing days, I set myself a timeline (and a budget—I was broke!). I prayed and asked my Creator to show me, each day, one sign that I was on the right path. I decided to try surrendering for a year and then, if my life was worse off than it had been before, I'd go back to my old ways.

Of course, I never went back. There were constant signs that I was doing the right thing. I got checks I never expected. I felt peace when I didn't imagine I would. I trusted my intuition, and I asked for help along the way.

When I'd receive a message from someone who thanked me for something I'd written, I took that as a sign that I was doing the right thing. When Kim Kardashian tweeted about me, that was a sign. When Tony Robbins invited me to his seminar, that was a sign. When Oprah invited me to participate in *SuperSoul Sunday*, that was a sign. But those big things would have never happened without paying attention to the small confirmations along the way when I was early in my journey.

I kept surrendering. I kept being courageous, even in the face of obstacles. I had stared death in the face, and I knew, without a doubt, that I wanted to live a happy, fulfilled life. And so must you.

When we surrender, we must let go of control. This does not mean that we stop trying to make things happen, but we do stop trying to be the manager of The Universe. When we release control of our circumstances, outcomes, and other people, we take a leap into a greater world.

So who or what do you need to surrender?

Make a list in your journal of your fears and sources of stress, which you will now offer up to your Creator.

Create a New Behavior

Next we must create a daily behavior of connecting to your Creator. This is sacred time, but it doesn't have to be a long time.

If you connect to your Creator in church, awesome. If it's on the yoga mat, that's awesome too. If it's in nature, awesome. There's no right or wrong way to connect. What's important is that you take the time to do it.

What habits make you feel most connected? For me it's as simple as listening to 10 minutes of Kundalini Yoga mantras or meditating during a bath. Morning weights and A.M. cardio are my therapy. Your method of connecting doesn't have to be fancy; it just has to make you feel good.

Make a list of things you can do to feel connected to your Creator:

When I connect to my Creator, I have two prayers that I say to myself:

1. Please take all that I cannot control and do as You will. I surrender my will to You here. Take this from me and use it as You will.

2. Give me the courage to follow Your direction. I will be Your humble servant in each moment and with each choice.

To begin the process of developing a relationship with your Creator, look back at the list you made above and choose two ways of connecting that you can create a daily morning and evening habit around. I promise the time you invest in this will be time well spent. This will be the best relationship of your life, and it will always be there for you.

Today's affirmation: I am connecting to my Creator's will. In this place of surrender, I rest with ease.

Today's prayer: Dear Creator, help me trust You even more. Show me Your will. Comfort me when I am scared. Show me that I am not alone. Give me the strength to courageously follow Your whispers and show me that I am on track. Speak to me in ways that I can understand. I surrender my entire life to Your will. Take me, dear Creator. I'm Yours. Use me as You wish. I am a vessel for Your love, Your will, and Your power here on earth.

DAY 20:
DO UNTO OTHERS

"Do to others as you would have them do to you."

– JESUS (LUKE 6:31)

This quote from Jesus is a well-known mantra. We all know it as the Golden Rule.

Today I'd like you to see the Golden Rule in a new way. During the past two days we talked at length about how to treat yourself and how important it is to consciously spend time connecting with your Creator. Most people, when they see this quote, focus on how to treat others. And yet the wisdom of this quote goes deeper than we might initially see. The real question is: How do you want to be treated, and, most important, how do you want to treat yourself?

Oftentimes, you can hear the deepest thoughts people have about themselves come out when they are in an argument. The names we call people when we fight are generally a reflection of the deepest conversations we have with ourselves. The next time you are in an argument with someone, take a moment to pause and listen to their words. What they are saying about you is really a projection of their deepest insecurities about themselves.

As we begin to change the way you engage with others, I want to first remind you of what we talked about two days ago when it comes to your self-care. Your love and caring (or lack thereof) for your Self will come out in your relationships with others. It was very helpful for me to realize that all the triggers, fights, and moments of pain in my relationships all stemmed from my own relationship with my Heart and Self.

As you engage in new relationships, remember your commitment to your Self and your Creator as the primary places you turn to for spiritual sustenance. This will be easier to do with new people that you meet. It will be harder to do when you try to redefine the major relationships in your life.

Lean into Courage

Changing your relationships with family members, a significant other, friends, and colleagues can prove challenging. I've had to do an intervention with my mother, break up with business partners, set boundaries with colleagues, and even disappoint clients. One of my SPs is making sure everyone is happy. The problem is, that's an impossible standard. In speaking up, I had to confront the fear within myself that said, "You will be abandoned if you upset others." And I proved that SP wrong.

The truth is that we grow together or we grow apart. We may be afraid to truly transform because we know that when we truly commit to a life change, we are renegotiating our power with the world, and the effects of renegotiating our power is unknown. We fear change, because change can be deadly. This is why we must always have courage when it comes to renegotiating our power with others.

When we surrender our will to our Creator's will, we are also surrendering control of how other people will respond to our growth. The hard truth is you are going to lose people in your life. Some people won't like the "new" you. Some will be threatened by it.

No matter how people react, your job is to maintain self-love and a connection with your Creator, and have compassion for others. If people are threatened by your growth, do not judge them. Instead love them. Have compassion for them.

We make unconscious agreements with the people we are relationships with as those relationships develop over time. When we grow, we begin to renegotiate our power and the power of that relationship. When this happens to the people close to us, their world can be rocked. So be compassionate and loving toward those who are scared. But remember to not back down. Just because someone is scared or threatened by your newfound empowerment does not mean that you have to stop being empowered.

It's time for change, baby.

So let's get clear on how you are going to renegotiate your power with other people. There are four categories of people you must become aware of:

1. Primary Relationships

2. Professional Relationships

3. Superficial Relationships

4. New Relationships

Let's look at each of these categories one by one.

Primary Relationships

Who do you need to renegotiate power with in your primary relationships? Is it your spouse? Your child? Your best friend? When I talk about renegotiating power, this could mean setting boundaries, apologizing for something you did, or redefining commitments you've made to them. It could even mean cutting people out of your life who do not support your Purpose. This isn't necessarily a bad thing. When we free up energy in our primary relationships, we create massive space in our lives and we take a huge step toward claiming our power.

Remember, people treat you the way you teach them to treat you. You need to ask yourself how you want to be treated in your primary relationships, and then look at how can you start treating yourself that way so you can start setting an example for others.

As you think about renegotiating power in each of your primary relationships, ask yourself the following questions:

What scares me about renegotiating my power in this relationship?

If I do this, what is the worst-case scenario?

How long have I wanted to do this?

Have I been withholding love in this relationship?

Have I left things unsaid?

Do I need to apologize for something?

Professional Relationships

Renegotiating professional relationships can be scary because it affects how you are perceived in the world and also affects your livelihood. Making empowered choices when money is involved can be especially scary because we link our survival to our job and career. I acknowledge that and also want you to know that when you claim your power in your vocation, it's a game changer.

Once again, when I talk about renegotiating power, this could mean setting boundaries, apologizing for something you did, redefining commitments you've made, or setting a new schedule. It could even mean cutting people out of your life. As you think about renegotiating power in your professional relationships, ask yourself the following questions:

Who do I need to renegotiate power with in my professional relationships?

How do I want to be treated in my professional relationships, and how can I start treating myself this way now?

What scares me about renegotiating my power?

What is the worst-case scenario?

How long have I wanted to do this?

Also, with your professional relationships, ask yourself:

Have I been withholding love?

Have I left things unsaid?

Do I need to apologize?

These last three questions are important, even in professional relationships, because when we live in the energy of blame, we cannot claim our power.

Superficial Relationships

Superficial relationships are ones built around gossip, hatred (i.e., woman hating, man hating, etc.), or things aligned with your old hierarchy. It's time to end all superficial relationships. They drain your power.

Today, let's call your spirit back from these superficial relationships. Begin by asking yourself the following questions:

Who are the people that I have superficial relationships with in my life?

What superficial idea have these relationships been based on?

How have these relationships allowed my old hierarchy and SPs to stay in place?

How am I going to end these superficial relationships?

When am I going to do this? (Hint: *now.*)

New Relationships

One of my favorite things about leading retreats, seminars, and online courses is that I get to create new tribes or groups of people who support one another. It doesn't matter if it's an 11-day retreat in Bali or a 4-day seminar in Los Angeles, my events draw people who not only are awesome but who love to support others.

As you renegotiate your old relationships and clear away the superficial ones, you create a vacuum for new people to enter your life. That's a good thing, because when you find your new tribe, the most powerful thing it can do is to see you as you are, not as you used to be. Your new tribe can also see your potential in ways than you may not be able to.

Yes, there are people out there who will support the new version of you. There is the perfect tribe, relationship, business partner, client, and friend out there for you. But you have to be willing to show your real Self. You can't blame others for not seeing you if you are not willing to show them who you really are.

As you begin to create new relationships, have the courage to unveil the new version of you. Show people your Heart. Show people your Soul. This will create your Soul Tribe, your family of choice.

How can you create your new Soul Tribe? Maybe you can come to one of my events and make some amazing new friends. Maybe your new tribe is at your local yoga studio. Maybe you are feeling the call to travel. When I spend time in Bali (which is where I wrote this book), I am amazed at how many people from all walks of life come here with the same set of values. They speak different languages and have different-colored skin, but they all seem to value a Heart- and Soul-centered life.

As you think about creating new relationships, ask yourself the following questions:

How can I let the hurt of the past go and trust again?

How can I courageously share my real Soul Self moving forward?

How can I intentionally create a new Soul Tribe?

What am I most excited about in meeting my new Soul Tribe?

To where am I feeling called to travel?

Get as clear as possible as you answer the questions above. And then get excited. There's a whole bunch of people you've never met who can't wait to meet the real you! Have courage and put yourself out there.

Today's affirmation: I share my Soul Self with the world, and as I do, I meet others who see the real me.

Today's prayer: Dear God, please show me how my Soul Self can be supported. Bring me people who are aligned with this new and exciting version of myself. Give me the courage to open up to my new tribe. Give me the discernment to stop repeating old and disempowering patterns in relationships and instead create new relationships based on truth. You are my ultimate relationship. I know that as I surrender to You, more good will come. I surrender the outcome of all my relationships to You.

Part III

ORDEAL

"The ordeal is the sacrifice of ego."

– JOSEPH CAMPBELL

The ego gets a bad rap. In much of today's spirituality and self-improvement literature, the ego is the new devil. It's even been said that the ego is (E) dging (G)od (O)ut. What nonsense. Who do you think gave us our egos?

Every aspect of our being has something to teach us, including our ego. The ego is what creates our sense of separateness, our sense of what's yours and what's mine. We need our egos to help us survive. In fact, you can think of your ego as where your SPs come from.

The key here is to not allow your ego to determine your destiny. In this new phase of our journey, we want to thank our ego for keeping us safe and then begin the process of surrendering it to our Soul. In other words, the Ordeal you must now go through entails killing off old SPs that prevent you from living your Purpose.

The good news is that your ego and SPs have done their job. How do I know? Because you're alive and reading this book. They have helped keep you alive, and now it's time for your Soul to take over.

For this to happen, we've got to become aware of the patterns that will get in your way and hold you back as you begin the process of claiming your power.

Think of this as a road map of your freedom. There are going to be some bumps in the road. These bumps are inevitable; you need to become aware of them so that you can steer around them.

We will all face bumps in the road, as well as detours and all manner of distractions, because we are not static beings. We are on the road to becoming more each and every day. So as we grow, our awareness of what can hold us back must also grow. The good news is, you don't need to be fixed. There is nothing wrong with you.

Say it with me: There is nothing wrong with me!

All we've got to do is change a few patterns, take them from disempowering to empowering, and then create faith where there was doubt before. If you can create a few new empowering patterns and then run with them with massive faith in your Creator, you're going to be rocking it in no time.

Caution: Universal Patterns Up Ahead

I want to make you aware of the road ahead, so that you can prepare. To do this, I am going teach you in the coming days about four patterns that will either empower or disempower you, depending on how you relate to them.

It's so important to choose wisely because if you allow them, these patterns will keep you dead and cause you massive regret at the end of your life. On the other hand, if you create empowering relationships with these patterns, you are going to bust wide-open into a whole new world.

The patterns I'm talking about are called archetypes. Carl Jung defines an archetype as "images and thoughts which have universal meanings across cultures."[10] Basically, archetypes are universal patterns that influence our behavior.

You've got to learn to see the deadness of your life archetypally (or universally) and symbolically, rather than personally. When you take your spiritual journey personally and start to doubt yourself, you judge yourself unfairly. Remember, these archetypes are *universal* patterns, meaning everyone encounters them again and again. Time and time again, there will be separation, initiation, ordeal, and return in your life. You can't judge the seasons of your life as good or bad, but rather as something that happens to us all.

The sun rises; then it sets. There is fall, then winter, then spring, then summer. It's not personal; it's universal.

10   Saul McLeod, "Carl Jung," *Simply Psychology*, 2014. Retrieved from www.simplypsychology.org/carl-jung.html.

Your deadness is the same. It's not personal. It's a pattern that happens. Your circumstance is predictable. The rejection of your old ways is predictable, and your redemption is also predicable.

It's how God works.

Our job is to work with these universal patterns and see them for what they are. When you understand that your crisis, your deadness, is archetypal in nature, rather than feel badly about it, you realize you can learn from it. Each archetype we will talk about in this section has a lesson to teach you, which will help you continue your spiritual growth.

Like you have SPs that have held you back, you also have—you guessed it—survival archetypes that have held you back. In her best-selling book *Sacred Contracts*, Caroline Myss informs us that there are four Archetypes of Survival. In the days ahead, we're going to look at how your SPs relate to Myss's Archetypes of Survival. I am going to give you my take on her archetypes, but I highly recommend that you grab a copy of *Sacred Contracts* for an expert-level deep-dive into the concept.

Over the next phase of your journey, your logical brain is going to want to fight the changes that are happening. Notice the judging, the fighting, and let it go.

What's so exciting is that when you begin to see that your life circumstances are not personal, that God is not against you, and that those circumstances can be changed, you take a massive step toward claiming your power. Before we do, we've got to invoke an ordeal and sacrifice the old SPs, old relationships, limiting stories, emotions, and beliefs that are holding you back.

Into the belly of the whale we go. Let's begin.

DAY 21:
BRING IT ON, DEATH

"When I let go of what I am, I become what I might be.
When I let go of what I have, I receive what I need."

– LAO-TZU

Death is something that we, as human beings, tend to avoid talking about. But it's something we need to talk about because it is the fact that you have been dead (either emotionally or spiritually) for so long that has brought you to this place. Your SPs have kept you physically safe but *spiritually dead*. For the spirit to come alive, you must challenge these patterns and create true behavioral change.

I can't tell you how many times I've seen clients in agony because they were unwilling to let go of a relationship, job, eating habit, spending habit, need to be right, or whatever their pattern was. They were afraid to let it die so they became stuck, and a part of their spirit died instead. That is the kind of behavior that brought us to this place. We are all afraid of change, of letting things go that we rely on. We are afraid of letting sugar or carbs go, because if we do, what will comfort us then? We are unwilling to have difficult conversations and instead allow anger, frustration, and resentment to boil up within us. And we tend to surround ourselves with people who do the same. Then we all stay nice and dead together.

You will most likely feel a ton of resistance come up because today is when we are going to begin killing off the old SPs that no longer have a place in your life. Letting go is scary, but let me remind you that it is far scarier to live a life full of regret than to see what God has in store for you.

Dropping the Deadweight

Much of what we are going to let go of today has been deadweight in your life for a long time. What's more, you know that it has. All the things we've done together so far have been things you wanted to do by yourself for a long time. For whatever reason—maybe you lacked the courage or didn't have the right process to show you how—you were unable to go through with it before. You weren't convinced that you were allowed to let go, or that you could.

Hear me now: you are allowed to let go. On the other side, God is waiting to fill your life with such great abundance. But if you cling to scraps, you can't be given a feast. If you cling to crumbs of love, you'll never create space in your life for big love to find you. If you cling to a job that kills your Soul because you want the security, you'll never live your Purpose. If you keep letting what other people think drive your decisions, you'll always wonder who you are. You finally find out who you are when you let go of what and who no longer serve you.

As I am talking about these things, you are probably thinking about the things you need to let go of. Your Soul is shouting *yes*, but your brain is telling you why now is not the right time.

Hard truth time: there is never going to be a perfect time to let go, so *now* is always the right time.

If you knew the abundance, the love, the joy, and the wonderment that awaited you on the other side of this, you'd let go in a heartbeat. But because life hasn't shown you that more than what you currently have is possible, my words may seem naive or like bogus positive thinking. I hope you'll trust me when I say you have no idea what grandness awaits for you on the other side of making the courageous choice to let go.

By actively choosing to let go, you place your faith in God and allow something new to enter the vacuum that you have consciously created. Get excited, because you are about to invoke a process that most people must be dragged into kicking and screaming.

Shelter from a Divine Storm

Divine Storms get worse the more you hold on to what no longer serves you. This is Grace in action because your Creator has much more in store for you. If you don't choose to do this on your own, your life will become more and more intolerable until you are forced into a corner. At that point, you will have no choice. It will be grow or die.

Let's not let things get that bad. Instead of allowing a Divine Storm to get worse, let's rip the Band-Aid off now. Let's get about the business of living your Purpose.

One question I get asked a lot is, "Mastin, *how* do I let this go?" There is often desperation around the word *how*. The subtext when someone asks me this question goes something like this: "I have been trying for so long to let this go, but no amount of therapy, positive affirmations, talking about it, or meditation has helped."

When people ask me, "How do I let go?" what they are really asking is, "How can I change my past?" But you cannot change your past. When I talk about letting go, one way to think about it is to accept what happened to you, not to try to change it.

Thinking you must change your past before you can have a better future is a tricky survival pattern. You cannot ever change your past, but what you can do is change your *relationship* to your past. This is one of the great aims of this book. The quicker you can accept what has happened and let it go, the faster you will begin to live your Purpose.

Sound good? Then let's start working on letting go right now.

The Good in Letting Go

In your journal, I want you to write down the old patterns, relationships, and behaviors that you must let go of in order for you to live your Purpose. As you do this, remember to be bold. You either trust God or you trust the old SP—which will it be?

After you name the things you need to let go of in each category, I am going to ask you another question: Why are you are letting all this go— for what purpose? Answering this question will help your logical mind remember the benefits of letting go, even if you can't feel them yet.

For so long there has been a benefit to holding tightly on to your old SPs. Now we must focus on the benefits of letting go. Remember that the best way to hold on to your Soul is to let go of SPs.

Make a commitment to yourself and your Creator by writing down all the things you will let go of.

In my romantic relationships, I am letting go of:

I am letting all this go because:

In my family relationships, I am letting go of:

I am letting all this go because:

When it comes to my health and well-being, I am letting go of:

I am letting all this go because:

In my financial life, I am letting go of:

I am letting all this go because:

In my career, vocation, or business, I am letting go of:

I am letting all this go because:

In my creative life, I am letting go of:

I am letting all this go because:

In my spiritual life, I am letting go of:

I am letting all this go because:

If you're feeling scared or nervous right now, that's okay. By letting go of old patterns, you are creating space in your life for new and unknown things to enter, and that is scary. But it's also time. It's time to turn the outcome of your life over to your Creator. It's time to allow God to fill the space you've opened up in your life with new circumstances, relationships, outcomes, and benefits that are aligned with your Purpose and your power.

Today's affirmation: I let go of all the SPs that no longer serve me. I have faith in my Creator that something better is on the way.

Today's prayer: God, help me have the courage to let go of all that does not serve Your Purpose in my life. I am scared to rearrange my life. I am scared to let go. Be with me now, even more. Show me signs that I am making the right choice. I want to believe that You will support a more powerful and purposeful version of me. Show me signs that this is true. I am giving over control of my life to You. You take the wheel from here.

DAY 22:
THE BENEFIT OF LETTING IT ALL GO

*"We must be willing to let go of the life we've planned,
so as to have the life that is waiting for us."*

– JOSEPH CAMPBELL

Today I want to focus on why you have clung so tightly to all the old patterns and behaviors you named yesterday, and why it's a great idea to let them go. Your logical brain needs a day to catch up to your Soul.

Why did you hold on? What limiting beliefs were you carrying around with you that kept you stuck? How did you outsource your power to someone else? If you knew you needed to leave your relationship, what took you so long? If you knew that your job was sucking your Soul, why did you stay? If you felt in your gut like there was more to life, that you were meant to play a bigger role, why did you play small?

Perhaps you stayed in your relationship because you were afraid of being alone. Perhaps you stayed in your job because you had bills to pay. Perhaps you settled for crumbs in your life because you didn't know that you could have something bigger and better.

All those are good reasons, but they can no longer be the excuses that hold you back. One of the most important things you can ever learn in life is how to tap into your own powers of resourcefulness. You are truly unlimited. If your circumstances are currently limited, know that you also have the ability to seek out, ask for, and receive unlimited amounts of support.

Here's the thing: when you grow, you have to become more. That means you'll be putting your butt on the line. Chances are that until now you've put your butt on the line for everyone else and wondered why you've come up short. You have not yet begun to tap into how resourceful you truly are. The two main ways to access your resourcefulness are through vulnerability and receptivity.

That's right, you have to be vulnerable, and you have to be able to receive. These are things that most people aren't very comfortable being.

When I started my business, I spent two years couch surfing in the homes of various friends. I felt very anxious and vulnerable not having a home of my own, and receiving that kind of support from others made me question my own sense of worthiness. I thought to myself, *You're taking advantage of people*, *This will never amount to anything, so their good deeds will be for nothing*, and *You're not worthy of this kind of support*.

One day as I was out for a walk to clear my head, I looked at all the homes around me and saw they'd all "made it." I compared myself with them and came up lacking. I felt abandoned and alone.

When I walked back to the tiny room I was staying in, I scowled because it was so small. It felt like a prison cell. In one of my meditations, I asked the question, *Why a room this size? You are so abundant—why something so small?* The answer I got back was immediate: *Mastin, this room represents the size of your faith.*[11]

As I reflected on in my book *Daily Love*, the room felt like a prison cell. Slowly I began to see that the room wasn't my jail; it was my cocoon. I was transforming from a caterpillar to a butterfly, but I had to "die" first.[12] I also realized that I wasn't alone—I was deeply loved, and this was just the dark before the dawn.

Chances are you've had moments of vulnerability or receptivity, and you felt uncomfortable, and perhaps even unworthy as you asked others for help. Deep down what's really been holding you back is a feeling based on the perception of others and yourself. And what's caused you to create your Survival Patterns™ may have been a sense of unworthiness and powerlessness.

There are few absolutes in life, but I can tell you that this has been true for 100 percent of my clients to date. They feel powerless, so they choose patterns that helped them feel they had the power to survive. But that is not the only power we can have. We can also learn to exercise our power to receive, to be vulnerable, and to ask for help.

One caveat: life supports what supports more of life.

Let's be clear, I am not suggesting that you turn into a mooching parasite and take from people without ever giving back. What I am saying is that when you step out on faith to live your Purpose with the intention of serving others, you receive unexpected help and support. Your job is to let it in because, yes, you are allowed to ask for help, and, yes, you are worthy of it.

---

11   Mastin Kipp, *Daily Love: Growing into Grace* (New York: Hay House, 2014).
12   Ibid.

Accept the Help That Comes Your Way

Professor Brené Brown is famous for her research on topics like vulnerability and worthiness. One of my favorite quotes from her comes from her book *The Gifts of Imperfection*:

> Until we can receive with an open heart, we're never really giving with an open heart. When we attach judgment to receiving help, we knowingly or unknowingly attach judgment to giving help.[13]

You have to allow in the answers to your prayer. If you've been praying to God for help and, at the same time, not accepting the help that comes to you, it is you and not God who has kept you small. The truth is that the moment you utter a prayer, it is answered. Your job is to see everything that happens after your prayer as an answer, and to have enough self-love to receive the bounty that comes to you.

Many of us have been conditioned to believe that giving to others is the best and highest spiritual goal. However, this cannot be so if you are giving from an empty cup. We must be willing to allow in and receive the good in our lives so that we can become power-full enough to serve others.

What's so ironic is that the mentality that "only serving others is best" is a fantastic SP. Why? Because giving puts you in the power seat. When you are giving to someone else, you don't have to be the vulnerable receiving one. The goal is to open yourself up to receive as well as give, and create a flow of all things good.

The by-product of always giving and never receiving is that your life becomes filled with people who drain your power. You surround yourself with Soul parasites. You give and you give and you give, and nothing ever seems to come back to you. You may even complain that everyone else is more important that you, but you stay stuck and dead because you lack the energy to change.

However, lacking the energy to change is also a sneaky SP. It keeps you from having to face a frightening situation because the moment you decide to surrender your will to Divine will, the moment you decide to claim your power, the moment you decide to live your Purpose, you become vulnerable. You tap into your deep-seated feelings of unworthiness. Until

---

13   Brené Brown, *The Gifts of Imperfection: Let Go of Who You Think You're Supposed to Be and Embrace Who You Are* (Center City, MN: Hazelden, 2010).

now, you've decided to stay dead because any move toward empowerment threatens you by forcing you to show your real Self to the world.

What if the world rejects you? What if people don't like the real you? The fear that this SP addresses is the fear that you will be abandoned, and in that abandonment, you will die. Because the SP thinks that if the world rejects who you really are, you are psychologically dead.

So you don't risk it. You stay dead inside your shell, not showing your real self to the world. Then you wonder why no one seems to see you or why you feel so stuck.

This is the reality you've created for yourself, but even still, you've felt the calling of your Soul. To do more. To be more. To live more. To share more. To serve more. To receive more.

Do you dare? If you've come this far, the answer is yes. You *do* dare. You dare to let all that is familiar go and step into a strange and unknown new world where you'll be tested, challenged, and rewarded tenfold for your bravery.

Embrace the Fear of Vulnerability

Does your logical mind understand now? Let's take some time to get clear about why you've not been able to be vulnerable and to receive in your life before. This inability has held you back, but if we can shine a light on it and better understand it, then you can make different choices, ones that free you up to live your Purpose. With this in mind, write out your answers to the following statements in your journal:

I have been scared to be vulnerable in my romantic relationships because:

I have been scared to receive in my romantic relationships because:

I am ready to be vulnerable and to receive in my romantic relationships because:

I have been scared to be vulnerable in my career or vocation because:

I have been scared to receive in my career or vocation because:

I am ready to be vulnerable and to receive in my career or vocation because:

I have been scared to be vulnerable when it comes to my health and wellness because:

I have been scared to receive when it comes to my health and wellness because:

I am ready to be vulnerable and to receive when it comes to my health and wellness because:

I have been scared to be vulnerable about money because:

I have been scared to receive more money because:

I am ready to be vulnerable and to receive when it comes to money because:

Well done! That was some heavy lifting. One final question for today:

What support, help, and miracles have you been blocking that are already there?

Today's affirmation: Today I give and receive only what is good.

Today's prayer: O Divine Spirit, heal me. Allow me to receive Your abundant blessings and steadfast Love. Help me forgive myself for blocking all the goodness that You have been sending my way, and wipe my slate clean. Show me how to share my real Self with the world, the Self that You made me to be. Give me the courage to ask for help when I need it and receive that help fully. I know that it is in receiving Your Love and Abundance that I am able to give even more.

DAY 23:
IT'S TIME TO GROW UP

"The core issue of all the Child archetypes is dependency
and responsibility: when to take responsibility, when to
have a healthy dependency, when to stand up to
the group, and when to embrace communal life."

– CAROLINE MYSS

Welcome to adulthood. Today we are going to explore the first of the four Archetypes of Survival by Caroline Myss, which is the Child archetype. (Remember, for a deep dive into archetypes, I highly recommend Myss's book *Sacred Contracts*.)

You've probably heard the term *inner child* before. It's this weird psychobabble term people throw around, not really knowing what it means. They often use it as an excuse for their bad behavior, or for not taking responsibility for their actions. Put another way, we can easily use our "inner child" as an excuse to stay dependent on old SPs. However, when we heal our child, wonderful things happen, awe emerges, we see things in a new way, our minds open, and we can tap into being playful again.

There are many aspects of the Child archetype,[14] but today I am going to focus on only two: the Wounded Child and the Magical Child. You can think of the Wounded and Magical Child as different sides of the same coin. That is to say, once you've healed your Wounded Child, you can step back into the state of magic that we love about children, and that still exists within you.

The Wounded Child

We are all born into this world as open books. Fresh from Heaven, fresh from the Spirit World, we are born knowing everything we need to know about who we are. We are born curious. We are born in a state of awe. We

---

14   See https://www.myss.com/free-resources/sacred-contracts-and-your-archetypes/
appendix-the-four-archetypes-of-survival/.

are born without a wounded past. We trust everyone and anyone—until the moment when our first OI happens. That's the moment when the openhearted, creative, free, and good-natured parts of us start to shrink, and we begin to adapt to the expectations of our culture.

Over time, we are told that the awe-inspired, curious, and open-minded parts of ourselves are "naive" and "foolish" and need to be suppressed. We learn to value instead things like logic, hard work, and doing well in an educational system that expects all children to learn the same and be the same. Too often our schools take these little magical beings and turn them into followers, people who are told what is important, instead of encouraging them to decide for themselves.

Over time, more and more OIs stack on top of the first OI and we can get firmly entrenched into the Wounded Child archetype. It's a fantastic SP because if you remain wounded, you don't have to take personal responsibility. When you stay wounded, there is always someone else to blame.

You can find a lot of opportunities for low-level connection and commiseration with other people who are wounded, and you can make unconscious social agreements to stay wounded together. When you identify with your wounds, rather than your Purpose and your power, you are suffering from what Myss calls "Woundology," which I've covered earlier in this book. It's also impossible for you to live your Purpose if you are blaming others.

The Wounded Child archetype is where all your OIs are stored until you are ready to face them, feel them, and forgive them. When you come from a place of woundedness, you blame everyone else for your problems, your parents, your government, your peers—heck, even me!

You do this for good reason. Remember, all aspects of who you are have a good reason for being there. If you've experienced pain in your past, you've had to find some way of dealing with it. Without awareness or training, you took on the hurt of your past and made it not just your story, but your entire identity. You don't just see yourself as having experienced some wounding moment in your past; you have become wounded. You identify with what happened and you defend staying wounded.

When you operate as the Wounded Child, you also create relationships with people whom you turn into parental figures. You set them up to take care of you, but in doing so, you outsource your own self-care to them. Of course, no one can ever perfectly care for or nurture you except yourself, so time and time again you are let down by the people to whom you have given this power, and this perpetuates the victim cycle.

As we begin to bring your Purpose to life, look out for your Wounded Child. As you open yourself up to receive and become vulnerable, things won't work out perfectly every time. There will be hurt in your future. Instead of using hurt as a reason to stay small and wounded, you can give this hurt new meaning. View hurt like a scientist, examining it for evidence of the patterns and behaviors you no longer want to participate in.

The Wounded Child at Work in Your Life

If you've associated love with hurt up until now, just know that love doesn't hurt when you have it. Love nurtures you. Love protects you. Love makes you feel safe. And the first person who needs to give you that Love is you.

Myss says this about the Wounded Child:

> The Wounded Child archetype holds the memories of abuse, neglect, and other traumas that we have endured during childhood. This is the Child pattern most people relate to, particularly since it has become the focus of therapy since the 1960s. Many people blame the relationship with their parents that created their Wounded Child, for instance, for all their subsequent dysfunctional relationships. On the positive side, the painful experiences of the Wounded Child often awaken a deep sense of compassion and a desire to help other Wounded Children. From a spiritual perspective, a wounded childhood cracks open the learning path of forgiveness. The shadow aspect may manifest as an abiding sense of self-pity, a tendency to blame our parents for any current shortcomings and to resist moving on through forgiveness. It may also lead us to seek out parental figures in all difficult situations rather than relying on our own resourcefulness.[15]

Let's find out where in your life your Wounded Child is still running the show, or where it is likely to show up as you continue with this process.

---

15   Caroline Myss, https://www.myss.com/free-resources/sacred-contracts-and-your-archetypes/appendix-the-four-archetypes-of-survival/.

Answer the following statements in your journal.

My Wounded Child shows up in my romantic life by doing:

My Wounded Child shows up in my business, career, or vocation by doing:

My Wounded Child shows up in my health and wellness by doing:

My Wounded Child shows up in my relationship to money by doing:

My Wounded Child shows up in my relationship to God by doing:

We all have wounds, but as you look back at the answers you just gave, remember that you are not your wounds. Who you are is who you choose to be in *response* to your wounds.

To truly claim your power, you must relate differently to your wounds. You must begin to see them not just as something painful that happened to you, but as a catalyst for your spiritual growth. Show me anyone who has attained the level of mastery in any area, and I'll show you someone who has healed their wounds and used their suffering to empathetically serve others.

With that in mind, let's look at your wounds in a new light, through the lens of spiritual growth. I want you to ask yourself how your wounds have been a catalyst for you to grow. In other words, what good has or could come from your wounds? List them by category in your journal.

The spiritual lessons of my wounds in my romantic life are:

The spiritual lessons of my wounds in my business, career, or vocation are:

The spiritual lessons of my wounds in my health and well-being are:

The spiritual lessons of my wounds in my family relationships are:

The spiritual lessons in my wounds around money are:

The Magical Child

You can think of the archetype of the Magical Child as your original state, when you were in awe of all things. Myss describes this archetype as someone who "sees the potential for sacred beauty in all things, and embodies qualities of wisdom and courage in the face of difficult circumstances."[16] When you can truly sit in awe of the majesty of life, with all its hurt and joy, that's when you know you have arrived.

When you heal your Wounded Child and learn the lessons it was meant to teach you, you open yourself up to being childlike. This is what Jesus meant when He said, "Truly I tell you, unless you change and become like little children, you will never enter the kingdom of heaven" (Matthew 18:3).

Your Wounded Child will want to protect your Magical Child from the hurt of the world. Why? Because we are told to put away our magical nature as soon as we are born, and "fit in" to the world.

However, it's time to come out of your shell and show your magical self.

Carl Jung said, "The creation of something new is not accomplished by the intellect, but by the play instinct arising from inner necessity. The creative mind plays with the object it loves."[17] Another way to think about this is that your Wounded Child will keep you dead, but your Magical Child, who wishes to come out and play, must be allowed out to create something new.

When you are playful, when you are in your bliss, your joy, and your curiosity, that is when you are most connected to your Soul, and thus to God. When we look at people like Walt Disney, Steve Jobs, George Lucas, J. J. Abrams, or anyone who has truly created something "magical," it happened because they allowed that part of themselves to run the show—often against strong, continued critique.

Every circumstance of your life was first a thought. If you have allowed the thoughts of your Wounded Child to keep you dead in your life thus far, know that it is the thoughts of the Magical Child within you that will free you. Your Soul, your Heart, your Intuition, your desire to be free, to create, to grow, to inspire, and to play all stem from this part of you.

---

16   Ibid.
17   C. G. Jung, *Collected Works of C. G. Jung, Volume 6: Psychological Types* (Princeton, NJ: Princeton University Press, 1971), 197.

Celebrate the Magic Within

To get back in touch with that part, think back to when you were a kid. What did you do for fun? I made movies. I played the piano. I worked out. I put on plays. I helped people. I was clearly creative and a performer, but later my SPs kicked in. When I moved to Hollywood (a Wounded and Magical Child epicenter), I allowed my Wounded Child to numb my creativity.

I wrote about this at length in my last book, *Daily Love: Growing into Grace*. Instead of allowing my inner artist to shine, I became a talent manager in the music business, making sure to focus all my attention and effort on others. Although I worked with Grammy-winning artists and multiplatinum bands, I was never satisfied. Life had to send me many Divine Storms before I woke up from the trance of my Wounded Child and gave my Magical Child permission to create. Everything I've ever created, including this book, has come from the play instinct of my Magical Child.

When I am teaching, leading a seminar, or writing about spiritual principles, I am in a flow like no other. Time flies by. Magically, my attention deficit disorder disappears.

I've never met someone who has fully functioning symptoms of A.D.D. when they are fully connected to their Purpose. Perhaps another way of looking at A.D.D. is that if you have it all the time, you are not in your Purpose. That's because when you are in your Purpose, you have no problem paying attention. In fact, you wonder where the time went.

Most of what we call A.D.D. today is based on boxing ourselves into a life we weren't meant to live. Drugs alone cannot fix this. I have three types of A.D.D.—three!—and the symptoms go crazy when I am doing work that doesn't align with my Purpose. However, when I am in my zone of Purpose, eating healthy foods, and taking care of myself with exercise and meditation—the symptoms lessen. Hear me out: I'm not saying that living in your Purpose will cure your A.D.D. once and for all, but it certainly can diminish the effects in your daily life.

In the interest of transparency, I do take medication for my A.D.D. Drugs don't lead you to your Purpose. If you have A.D.D. like I do, they can enhance your performance of your Purpose. My rule of thumb is, Purpose first, drugs second. As of the writing of this book, I am no longer on Adderall and only take a moderate amount of Wellbutrin. I've been able to cut down on my medications because I work very hard at maintaining a healthy lifestyle and staying in the flow of my Purpose. But it wasn't always this way.

For me, no amount of Adderall, Wellbutrin, or success in my career managing other artists could replace the feeling of letting myself create. Even though I was living in Hollywood—one of the most creative places—I felt drained because I wasn't nurturing my creativity.

"Well, I'm just not a creative person," you might say. But the truth is *you are*. Something unique and special wants to be born through you, and only you can bring it forward. No one else can create from your perspective or with your unique ability. You have much value to add to this world. When you dedicate your life to adding the value that can only come from you when you are living your Purpose, you create a truly legendary legacy.

Nurturing Your Creative Side

In a world that values survival over trusting your creative instincts, your choice to become creative is a bold move. As you move forward, the Wounded Child will try to hold you back. It will try to convince you that all the pain you've been through will only be repeated when you put yourself out there.

But that's not true. The past is gone, and what you choose to create today will determine your future. So let's create your future through the lens of your Magical Child archetype. Begin by asking yourself that question again: When you were a child, what did you do just because you loved it?

Another way to think about this is to imagine you had all the money you would ever need, and you knew you could never make a wrong choice. If that were true, how would you answer the following questions?

How would you allow yourself to play?

What would you love to create?

What would be your biggest dream?

Who would you love to inspire?

Can you think of any role models who have done something similar?

Answering these questions will put you in direct contact with your Soul and the play instinct, which is your zone of genius. As you do so, watch out for old patterns and your Wounded Child, which may try to creep in with whispers like, "You can't do that," "That's nonsense," or "That would never work." Instead let your Magical Child answer the questions honestly. Let yourself play, have fun, and imagine.

And no matter what, trust yourself.

Today's affirmation: I allow my Magical Child to play, knowing that the more I imagine, dream, and create from my Soul, the larger my life will become.

Today's prayer: Dear Creator, give me the courage to follow Your intuitive inspiration. Give me guidance on how I can best connect with my Magical Child and let it out to play. Give me a balm for my Wounded Child that will allow it to forgive the past and learn the lessons it's meant to learn. Give me the freedom to create a brand-new and inspired life—a life of Your Purpose. A life of joy. A life of my Soul made manifest on earth. Guide me, and I will obediently follow the signs.

DAY 24:
TAKE RESPONSIBILITY FOR YOUR LIFE

"We may like to play the Victim at times because of the
positive feedback we get in the form of sympathy or
pity. Our goal is always to learn how to recognize these
inappropriate attitudes in ourselves or others, and to act
accordingly. We are not meant to be victimized in life, but
to learn how to handle challenges and outrun our fears."

– CAROLINE MYSS

Today we are going to cover the next archetype we need to become aware of, which is the Victim archetype. We covered the difference between being victimized (i.e., something bad happened to you) and being a victim (i.e., the bad thing that happened has become your identity) earlier in this book. Now, I not only want to remind you of this tendency, but also expand your understanding of this archetype so you can begin to master it.

The word *victim* makes this archetype sound like it's only a bad thing, but there is an empowered version. You have two choices for how you relate to this archetype: you can blame or you can take responsibility.

When you begin to make forward momentum in your life, you will be faced with the challenges of the disempowered victim archetype. Those challenges come in the form of jealousy, envy, and blame, and in making your problem big and yourself small. If you feel small in the face of your circumstances or problems, remember that God is bigger than any problem you have. The feeling of powerlessness can only come if you truly believe that you are disconnected from your Creator. When you know, act, and believe that God is with you in every moment, you cannot be a victim. You cannot be powerless. In fact, you become very powerful. But without God, without our Divine Creator and our connection to something greater than ourselves, we are truly powerless. That's why it's so crucial to get in sync with the larger Divine forces of life.

Think of it this way: you are but a drop of the Divine, yet your Soul desires to make waves in this lifetime. A drop cannot, in and of itself, make waves. However, if that drop was to join a larger body, say an ocean, then that drop can become part of a wave with much greater power than it has on its own.

When you align with your Soul, you set yourself up for miracles and synchronicities to happen. But living in this state of connection to something greater cannot happen if you let your disempowered victim out to play. Following are some questions to ask yourself to see if the disempowered victim is running the show:

Do you blame anyone (or anything) for the way your life currently is, or for not having what you really want? If so, who?

Who are you envious of?

Are you intimidated or jealous when others seem successful but you don't?

Do you have a hard time celebrating the success of others?

How much time do you spend feeling sorry for yourself and the circumstances of your life?

Who or what do you compare yourself to?

Who or what do you feel small in the presence of?

These questions require rigorous honesty. They are also worth revisiting from time to time as you grow. With awareness, you will get better and better at not being a victim and instead realize that when the empowered side of the victim archetype shows up, you've harnessed some major spiritual mojo.

The Empowered Victim

At one time or another we've all been victimized. For some of us, this victimization has been subtle; for others it has been dramatic and traumatic. Either way, an inevitable part of our spiritual growth will be to step into an Empowered Victim archetype.

The empowered version of this archetype allows us to identify situations where we've set ourselves up for victimization and do something about them. The Empowered Victim is the part of us that says, "Enough," when we are in a toxic relationship and decides to leave.

The Empowered Victim says, "I am 100 percent responsible for my choices, my circumstances, and how I choose to respond to the uncertainty of life."

The Empowered Victim does not shame himself or herself for once being disempowered, but rather says that everything has happened in perfect time and for a reason.

The Empowered Victim has the courage to feel and process the negative emotions of trauma and get to the other side.

Most important, the Empowered Victim wants to stop, prevent, and heal the victimization of others.

One of the greatest insights that my clients who have suffered from profound trauma come to is that, while we cannot make what happened to them right, we can find meaning in their suffering. They come to realize that their past, their trauma, and all that they've been through have given them a unique perspective and empathy with which to relate to others who are being victimized. These are the experiences that allow them to be part of the process of stopping the victimization of others.

My friend Kris Carr, who was diagnosed with a rare and currently incurable form of cancer, articulated this idea best when she said, "I wouldn't want to call my cancer a gift, because I wouldn't want to give it to you, but I would call it a blessing." Kris did not allow her diagnosis to become her identity and instead views it through the lens of the empowered victim. She took her power back by becoming the C.E.O. of her "Crazy Sexy" life, turned her pain into Purpose, and is now inspiring literally millions of people with five best-selling books, an award-winning film, and a thriving online community (www.kriscarr.com). Kris has my utmost love and respect for living this amazing example each and every day.

It can be this way for you too. Your wounds can lead you to your Purpose. You can find much wisdom within your pain. You can find meaning. Then you can use that meaning to not only improve your life but also the lives of others.

Another great lesson that the Empowered Victim teaches is that whomever you are jealous of is a living, breathing example of what is possible for you. You are only jealous of people who have something you don't. In all honesty, I still get jealous of people who have something I want! But now, whenever I notice jealousy, I turn those people into my mentors. And instead of thinking negative thoughts, I pray for them, wish them well, and thank them. Instead of feeling badly about that, I can see the deeper truth, which is that in those people, *I am recognizing my own potential.*

Once you understand this truth, you can begin the process of unleashing in yourself what you see in others. Let's take some time now to step into your empowered victim by answering the following questions.

How could the wounds of your past be turned into a blessing today?

How can you help others because of this blessing?

What will your life look like when you no longer accept that you are a victim?

Who in your life keeps you stuck in your victim story?

When would be a good time to end these relationships?

Who are you jealous of?

What do you think they have that you don't?

How can you begin to create more of this in your life?

How can you celebrate the successes of others?

Very good! Today you are no longer a victim. Instead you are a powerful creator.

Today's affirmation: I am the creator of my destiny. I recognize my own potential.

Today's prayer: O God, help me find the blessing within my current circumstances. Allow me to embody that which I am jealous of in others. Help me create relationships based on abundance, acceptance, and the power of my Soul. Help me heal the part of me that feels powerless without You. Show me how to stop comparing myself with others and instead stay in my own lane. Allow me to take my power back. Keep me safe. Show me the pathway to freedom.

DAY 25:
HOW YOU GET IN YOUR OWN WAY
AND HOW TO STOP

"This may be the most difficult of all the archetypes
to understand, because its name is associated with
betrayal. Yet the purpose of this archetype is not
to sabotage you, but to help you learn the many
ways in which you undermine yourself."

– CAROLINE MYSS

In the above quote, Caroline is talking about the Saboteur archetype, which is that part of us that gets in our own way. Why do you get in your own way? By now you know: survival. Your old SPs block your growth because growth is scary and uncertain, and requires risk. Self-sabotage is really a form of self-protection.

You've been doing the best you can in your life to stay safe, but now we are rocking the boat and diving straight into the sea of uncertainty. This isn't easy, so be kind to yourself today. It makes sense that after you've been through challenging times, you wouldn't want to repeat those hardships. However, if you allow the disempowered Saboteur to creep in, you will get in your own way again and again.

The Saboteur is responsible for all those times when you *almost* made it and then, out of nowhere, you had to start from scratch. It's the part of you that is afraid that change, transformation, and growth will destroy you, rather than set you free. Why? Because your Saboteur compares what's possible in your future with what's happened in your past. The disempowered Saboteur says, "Not so fast—if you really make this change, if you really become big, if you really let go, then it'll all be over."

Here's the ironic truth: the life you are currently living is already the rock bottom that you fear.

Seem harsh?

Let me say it a different way: the circumstances you are living are the circumstances that you fear. You are currently living within the prison of your greatest fear, afraid that if you make a move toward empowerment, your greatest fear will come true even though *it has already come true*.

What do I mean?

If there is an outcome you're afraid of, and you do not take action because you are afraid, then you produce the outcome you are afraid of. Your inaction, powered by your Saboteur, actually creates the circumstance you fear. For example, if you're afraid that you will be in rejected in a relationship so you don't put yourself out there, then you end up alone, just like you would have been if you had been rejected.

That may sound bad, but really this is a moment to celebrate. If you are already at rock bottom, if you are already living the circumstances you fear most, the only place to go is up.

The Disempowered Saboteur loves you right where you are. Safe. Secure. Dead. It fears change. We need to become aware of this archetype so that we can stop it from getting in our way. You can spot where in your life the Saboteur archetype is disempowering you by asking yourself the following question:

What change do you fear most?

When you get courageous and follow your fears, you find that the areas of greatest fear are also the areas most associated with your Purpose and power. So our goal, our aim, our cure for the disempowered Saboteur, is that each and every time you feel scared and resist transformation, you rip off the Band-Aid and face that feeling. Meet your fear head on.

A funny thing happens when you face or name your fear; it lessens its power. Just like the case of Voldemort. Once Harry Potter found the courage to say Voldemort's name, he discovered that it was not his enemy's name that gave him power, but the fear of *not saying his name* that gave him power. That discovery put Harry on track to ultimately defeating Voldy. As it will be for you and your personal nemeses, whatever they may be.

So let's take some time now to explore your fears and what they are telling you about your power and Purpose.

Where is there the greatest resistance in your life?

What fears are you afraid to name?

What outcomes do you fear most?

What's the worst-case scenario you can imagine if, instead of letting your fears stop you, you pulled off the Band-Aid and claimed your power and Purpose?

Ahhhh, that wasn't so hard was it? When you get your fears out on the table, they begin to lose their power and you begin to claim yours.

This is the gift of the Saboteur archetype. It enables you to see your greatest fears and reestablish your relationship with them. Instead of allowing your fears to hold you hostage, you face them and are set free.

Fear contracts the body. Your Soul expands it. That's the way life works—expansion followed by contraction followed by expansion. It's a predictable pattern. As you take more and more risks, the stakes get bigger and bigger, which means the fears also get bigger and bigger. People who allow themselves the opportunity to play big must face their Saboteur time and time again, with more courage, more tenacity, and more faith each time.

Instead of allowing your Disempowered Saboteur to guide you, allow your faith to guide you. God is bigger than the fearful part of you that wants to remain small. And you can be sure that each time you take a risk on behalf of your Soul, you will either learn a powerful spiritual lesson that will change you forever (and for the better) or you will emerge victorious. Sometimes you even get both.

The Empowered Saboteur

Once you face the fears of your Disempowered Saboteur, you can start to have a positive relationship with this archetype. The now Empowered Saboteur gives you courage and exposes your ability for growth. Your Saboteur can also bring you closer to God because that's what the experience of faith is all about. One of the coolest spiritual lessons of the Saboteur is that with God, all things are possible. So let's begin the process of surrendering your fears to God by asking yourself the following question:

What fears and outcomes would I like to surrender to God?

Remember, the areas of life in which you are dead are the areas in life in which you have little courage or faith. Once you've surrendered your fears, it's time to expand your faith with courageous action. Ask yourself the following questions in your journal:

What courageous action can I take in my romantic life?

What will the ultimate benefit of this action be?

What courageous action can I take in my financial life?

What will the ultimate benefit of this action be?

What courageous action can I take in my business, career, or vocation?

What will the ultimate benefit of this action be?

What courageous action can I take in my health and well-being?

What will the ultimate benefit of this action be?

What courageous action can I take with my family?

What will the ultimate benefit of this action be?

These are powerful questions with answers that will amaze, scare, and excite you. Remember, the Disempowered Saboteur can only comprehend a future based on your limited past. But God has the ability to make all things new, to expand your horizon, and to create, present, and organize synchronicities in your life that you can't yet imagine.

Stay curious. Stay childlike. Stay open. As you begin to take these courageous actions, a new version of life begins to unfold. Your Purpose will feel scary at first. Yet, with time and persistence, your life opens up to new and higher levels of living.

A great way to prevent the Disempowered Saboteur from taking over is through a mentor—someone who has walked the path before you, who knows the road ahead, and who can help you stay courageous and on course. No one, and I mean no one, makes this journey alone.

My first mentors were my parents. I learned through my mother's resilience to overcome chronic pain. And I learned through my father's unwavering commitment to his wife to not move or change, as the love of his life was incapacitated for years.

Then I started watching free videos from Tony Robbins and Eckhart Tolle on YouTube. I bought tons of books.

I found business mentors, Jeff Walker and Peter Katsis; my Kundalini yoga teacher, Tej Kaur Khalsa; authors whose books and courses really resonated with me; my therapist, Trinka Terra; and professional speakers I admired, including Tony Robbins. Each form of mentorship took me a step further. And as I decided to raise my game, I had to face my own survival pattern around money and invest in higher-level guidance.

The mentors I work with today don't come cheap, but I consider them to be an essential investment in my future and the best money I invest each year. So, take a moment to think about the ultimate life that you want to live. Who already has a life like the one you want? If the people who come to mind are famous or hard to get to, buy their books, read interviews with them, begin to absorb their thoughts, and take immediate action on what you learn.

The Disempowered Saboteur loves spiritual entertainment. The Empowered Saboteur takes it a step further and turns spiritual entertainment into spiritual growth through the virtue of courage. Begin to do that now by making a list in your journal of the mentors you would like to hire, learn from, or read about.

Mentors in my romantic life are:

Mentors in my career, vocation, and business are:

Mentors in my spiritual life are:

Mentors in my health and wellness are:

Mentors in creativity are:

Mentors in family life are:

Yogi Bhajan once said, "Consciousness is not taught, it's caught." That's why I believe it's so important to find the best mentors that you can and keep upping your game. By surrounding yourself with people who are further down the road than you are, you allow yourself to follow in their footsteps.

One point of clarity: A lot of people ask me how to get influential people to help them. The simple (but not easy) answer is to find a way to become valuable to them. The best way to get help is to provide it.

Also, when you truly begin to live your Purpose out loud, people will notice. So serve others, help others, and do your thing. When you do, you will stick out from the crowd in a big way.

Today's affirmation: I am a Divine Child connected to my Divine Source. I will begin each day anew.

Today's prayer: Divine Source, help me have courage. Show me how to keep going when I want to stop. Give me a sign today that I am on track and on course. Help me remember who I really am when I forget. Bring me all the tools, resources, mentors, and guides I need to stay supported and connected to my Purpose. I am open to receiving guidance. Help me find and create the best support group possible. Help me find my Soul Guide and my tribe.

DAY 26:
HOW TO STOP SELLING YOUR SOUL

"None of us thinks kindly of the term 'prostitute,' and yet from this archetype we learn the great gift of never again having to compromise our body, mind, or spirit . . . The Prostitute archetype engages lessons in the sale or negotiation of one's integrity or spirit due to fears of physical survival or for financial gain."

– CAROLINE MYSS

Today we cover the fourth, final, and perhaps most provocative survival archetype in Caroline's arsenal. That is the Prostitute archetype.

The word *prostitute* can easily offend and trigger people. When you read it, you may have even wanted to put this book down. Don't. Understanding this archetype will cause you to confront some uncomfortable but critical things about yourself.

For example, the great question of the Prostitute is: *How much is your Soul worth?* While some people sell their bodies and are shunned for it by our culture, many, many more sell their Souls for a salary and a 401(k).

The Disempowered Prostitute archetype is one of the greatest sources of leaked power. This aspect of the Prostitute will drive you crazy trying to control others. It will drive you to seek financial gain, rather than spiritual knowledge. It will keep you in jobs that suck your Soul, romantic relationships that lack intimacy, power struggles with business partners, and other situations of financial stress. The phrase "selling your soul to the devil" aptly describes the Disempowered Prostitute. In this case, however, the "devil" is your old SPs that keep you dead.

You need to get clear about what your choices are costing you because when you lose power through your Disempowered Prostitute, you are left with very little—if any—to bring your Purpose to life. If you are playing small, making everyone else more important, and selling yourself for far less than you are worth, then you will have no power of manifestation in this world.

All your SPs and limiting stories surrounding money exist here. You can hear the voice of the Disempowered Prostitute in comments like:

"Rich people had to take advantage of other people to get there."

"The 1 percent controls the 99 percent."

"Rich people are evil."

"I'm not worth investing in."

"Investing in personal growth is a luxury."

"Money doesn't grow on trees."

"The only thing I need is a job that pays my bills."

"I could never charge for my services, especially if they are of a spiritual nature."

Money SPs are some of the most gripping, powerful, and limiting patterns there are. Why? Because the reality is, if you live in this world, you need money to survive and thrive. There is a price tag for every day that you are alive. You have rent or a mortgage to pay, heating bills, gas bills, grocery bills, and so on.

Then there are the other things we spend our money on. The status symbols. The fancy car. The house that's bigger than what we need. The clothes. The bling. When it comes to money, we can easily imprison our Souls with the bondage of material things. One of my favorite quotes on this topic is from the great film *Fight Club*: "The things you used to own, now they own you."

One of the most powerful moments of my life was when I had to decide between going back to my career in the music business or moving forward into the great unknown of becoming a spiritual teacher. I'd been involved with music for years at this point, but I knew the temptation for an unhealthy lifestyle would be strong.

In a moment of clarity, I chose the unknown path, which meant the first thing I had to do was downsize. I left behind my luxurious lifestyle and moved into an eight-by-eight room to pursue my dream of becoming a successful entrepreneur who inspired and improved the lives of others.

Trust me: it wasn't a glamorous time, but it was worth it. Even though I was massively limited on funds, even though I had no idea where my next means of financial support would come from, I knew that my Soul was worth more than any amount I might be paid for a job I didn't love.

You might think that someone like me who has "made it" has also had it easy. However, the process of *making it* took years for me, as it has for most successful people. Even today I have to check in with my

Prostitute archetype regularly because the bigger the game that I play, the more this fella likes to cause trouble.

Even when I decided to go after my dream and get out of the music industry, I had several limiting stories surrounding money. I was worried I'd never have enough. I worried if I found my purpose I wouldn't have any money. I thought I didn't deserve to make enough money to live the life I dreamed of living. So I was worried when I had money, and I was worried when I didn't have money!

You've got to begin to change your thinking around money. This is an area of our lives with so many limiting stories and beliefs, but the simple fact is that money is just energy. Pure and simple. Money isn't evil. It isn't bad. It can be lost, created, grown, shrunk, and exchanged. Most important, like all energy in The Universe, money likes to flow.

As you grow, the flow of money grows too. The challenge is that there may be more and more zeros at the end of the checks you write or the credit card bills you receive. And many times you will have to beg, borrow, or steal (kidding) to live your dreams.

You Can't Do It Alone

Everyone who has made it has made it because of the help of others. No one has done it alone. When I was starting out, many friends helped me just get through another day. My time couch surfing, before my business became successful, brought me into the present moment. All I could focus on was today—not tomorrow and certainly not yesterday. Moment by moment, day by day, I was guided, protected, and taken care of by my Creator. And miracles would happen. I would get random checks in the mail from subscribers thanking me for my help just when I needed them.

One of the greatest gifts we can receive is confirmation that we are on the right path. Little moments give us this confirmation. For me it could be a supportive tweet or e-mail from someone who was touched by my work, or a sign on a bumper sticker with the exact message I needed to hear. Back then, receiving unexpected (but greatly needed) checks in the mail were confirmation to me that I was on the right path. When you are open to and looking for confirmations that you are on the right path, they start showing up.

At the same time, I was stuck with a persistent limiting belief of this archetype: I believed that investing in myself, my education, and my growth was the last thing I should do. Personal growth seemed like a luxury.

In the early days, I was able to get into Tony Robbins's epic Date with Destiny seminar as his guest. Still, I had to pay for my room and food, which felt like a lot at the time. When I arrived at the seminar, I received an invitation to come to his Business Mastery program—this time as a paying guest. My whole soul *knew* I had to be there because this would be the experience that busted me wide-open. My Heart said yes and my SP said no. I really felt like I needed to go—the problem was I'd have to spend half of what I had left in the bank to attend, and the other half to get to the seminar and stay there.

After much mental turmoil, I decided I couldn't do it. It was worth it—I knew that, but *I* wasn't worth it. As fate would have it, during the Date with Destiny seminar, I ran into a man I had come to know who happened to be a billionaire—something that seemed so out of reach to me in this lifetime. We had lunch, and I talked to him about how I wanted to go to the Business Mastery program but couldn't afford it. I said I didn't have enough disposable income to attend.

The truth was, I had the money, nearly the exact amount, but I was scared to spend it all, and I was justifying my decision not to with this limiting story. The man I was talking to caught on to this right away and said to me, "Mastin, the money you invest in yourself and your growth is not disposable income. It's mandatory if you want to be successful. Do you have enough money to attend?"

"Uh, yes, just enough," I said.

"Then you must go," he said. "Life will open up when you play a bigger game."

That was it. He called my bluff. For an hour or two, I debated whether or not to take his advice. Then I had a thought that ended up being one of the most important realizations of my life. I thought to myself, *Who are you going to believe right now? You or him? He's a billionaire. He has no vested interest in you going to the seminar. But you did just get free advice from a billionaire and you're thinking about not taking it . . .*

I paused and considered the idea that a billionaire's thoughts in this moment of my life might be more valuable and accurate than my own, especially a billionaire at a Tony Robbins event. I decided, in a terrifying and sobering moment, to trust his advice and go to Tony's program. It was really a choice between investing in myself or staying small and retreating. The right choice may sound obvious, but it was a massive leap for me, financially and emotionally.

But I did it. I went to the seminar, which changed my life and my way of thinking about business. What changed even more was my relationship with money. I was now allowing it to flow in and out of me even though I had massive SPs and limiting stories surrounding it. And that changed me. By investing in myself beyond what I felt was comfortable, I opened up a door for new energy and possibility to come in.

What I learned by stretching to go to this program was this: when something is an intuitive *yes* in your Heart and it scares you, it's the right choice. Growth will always scare you.

What's so magical is that a week after the seminar, I got my first big ad check from an advertiser on my blog, which was *twice the cost* of the seminar and all the associated expenses. So within a week I doubled my money.

I believe that by taking the leap to invest in myself and backing it up with courageous action, I created a vacuum that called in that ad check. I know in my bones the check would not have come if I hadn't made the first move.

This is the deep lesson of the Disempowered Prostitute. Can you trust your Intuition, your Heart, your Soul, your Spirit, and God more than your current circumstances? Are you willing to invest in your growth, to stretch beyond those circumstances? I hope you'll say yes.

Take Back Your Power!

One of the great truths in life is that when you try to change, the thing you want to change will be the very thing that tries to stop you from changing. That's why we need to catch ourselves, to take notice of our limiting beliefs and SPs, so that we can challenge them and grow beyond them.

When you begin to experience a larger version of your life, you will see that each time you grow and stretch yourself, you will be supported. You are resourceful and faithful enough to become more. So let's take your power back from the Disempowered Prostitute and step into a faithful life where you no longer sell your Soul. Begin by answering the following questions in your journal:

Where in my life am I currently selling my Soul?

Where in my life have I decided money is more important that faith?

How have I made financial security more important than faith in my career, vocation, or business?

How have I made financial security more important than faith in my romantic life?

How have I made financial security more important than faith in my health and well-being?

How have I made financial security more important than faith with my family?

How have I made financial security more important than faith with my creativity?

How have I made financial security more important than faith with my Spirit life?

Why is now the right time to invest in myself?

Who do I want to work with as a coach, mentor, or teacher?

How can I stretch and become even more resourceful so I can work with this person?

How can I open up even more to receive the good that is coming to me?

What fears around money do I need to place in the hands of God?

What products or services could I start offering to the world that I've held back until now?

What would I have to believe to feel good about receiving abundant financial compensation for these products or services?

Today's affirmation: I invest in myself and create new energy and opportunities as a result.

Today's prayer: Dear God, please help me soothe my money fears. Show me where in my life I have sold my Soul and help me call it back. Help me feel supported as I stretch financially. Help me take my next step in faith, knowing that even though I can't feel it yet, You will provide for me. Show me how I can be even more resourceful than I thought. Guide me and allow Your wisdom, abundance, and Love to fill my Heart. Aid me in receiving all the financial abundance You intend for me in direct proportion to my ability to serve Your children.

DAY 27:
BRAVE THE STORM

"The big question is whether you are going to be able to say a hearty yes to your adventure."

– JOSEPH CAMPBELL

On any journey, there are two opposing forces that, until recognized, will keep you dead. They are the need for survival and comfort, on one side, and the pull of your Soul's calling, on the other.

Your survival instinct wants to keep your Soul dead. It wants everything to remain the same, to maintain the status quo, in order to keep you safe. At the same time, there is a deep calling within you in for growth, for change, and for the thrill of the adventure. You've most likely taken two steps forward for every two steps back, caught up in the dance of these two forces without even realizing that you were being pulled in opposite directions.

Yes, you need to survive—to eat, breathe, sleep, shelter, and so on— but we are raising our standards here to something much more vital. We are choosing, in the face of fear, to follow our Soul's calling. There is an unseen and magnetic force within you pulling you forward. You can resist it. You can deny it. You can try to explain it away, but there it remains.

Which force are you going to let drive the ship from now on? I know it's nice to feel safe and cozy and comfortable, but you cannot measure God's Love based on how comfortable you are.

God is interested in your personal growth and development. Your Soul is longing to pursue its own evolution and Purpose. So right now, as we are winding up the Ordeal phase of your journey, you get to ask yourself: Will I continue forward or will I shrink back?

Remember that six-month commitment you made earlier? We've probably all heard that it takes 10,000 hours of work on one area to be an expert. But in my work with thousands of clients, I've noticed that it takes six months of sustained effort to make a change, and so the new patterns and behaviors will stick. Sure, it seems like a long time. But wouldn't you rather devote six months to a new life rather than stay stuck in your old life for the next 20 years?

After consciously invoking the habits, patterns, relationships, and beliefs that have been holding you back, and then bringing to your attention how archetypal energies are keeping you dead, you are surely beginning to feel like your life is turning upside down. My great wish for you is that you accept this and you keep journeying with me, that you leap into the wild abyss of the unknown and allow a miraculous turn of events to come your way.

Don't stop a miracle in progress. Your SPs will speak the loudest just before your greatest breakthrough occurs. So today, as we consciously kill our disempowered relationship to our archetypes and create a vacuum, stay the course. You owe it yourself to brave the storm.

A Small Start to Something Big

I want us to look now at how you can either hold yourself back or move forward. With that topic in mind, I want to share a story that will bring you hope, inspiration, and peace of mind.

My clients and people who attend my events often ask me, "Mastin, how did you become successful?" Many of them seem to expect a simple, easy, no-hard-work-required answer that will create instant success in their lives.

Anyone who is successful knows that this is not how it works.

My answer is always the same: My success started the day I made my own bed. Typically this response is met with looks of confusion, so I explain further, detailing more of the story I first shared with you in the introduction.

When I was a manager in the music business, I used to be addicted to cocaine. Drugs are bad. Cocaine is bad. But I did it because I wanted to be in a relationship with a certain girl who also did cocaine. Cocaine was the glue that brought us together.

After a couple of years of hard use, I hit a rock bottom. Lost my dream job. Lost the girl. Lost my significance in the music business. Lost my identity. I didn't know any of the stuff I'm writing about in this book today.

After a particularly hard night of bingeing and snorting cocaine, I had a spiritual experience, a moment of clarity that showed me I needed to quit cocaine. It was a moment of Divine intervention. I was still cutting the line of cocaine when I heard an audible voice within me say, "If you do that line you're cutting up right now, you'll die."[18] I also had an overwhelming sense that this voice was telling the truth.

Something within stopped me. You could call it my Soul, God, or a Divine presence, but something would not let me continue to kill myself. I quit cold turkey that night and never looked back (though I still dream about doing coke from time to time, even today, 12 years later).

A couple of days after quitting, I was feeling like crap when I suddenly had this awareness: I had been using cocaine to feel better because without it I felt powerless and dead. I realized that in order to make progress, I needed to make it my intention to feel as good off the drugs as I did on them.

The next day I woke up with sober eyes and looked around my apartment in Santa Monica. It was a mess. A total disaster zone. The thought of cleaning and organizing it all was overwhelming. So I did what I could with what I had. I simply made my bed—something I hadn't ever done before. That night when I came home, the apartment was a mess, but the bed was made. It provided a tiny bit of peace—an oasis amid the storm. I felt a little bit of comfort from this, as if someone cared enough about me to do this small thing for me. It felt like I had a motherly presence taking care of me, except that I had actually given this gift to myself. That made me want to give myself this gift every morning.

After that I decided to clean my bedroom. The next day it was the living room. Then the kitchen. Pretty soon the whole apartment was no longer a dark, messy, shame-inducing drug hole. It was a clean, light-filled space. And in that place, I could finally think clearly. It was that thinking that eventually led to my success.

So, how did I become successful? It literally started with making my own bed.

The idea is that when you focus on small, measureable results, rather than trying to do everything at once, you put yourself on the fast track to success. Poet Christopher Morley explained it best when he said, "Big shots are only little shots who keep shooting." Or, as I like to say, a master is a beginner who kept beginning.

---

18   Mastin Kipp, *Daily Love: Growing into Grace* (New York: Hay House, 2014).

The best way to fast-track your soulful success is to create small, achievable goals, while keeping the bigger vision in mind. When Oprah Winfrey first started her OWN Network, it didn't take off right away. She and her executive team turned OWN into what it is today by focusing on what they called "the next thing." If this method worked for me, a poet, and Oprah, then it can work for you too.

So let's start small. Let's brave the storm one step at a time. Your desire to stay safe and secure can be slowly outsmarted if you break down your progress into bite-size pieces that you can focus on and achieve one at a time.

First Things First

Let's start doing that right now by looking at two things. First, the vision or outcome you want to create in each area of your life. And second, one simple, grounded step that you can take to start bringing that vision to life.

One caveat: we want *grounded action steps* here. Not broad concepts.

When I work with clients on this process, many of them make the mistake of writing out concepts versus actual steps. For example, if you are ready to start taking better care of your health, you might say that you next step is to "love yourself" or "take better care of yourself." But that's not grounded or specific enough. Instead you might say, "I am going to drink half an ounce of water per pound of body weight each day." Or, "I am going to do cardio exercise for 20 minutes three times a week." Or, "I'm going to stop eating products with high-fructose corn syrup."

We want specifics here. Actual steps and actual timelines. So as you answer the questions that follow in your journal, be on the lookout for broad concepts when what you really want is grounded actionable items and set dates as to when you will accomplish each step. Let's go.

The biggest outcome for my romantic life is:

My next baby step is:

I will take this step by:

The biggest outcome for my health and well-being is:

The next baby step is:

I will take this step by:

The biggest outcome in my career, business, or vocation is:

My next baby step is:

I will take this step by:

The biggest outcome in my financial life is:

My next baby step is:

I will take this step by:

The biggest outcome in my creative life is:

My next baby step is:

I will take this step by:

The biggest outcome in my spirit life is:

My next baby step is:

I will take this step by:

This process will satisfy the dreamer and visionary in you while also allowing you to make tangible, achievable progress, baby step by baby step, in a defined amount of time. These baby steps should feel both manageable and a little scary at the same time. As you plot out your steps, remember that you are beginning the process of your inevitable resurrection.

Today's affirmation: I see the larger vision and ground that vision by making one small step toward realizing it each day. I celebrate every step along the way.

Today's prayer: Creator of All, show me what my next small steps are. Give me the courage and clarity to take these small steps. Aid me, each day, in taking one baby step a day. Give my signs that I am on the right path. Put up obstacles to the pathways that will keep me dead, and open doors toward opportunities to bring my Purpose to life. My life is in Your hands. Show me my next grounded steps, and I will take them with passion, vigor, and faith.

DAY 28:
WHY HUMILITY IS ESSENTIAL FOR YOUR JOURNEY

"Humility is the ability to remain approachable."

– GURU PREM

You can tell how spiritually advanced someone is by how loved you feel in his or her presence. Every time. Spirituality has little to do with the rituals people engage in or the books they read, and far more to do with how they act and how loving they are.

Spirituality is, in fact, the measure of how loving you are.

There are two truths that are paradoxical in nature, and, as always, how you relate to these truths that will determine how far you go. On one hand, you are a unique, special, and Divine Child of God. You are perfectly made and your Soul is not flawed. On the other hand, you are a speck of a speck of a speck, a teeny tiny little spot in an infinite universe that is so much larger than you that you are almost nothing.

So, you are Divinely Special and you are almost nothing.

Both these things are true.

Embodying the balance between these two truths creates a healthy relationship with your ego and allows your Heart and Soul to lead. It also gives you the self-esteem you need to create the life of your dreams, as well as the humility to know you're no more important than anyone or anything else. Humility makes you approachable so you can actually connect with people.

All the great people I've met, the ones I truly want to be like, have this same combination of traits. They have enough self-esteem to believe they can be successful, combined with a profound humility that keeps them approachable and teachable. It's important to remember that the same balance is necessary to the growth of everyone you meet, from beggar to queen. Gandhi said this about it:

The seeker after truth should be humbler than the dust. The world crushes the dust under its feet, but the seeker after truth should so humble himself that even the dust could crush him. Only then, and not till then, will he have a glimpse of truth.[19]

Not getting this right can stop your progress dead in its tracks. Why? Because you won't ever be successful or live your Purpose if you don't first believe that you can. And nobody likes being in a room with someone who thinks he is the only special person, which means he is allowing his ego to drive the ship, rather than his Soul.

When someone feels deeply that she needs to be special in this world, one of the most common reasons is because she is coming from a past where she was not nurtured or supported, where she didn't feel important. If this is true for you (as it once was for me), you need to have love and compassion for yourself. If you feel as if you are worthless and powerless, then for a time narcissistic qualities may be needed to find your power. However, you must eventually bring them back into balance with your Heart.

It is equally destructive to remain overly humble about your gifts. While the most successful people in the room act humbly, they also take bold and decisive action. In many ways, their actions speak louder than their words.

On the other hand, pretending to be the most special person around is a fantastic SP because you feel a sense of greater importance than everyone you meet. This pattern protects your Heart and vulnerable self, but it creates unnecessary competition and stress and causes all kinds of violence and misuse of human will. Like David Hawkins is quoted as saying, "A fall in consciousness can happen when the (spiritual) ego of the receiver claims authorship of the effects and achievements of the Divine spirit."

Too much humility is also a great survival pattern. It allows you to hide and not get into the arena. Brené Brown summarizes this perfectly in her book *Daring Greatly*:

When we spend our lives waiting until we're perfect or bulletproof before we walk into the arena, we ultimately sacrifice relationships and opportunities that may not be recoverable, we squander our precious time, and we turn our backs on our

---

19 Mohandas K. Gandhi, *Autobiography: The Story of My Experiments with Truth* (Mineola, NY: Dover Publications, 1983), ix.

gifts, those unique contributions that only we can make. Perfect and bulletproof are seductive, but they don't exist in the human experience.[20]

Many spiritual seekers and teachers with good intentions can get trapped between these two extremes. There is a sweet spot between knowing that you are special and remaining humble that opens a door to a world unknown by many. A world where you can have it all. A world where you can attract amazing people into your life to assist you with your Purpose. A world where you set the example and bar for others. A world where you can seemingly create magic out of thin air with your every desire because you are so in rapport with both your massive Divine nature and your smallness that it is a joy to be in your presence.

This is the dance you must learn if you are to claim your power.

Where Are You Now?

Grab your journal again and let's find out if you've been acting a little more special than you truly are or if you've been hiding in the humility hole a little too long.

Do I believe I have to be the most special person in my romantic life?

Do I believe I have to be the most special person in my health and fitness routine?

Do I believe I have to be the most special person in my career, business, or vocation?

Do I believe I have to be the most special person in my family?

Do I believe I have to be the most special person in my spirituality?

Have I been too humble in my romantic life?

Have I been too humble in my health and wellness?

Have I been too humble in my in my career, vocation, or job?

---

20   Brené Brown, *Daring Greatly: How the Courage to Be Vulnerable Transforms the Way We Live, Love, Parent, and Lead* (New York: Avery: 2015).

Have I been too humble in my family affairs?

Have I been too humble in my spirituality?

Based on your responses to the previous questions, answer the following:

What action can I take to find more balance in my romantic life?

What action can I take to find more balance in my career, vocation, or job?

What action can I take to find more balance in my health and wellness?

What action can I take to find more balance in my family affairs?

What action can I take to find more balance in my spirituality?

Finally, ask yourself this question:

Who is someone I can trust to call me on these patterns the next time they come up?

Today's affirmation: I am living my Purpose.

Today's prayer: Dear God, help me feel special. Help me feel unique. Give me the courage to boldly live my Soul's Purpose on the earth. Give me courage to speak my truth, to share what I know, and to be who You made me to be. Give the humility to be less than dust, to always remain approachable, and to know that all gifts, success, and good deeds are by Your design. I give You all the credit.

DAY 29:
THE PRICE OF INACTION

"He who rejects change is the architect of decay.
The only human institution which rejects
progress is the cemetery."

– HAROLD WILSON

So far in this book we've found your Soul's Purpose and your emotional blueprint, and you've created your new hierarchy. I've warned you about all the different ways you might get in the way of your own progress as you continue down your spiritual path. Yet your SPs can be so strong that you still won't change.

Have you ever met someone who knew what to do, had the tools to do it, but still didn't transform? Perhaps that's been you.

Today we have to go back to the beginning of our journey and remember our success formula:

Intense emotion + belief + action = result

You may have the belief, you may know the actions you need to take, but you don't have the correct intense emotion around these things. Before or during any major change, the intense emotion my clients tend to feel is fear—fear that they do not use for growth, but rather as an excuse to stay dead.

We need to create intense emotion within you, enough to unleash the transformation promised in this book. Without that intense emotion, channeled in the right way, you'll stay dead and this book will just become just another example of spiritual entertainment. So, let me twist the knife in your SPs one final time as we round out the Ordeal part of our journey.

Let's be really honest with each other here, okay? If you were to die today, having lived a life where your SPs ran the show, what would your obituary say about you?

Before you put too much thought into that question, I want to share with you a powerful example of the suffering that awaits you if you do not change. This is from the PBS documentary *The Power of Myth*,[21] in which Bill Moyers interviewed Joseph Campbell.

BILL MOYERS: Follow your bliss?

JOSEPH CAMPBELL: Your bliss, where the deep of sense of being in form and going where your body and soul want to go, when you have that feeling, then stay with it and don't let anyone throw you off. Have you ever read Sinclair Lewis's *Babbitt*?

BILL MOYERS: Not in a long time.

JOSEPH CAMPBELL: Do you remember the last line? "I've never done a thing I wanted to in all my life."

BILL MOYERS: Quite an admission.

JOSEPH CAMPBELL: That's the man who never followed his bliss. Well, I heard that line. I was living in Bronxville when I was teaching at Sarah Lawrence. Before I was married, I used to be eating out in the restaurants of the town for my lunch and dinners. And Thursday night was the maid's night off in Bronxville, so that all the families were out in the restaurants. And one fine evening, I was in my favorite restaurant there. It was a Greek restaurant. And at a table was sitting a father, a mother, and a scrawny little boy here, about 12 years old. And the father says to the boy, "Drink your tomato juice." And the boy says, "I don't want to." And the father with a louder voice says, "Drink your tomato juice." And the mother says, "Don't make him do what he doesn't want to do." The father looks at her, and he says, "He can't go through life doing what he wants to do." Said, "If he does only what he wants to do, he'll be dead. Look at me, I've never done a thing I wanted to in all my life." I said, My God, Babbitt incarnate. And that's the man who never followed his bliss.

---

21   See https://en.wikipedia.org/wiki/The_Power_of_Myth.

You may have success in your career and in other areas—but what good is it if you've never done a thing you wanted to in all your life? What's so ironic about the father in Campbell's story is that he said if his son did what he wanted to, he'd be "dead." His choice of words tells us a lot about the source of this advice.

Obviously we don't know this father, but there is a high likelihood that he was dead in his own life. Remember, dead people give you advice to keep you dead. But you don't want to be dead any longer.

Writing Your Obit

It's time to grow, so be honest with yourself and write out your obituary in your journal as it would stand today.

If I died today, my obituary would say:

Great, how does that feel? You might feel a little depressed, uncomfortable, or proud as you remember some of the great things you've done.

My hope is that we are starting to awaken some of that intense emotional energy you need to transform your life. So look at this obituary and ask yourself: *Is this the legacy I want to leave on this planet? Is there something unique that is still within me that yearns to come forward?* Maybe it's a book, or a company, or a child, or a business, or a work of art.

And finally: Have you aborted the process of your Soul's evolution on this planet because you were afraid?

The only answer to this question is, of course, yes.

Now, for a moment, step into your imagination, that genius part of your Soul that loves to play and create and dream. And dream with me about your future life. Imagine that you lived a great while longer, long enough to bring forward your unique gift. Long enough to leave your mark. To make your impact. To help other people. To heal your wounds. To forgive. To let go. To connect with your Soul and to do something that truly has meaning.

Step out with me and see all the people you don't even know yet that you could positively affect. Think about all the inspiration that you could bring to the planet. Think about how all the relationships in your life will change for the better and how your liberated self inspires others to liberate themselves. See all the ripple effects of a well-lived life lived from your Soul's Purpose. See yourself taking risk after risk. Becoming bolder and bolder. Stretching. Going further than you could ever imagine.

Picture the greatest life you can imagine, and then picture yourself on your deathbed after having lived that life. How do you feel about yourself now? What does God say to you when you return home after a well-lived life? What scars are you proud of? How have you left this planet a better place than when you found it?

Write your new obituary:

Your new obituary is a lot different, isn't it?

This life is *more than possible* for you. It is inevitable if you practice what you are being taught in this book each and every day. When you return to your Soul and put your faith in God, all blocks are cleared, mountains moved, and the wasteland of your life is restored to an abundant and fruitful paradise.

You must take this journey. You must do it for yourself and for those whom you are meant to help. You cannot be like Babbitt and live an unlived life. You must do whatever it takes, make all sacrifices that need to be made, and make the bold and courageous choices needed to bring your Purpose to life.

No one is coming for you. You must save yourself. You can do that by choosing to remain open to Divine guidance. You must surround yourself with mentors and a community that lifts your spirits. And you must not delay. Begin at once. Make it big. Make it bold and watch miracles come. You no longer need to be jealous of others or delay in your attempt to live a bigger life. You've got all you need within you to make the leap. Now is your time.

Today's affirmation: I will take risks and live a life that is bigger each day than it was the day before.

Today's prayer: O Creator, help me respect myself. Give me the courage I need to arrive at Your doorstep at the end of my life fully used. Give me the ability to trust myself, my body, and my Soul. Aid in my attempt to live a purposeful life. Support me when all seems lost. Guide me when I am in a fog. Show me the way. Open doors. Give me the courage to start now.

DAY 30:
SURRENDER ALL THE RESULTS TO GOD

"When you trust in yourself, you trust in the
very wisdom that created you."

– WAYNE DYER

We have come to the end of your Ordeal. We have hit the point of your surrender. The point at which you leap, let go, and trust God with all your Heart, mind, and Soul. Remember, when you trust your Heart and your Soul, you are also trusting God.

Tomorrow we begin a new phase of your journey—the journey back home so you can channel your Purpose in a powerful way. Starting tomorrow, we really bring your Purpose to life.

We've journeyed far together, so today is about taking a moment to breathe, pause, and celebrate how far you've come. You are crossing a threshold and becoming a new person. You are becoming a person who has claimed their power and will begin to show others how to do the same. So today we make a vow together: from this moment forward, you turn your whole life over to your Creator's will. And when your old SPs try to creep back into your life and stall your growth, you will pause, notice them, and then keep going.

It's time to surrender. Remember, *surrender* doesn't mean giving up. It means giving in to something greater.

Your best thinking is what killed you, so now it's time to change. It's time to become humble enough to allow God to work for and through you. Why? So that you can come back to Love. Love of God, love of yourself, and love for others. As the great poet Rumi said, "Looking at my life, I see that only Love has been my soul's companion. From deep inside my soul cries out: Do not wait, surrender, for the sake of Love."[22]

What you are surrendering to is a greater outcome. You are allowing yourself to be made new. You are leaving behind that which is old and no longer serves in order to create space for something new, unknown,

---

22 *Rumi: Whispers of the Beloved* (HarperCollins Publishers, 1999)

and exciting. That thing is coming, and your job is to open up and let it in. You can celebrate today because redemption is on the way. Do something extraspecial for yourself today, whether it be pampering yourself with a massage, spending extra time in meditation or prayer, choosing a healthy smoothie instead of a cupcake, or taking an extralong walk. You've earned it! And your body and Soul will thank you for a gift of love.

Sweet Surrender

Today, what outcomes are you going to surrender? You cannot control how life unfolds, but you can choose how to respond to what happens. You can respond in a way that allows for even greater things to come. Today is a day to remind yourself why you want to surrender, to remind yourself of all the greater things you are hoping for, aiming for in your life. Do that now by answering the following statements in your journal:

Today, I surrender the outcome of my romantic life because:

Today, I surrender the outcome of my health and well-being because:

Today, I surrender the outcome of my business, career, and vocation because:

Today, I surrender the outcome of my family dynamic because:

Today, I surrender the outcome of my creativity because:

Today, I let go of control because:

Fantastic. You've set yourself up for your rebound. Tomorrow we begin. Today we celebrate!

Today's affirmation: I allow God to determine my direction. I am God's passenger.

Today's prayer: Dear Divine Source, help me trust in your wisdom, timing, and outcomes. Give me freedom. Help me let go of control. Allow me to be flexible so You can do your great works in my life. I surrender and accept what You have in store for me knowing that it is far greater than anything I could ever imagine for myself. I am Your passenger. Take me, O God, where You will.

Part IV

THE JOURNEY HOME

"The return and reintegration with society, which is indispensable to the continuous circulation of spiritual energy into the world, and which, from the standpoint of the community, is the justification of the long retreat, the hero himself may find the most difficult requirement of all. For if he has won through, like the Buddha, to the profound repose of complete enlightenment, there is danger that the bliss of this experience may annihilate all recollection of, interest in, or hope for, the sorrows of the world; or else the problem of making known the way of illumination to people wrapped in economic problems may seem too great to solve."

– JOSEPH CAMPBELL

You've come a long way, and I am proud of you. The work you've done has been challenging. Many, who are not so determined, have turned back by now. But not you.

As Campbell states above, the hardest part of the journey is the return to the ordinary world. You have had aha moments. You have had breakthroughs. You understand yourself in a way that you didn't a month ago. You have a new vocabulary, new insights, new awareness, and a new identity. You may even be in a state of bliss or flow around your new-found sense of freedom and self-knowledge. After all this, it is normal to experience both the fear of returning to your old life (your relationships, circumstances, and career) as a changed person, and the fear embracing the new life (the unknown) that you're stepping into.

There are two parts to every journey that many people fear. The first is the call to adventure, the call to step outside your current patterns and embrace the dark, mysterious unknown. At the start the journey represents both possibility and the unknown. There's so much you don't know and yet tons of curiosity about the answer to the question, "What if?"

The second part of every journey that is feared is what's called the "Refusal of the Return," meaning that once someone goes on a journey and finds bliss, they don't want to go back into the world because the world is too harsh for them. But, in order to make the journey complete, return we must.

After enough Divine Storms you go on the journey. The way is unknown, but you meet allies, friends, and a new tribe. You find yourself transforming, shedding old layers, and gaining clarity. You begin to come home to yourself. Little by little, the old, dead version of you dies, and a new, Soul-centered version of you is born. You are beginning to see that the world, God, and all life will support this empowered version of you.

Like a child who has just begun to walk, you've taken your first step into a larger world. It's scary, exciting, and wonderful all at once. And what you really love is this feeling—the feeling of knowing your Purpose. Knowing your hierarchy. Creating habits of self-love and self-care. Connecting with your Creator. Finding out who you really are. Boundaries have been set, and you are becoming new.

That fear that you first felt when you embarked on your journey can come back upon your return, when you have to start integrating this new you into your old life. Perhaps you fear repeating old patterns in a relationship. Perhaps you're afraid of going back into the world and meeting its pain. Perhaps you fear you will lose that special feeling, lose your Purpose, and lose yourself. You fear deep down that this new version of you won't be accepted by your old tribe, and you may end up alone. You may wonder if you are going to slip back into your old hierarchy and if the archetypes will get the best of you. You may feel that this moment is fleeting and that you will just end up going back to the "real world" and that our time together will have been some fantasyland.

Every hero or heroine fears the return. But we must, if we are to fully realize our Purpose, bring what we've learned back to the world. We owe the world our light, even if it has only shown us darkness. The world needs you to shine, to glow, to succeed, and to demonstrate that, even in the face of sorrow, joy can be found.

DAY 31:
LET'S MEET YOUR HEART

"The journey of life is for the heart to usher the
mind into the zone of revelation."

– JOSEPH CAMPBELL

Your guiding light, your barometer, your compass, your decision maker from now on is your Heart.

Yes, your Heart.

It has a voice, a direct line to the Divine. And when you tap into your heart, life begins to expand. You can break through barriers and see opportunities you never saw before. Your Heart can even help you solve problems, answer questions, and create a better life than you've ever imagined.

I have taught the process of Kipp Heart Therapy (which will guide you to literally talk to your heart) to thousands of clients all over the world.

I lead a powerful retreat called Enter the Heart in places like Bali and Maui, where clients come to learn this in-depth process directly from me. There is nothing like a sacred environment to evoke the wisdom of your Heart. Today is a great day to take this book to a place you hold sacred because I would like to ask that you read these words with the intention of finding the sacred.

At first, asking you to "follow your Heart" can seem like bad advice. When many of my clients are first introduced to the idea of trusting their Hearts, they say something like, "Mastin, I trusted my Heart in the past and got burned, so I've learned not to trust my Heart."

What really happened, however, is that these clients thought they were following their Hearts when really they had a hierarchy that didn't serve them. Put another way, they didn't follow their Hearts; they followed their codependency or their addiction. They followed their old SPs. They made someone else the source of their emotional wealth and paid dearly for it.

When you follow your Heart, you live within a healthy hierarchy and never give someone else your power. Following your Heart is the opposite of what you've done up until now. When you love yourself, you can never make a wrong choice.

The other thing I hear when I talk about listening to your Heart is that it's just some naive Disney or Hallmark idea. That it's silly, shallow, or for kids who watch *Frozen*, but doesn't have any real-world practicality. Nothing could be further from the truth.

Your Heart contains the deepest wisdom you have. Your Heart is the keeper of your Intuition, your Soul, and it is your Divine connection. The Heart always knows the truth, always knows what your next step should be, and speaks in very simple terms. Your Heart also whispers.

Your mind is loud. Irrational fear and old SPs speak much louder than your Heart. Your Heart is the cool, calm feeling you have within you. Your Higher Wisdom.

Your Heart is what called you to this book. It's what kept you reading. It's what made you feel like you are guided.

Oprah Winfrey once told Piers Morgan, "Everything I'm saying, whether it's in my magazine, whether it's Gayle on the radio, whether it's the *Oprah Winfrey Show* and everything now about the channel OWN, is about opening your space, your heart space, so that you can love more."[23]

The decision to love, the decision to live your Purpose, the decision to rise above your current SPs, and the decision to be courageous in the face of insurmountable odds all come from the wisdom of your Heart. Finding and listening to your Heart is serious business.

Listen to Your Heart

If you have been living in your head, in a place of stress, high cortisol and adrenaline levels, and in constant fight-or-flight mode, then it is difficult to hear your Heart. Remember, it whispers. The good news is you don't need to meditate for 10 years, go vegan, or do yoga to hear your Heart. These things are all well and good, but there are many people who may look like they are living in their Heart space when they really aren't.

The cornerstone of the new model of transformation is making the jump from our brain to our body. Dr. Candace Pert reminds us that "your body is your subconscious mind."[24] That means the Heart space, the subconscious, and the wisdom you are looking for are within your own body.

---

23 *Piers Morgan Tonight*, Interview with Oprah Winfrey, CNN, January 17, 2011,
http://transcripts.cnn.com/TRANSCRIPTS/1101/17/pmt.01.html.
24 Candace Pert, *Your Body Is Your Subconscious Mind*, Audio CD, unabridged (Sounds True, 2004).

At the top of this chapter, Joseph Campbell was quoted as saying that the "Heart ushers the mind into the zone of revelation." What Campbell meant by this is that the Heart is connected to a larger amount of wisdom than we can mentally and consciously understand. When you follow and trust your Heart, it will blow your mind. That's because your Heart is God's voice within you.

Jesus said in Luke 17:21: "Neither shall they say, Lo here! or, lo there! for, behold, the kingdom of God is within you."

In the Gospel of Thomas, you can find the same wisdom. Jesus said: "If you bring forth what is within you, what you bring forth will save you. If you do not bring forth what is within you, what you do not bring forth will destroy you."

Saint Francis of Assisi said, "The One you are looking for is the One who is looking."

Time and time again, when I lead my clients through Kipp Heart Therapy, they report a sense of connecting to that part of themselves that they have been looking for. What's so impressive is not just this experience, but the physiological changes my clients go through. Their faces become lighter. Their bodies relax. They are more centered, more certain, and more in touch with their own wisdom.

The whole purpose of this book is not for you to follow me but for you to learn how to follow the guidance coming from your own Heart. Everything we've done up until now has been preparation for this moment when you discover your Heart.

So start tapping into the wisdom of your Heart. First, let's try some "Heart Focused Breathing," as HeartMath calls it.[25] This is what you do:

1. Find a sacred space where you are away from all Internet connections, phones, things, and people that can disturb you.

2. Sit down and place your hands over your Heart. Close your eyes and focus on your Heart. Inhale deeply and exhale deeply. Your breaths should be intentional and focused. As you breathe in, focus on your Heart; as you breathe out, focus on your Heart.

3. After 5 to 10 minutes have passed, come back to this part of the book.

---

25   See https://www.heartmath.org.

Now that you've done your Heart breathing, the next step is to begin your Kipp Heart Therapy.

Leap into the idea that your Heart is a consciousness, a personality, a thing that you can talk to. However, the Heart "speaks" through feelings. If you are used to thinking more than feeling, it can be hard to hear your Heart at first. My Heart Meditation, which you can access at http://thedailylove.com/this-is-how-to-follow-your-heart/, can be helpful with this.

When you ready to listen to your Heart, I want you to ask it some questions. Start by closing your eyes and focusing on your Heart. Then ask your Heart out loud:

"Heart, show me where you are."

Repeat this question a few times and notice what you notice.

Then ask, "Heart, show me yes."

Ask that question a few times and notice what you notice.

Next, ask, "Heart, show me no."

Once again, notice what you notice.

If you find yourself overthinking, doubting, or judging yourself, you've gone back into your mind and your old SPs. Thank them for showing up, but then ask them to take a seat. Trust your body.

Oftentimes people report feeling their Hearts in their legs, hands, shoulders, or bellies. The feeling of your Heart doesn't have to start in the center of your chest, so don't worry if it doesn't. It could be found anywhere in your body at first.

After you've asked these three questions a few times, you will get a feeling response. What I've generally found with my clients is that a yes is a speeding-up or expansion feeling and a no is a slowing-down or a contraction feeling. Of course, this is just the general reaction, so don't worry if something different happens for you.

As you focus on your Heart, you will get information. Typically it's in the form of yes/no or single-sentence ideas. (Once again, you can further practice talking to your Heart by doing my Heart Meditation.)

The following are examples of some great questions to ask your Heart. Make sure to ask these questions *out loud* and notice what comes. Trust what comes, even if—and especially if—it makes no sense. If you are worried about "making things up," don't be. Trust what comes. This is the deepest wisdom within you.

Romantic Life Questions

If single:

Heart, what can I do to attract the love of my life?

Heart, how can I love myself even more today?

Heart, what really makes me attractive?

Heart, what is the best way for me to find love?

Heart, how can I be courageous in my dating life?

Heart, when will my love show up?

Heart, what should I do until my love arrives?

Heart, how can I trust myself to make the right choice?

Heart, what is the spiritual message of being single right now?

Heart, what am I learning as a single person?

If in a relationship:

Heart, how can I love my partner even more today?

Heart, what is the best way for me to resolve this fight or disagreement?

Heart, how can I live my Purpose in my relationship?

Heart, what is my next step in my relationship?

Heart, what needs are not getting met in my relationship?

Heart, how can I ask for those needs to be met?

Heart, how I can I meet the needs of my partner even more?

Heart, what is the spiritual lesson in my romantic relationship?

Heart, is there anything else you want me to know about my relationship?

Heart, where am I holding back in my relationship?

Heart, what is the next risk I can take in my relationship?

Health and Well-Being Questions

Heart, what's the best way to nourish my body today?

Heart, what is the best kind of exercise for me today?

Heart, how can I live my Purpose with my health?

Heart, what is the best food for my body?

Heart, what am I eating or consuming that is not good for me?

Heart, how can I love my body even more today?

Heart, what does my body need to thrive today?

Heart, how can I heal [insert your pain or sickness] the fastest?

Heart, what is the best environment for me to be in for optimum health?

Heart, what habits should I give up that are making me sick?

Heart, what is the next risk for me to take to become well?

Business/Career/Vocation Questions

Heart, what is the best career for me to live my Purpose?

Heart, what is the ideal way for me to be of service in my career?

Heart, what changes do I need to make in my career or business?

Heart, what am I worth in this career or business?

Heart, how can I earn what I am worth in my career or business?

Heart, how can I set healthy boundaries in my career or business?

Heart, what is my mission in my career or business?

Heart, where am I holding back in my career or business?

Heart, what is the next risk for me to take in my career or business?

Spirituality

Heart, what is the best way for me to connect to God?

Heart, are you how God/Spirit/Divine talks to me?

Heart, what are the best spiritual practices for me?

Heart, how can I live my Purpose in my spiritual life?

Heart, how can I improve others' lives with the greatest impact?

Heart, what is the next step for me to take to live my Purpose?

Heart, what is God's will in my life?

Heart, how often should I talk to you?

Heart, how can I have even more faith?

Heart, what do I do when I am scared to take action?

Heart, what is my next courageous action step?

Talking to your Heart, like any relationship, grows with time, attention, and love, so keep working on this. I highly suggest talking to your Heart and doing the Heart Meditation daily.

The Heart speaks in simple terms, but its answers demand all our courage. Summon your courage because this connection to your Heart is the connection you've been seeking for so long.

You are now returning home. Home to your Heart. Home to yourself. Home to your inner wisdom. It's as if you are looking in a mirror that shows you a reflection of your Soul as it beckons, "Come home to me. We've got work to do."

Today's affirmation: I follow my Heart's guidance with faith. Everything I need is within me.

Today's prayer: Dear God, speak to me through my Heart. Show me how to build an even closer relationship with You. I yearn to feel connected to You. To take action on Your will in my life. To feel fully alive, on Purpose, and in my flow. Give me clarity. Give me courage. Show me my next step. Help me stay connected to You in the Heavens and grounded firmly here on earth. I am Your servant; speak to me through my Heart.

DAY 32:
GOALS WITH PURPOSE

*"It is good to have an end to journey toward;
but it is the journey that matters, in the end."*

– URSULA K. LE GUIN

Have you ever set a goal, reached it, and then thought . . . is *this* all there is?

The problem with most goal-setting processes is that they tend to lack Purpose and meaning, and they don't tap into the true reason why we set goals. The reason we set goals is to feel a feeling. What feeling? Your top two emotions, of course!

My top two emotions, as I mentioned before in Day 12, were belonging and connection. (They've since changed to nurturing and excitement. Remember, this is an evolving process, and as you transform, your top two emotions will change as your needs change.)

In the past, when I was emotionally in debt, I would set goals that I thought would make me happy only to end up short. I set goals to get money, relationships, success—you name it. But I was setting goals according to the hierarchy of "others, others, others." I was also coming from a place of feeling special without much humility.

This created massive disruption in my early career in the music business. I wanted to be special, and I wanted everyone to belong and connect to me. I didn't know a thing about Purpose. I didn't know a thing about why I set goals. I did it unconsciously. Looking back, I am grateful for the Divine Storms that came in and wiped away old patterns that didn't bring the emotions of Purpose into my life.

Outside a major tragedy, negative emotions on a day-to-day basis are subtle signs that we are not fully living our Purpose. To set Purpose-driven goals, you must make it your aim to align everything in your life with your top two emotions.

Since my top two emotions were belonging and connection, when I set goals, I used to ask myself questions like: Where do I feel like I truly belong? How will I feel most connected? My answers would determine my goals.

Now this is not how most people set goals. They determine what thing they want, figure out what they need to do to get it, and only then stop to think about how they feel as a result. That's why so many are left feeling empty, even when they achieve the things they thought they wanted. This happens because you cannot stress yourself to peace. You cannot lack yourself to abundance. You cannot strive your way to Purpose. If you are coming from a place of stress, lack, or striving, you are setting yourself up for a Divine Storm that will get larger and larger until you pay attention.

Let's not go there. Instead let's find out what you *really* want based on your emotions of Purpose and your new hierarchy. To reorganize your life in this way will take courage, boldness, and faith. This day will be a longer day than most because this is a visioning process. But it's important to get us to the next level, and to do that, we need to understand your life goals.

Setting New Goals

As you set goals with Purpose, you begin to change your life, from a life lived in emotional debt to an emotionally rich life. This emotional richness will pour into every area of your life. As you improve one area of your life, every other area will improve.

It's well documented that the best way to keep making progress toward your goals is to break them down into smaller pieces. This allows you to know the exact next steps you need to get the feeling you want, as well as have a sense of control in this new, unknown world of your Purpose. You also want to make sure that your goals are realistic and stretch you. Yes, you can create any life you want.

Let us talk financial goals for a moment. I know that you are not motivated *only* by money, but it makes for an easy-to-understand example.

Let's say that you want to start a business that makes $1,000,000, but until now you've made $0 and you have no previous entrepreneurial experience. Is it even possible that you can make $1,000,000 or more?

Yes.

But you have to start by making the first $10,000. To go from $0 to $10,000 is hard, but not as hard as going from $0 to $1,000,000.

Once you've made it to $10,000, it's a little easier to go from $10,000 to $100,000. Then it's the turn of a few knobs to go from $100,000 to $1,000,000. You *can* get there if you go step-by-step, bit-by-bit.

Part of the joy of setting goals with Purpose is that you dream as big as you can dream. However, you must take baby steps to get to your goal. You should also celebrate each advancement along the way.

The first part of any new process is the hardest. You don't have any proof that your dream or goal is possible. Your logical brain can only compare what's possible for your future with what has already happened in the past. That's why the beginning is so hard.

The hardest day to go to the gym is the first day.

The hardest day to start your business is the first day.

The hardest moment to say "I love you" is the first time.

Know that you are in the hardest part of your journey. To choose to begin and then actually begin is the hardest part. The rest is manageable. Your highs will get higher, and your lows will get higher.

The second-hardest part of your journey is deciding to keep going when you want to quit. You will want to quit, probably more than once—maybe even often. The simple-but-not-easy coaching on this is *don't*. Your job throughout is to give yourself the gift of not quitting. Don't stop. Keep going.

Today, all you have to do is decide that you will begin. Then, each day after this, decide to begin again. You only have to take this one day at a time. At any given time, each of us only needs to do the next thing. Bring your attention, your awareness, into the present moment so that you can bring your Purpose to life one moment at a time.

So, let's create your ultimate vision and then set realistic goals for how you can get there. Our aim today is to help you get clear on your big vision, to break it down into manageable next steps, and then to give you a sense of control so that you can take those steps, while also feeling like these Purpose-driven goals challenge you and that you are invoking the spirit of a worthy opponent.

One more piece of coaching before we get started: the worst advice you can take is proximity advice. That is to say, advice from the people closest to you who have never done what you are trying to do.

Sure, you love your mom, but your mom may have never started a business. And Mom has her own SPs to contend with. On the subject of starting your own business, you would probably get very different advice from your mom than you would from, say, Richard Branson. So, before you start talking to others about your Purpose-driven goals, make sure of two things:

1. *That they will support your choice.* Surround yourself with positive and inspiring people who will cheer you on. Separate from downers and people who say you can't do it.

2. *That they have been where you want to go.* The mentors or other people you take advice from should understand your journey and where you want to go. This is the difference between taking expert advice and taking proximity advice.

If you are blessed enough to have a family or tribe that supports your dreams and has produced the results you want to create, then by all means, fill them in. However, this is not the case for most people I meet. It's vital in the early stages of your dreams that you take good care of them. The beginning is when your dreams and goals are most fragile.

Let's start setting your goals with Purpose. Journal time again. We'll begin with a refresher:

Your top two emotions of Purpose are:

Your new hierarchy is: Self, Creator, and Others.

Now let's go through each area of your life and set goals based on these emotions and hierarchy.

Romantic Life

My top emotions are:

Goals that will allow me to feel this way toward myself in my romantic life are:

Goals that will allow me feel this way with God in my romantic life are:

Goals that will allow me to feel this way with my partner (or future partner) are:

What goals support a healthy hierarchy in my romantic life?

Career, Business, and Vocation

My top emotions are:

Goals that will allow me to feel this way toward myself in my career, business, or vocation:

Goals that will allow me feel this way with God in my career, business, or vocation:

Goals that will allow me to feel this way with others (team, clients, boss, etc.) in my career, business, or vocation:

What goals support a healthy hierarchy in my career, business, or vocation?

Health and Well-Being

My top emotions are:

Goals that will allow me to feel this way toward myself in my health and well-being:

Goals that will allow me feel this way with God in my health and well-being:

Goals that will allow me to feel this way with others (family, spouse, partner, clients, etc.) in my health and well-being:

What goals support a healthy hierarchy in my health and well-being?

Creativity

My top emotions are:

Goals that will allow me to feel this way toward myself in my creativity:

Goals that will allow me feel this way with God in my creativity:

Goals that will allow me to feel this way with others (family, spouse, partner, clients, etc.) in my creativity:

What goals support a healthy hierarchy in my creativity?

Look back at all the goals with Purpose that you came up with in the various areas of your life.

Make a master list of all your goals here:

Next decide which of all these goals are the three most important.

Write them down here:

Awesome. We are starting to make real headway here. Now we are going to take your top three goals and break them down into smaller pieces or next steps. Remember, we don't want broad concepts here; we want grounded action steps, complete with a due date.

Purpose Goal #1

My next step is:

How is this goal a worthy challenge for me?

Who can be a mentor to help me achieve this goal?

How does my schedule have to change to achieve this goal?

Purpose Goal #2

My next step is:

How is this goal a worthy challenge for me?

Who can be a mentor to help me achieve this goal?

How does my schedule have to change to achieve this goal?

Purpose Goal #3

My next step is:

How is this goal a worthy challenge for me?

Who can be a mentor to help me achieve this goal?

How does my schedule have to change to achieve this goal?

Before we finish, it's vital that we link your Purpose to a sense of contribution, growth, and deeper meaning.

Purpose Goal #1

Who will you become as a result of achieving your first Purpose goal?

What is your Purpose in achieving this goal?

Who will benefit from you achieving this goal?

Purpose Goal #2

Who will you become as a result of achieving your second Purpose goal?

What is your Purpose in achieving this goal?

Who will benefit from you achieving this goal?

Purpose Goal #3

Who will you become as a result of achieving your third Purpose goal?

What is your Purpose in achieving this goal?

Who will benefit from you achieving this goal?

Finally, create your support tribe. Who can you share your Purpose-driven goals with? Who will support you?

Name your support tribe here:

Who will *not* support these goals? Who would it be best *not to tell* right now?

Name them here:

Wow, what a big day! The future is bright. You are in control. You are growing. You are clear. You have met your next three worthy challenges, the next three worthy opponents you will face. You know who will support you as you take them on. You know who your mentors need to be to get you there. Well done!

The reason I limited your focus to three goals of Purpose is to help keep you focused on what is more important right now, on those goals that will solve your biggest pain and bring you the greatest sense of Purpose. This is how you will build momentum. You will see that as these areas of your life improve, so will the rest of your life.

The time to begin is now.

Today's affirmation: I set goals with Purpose and pursue them now.

Today's prayer: Creator, thank You for giving me the clarity to know what my Purpose and my goals are. Allow me to feel even more connected to You as I take a step out into uncertainty. Aid in my pursuit of these goals. Help me be proud of who I am becoming, as I create an even bigger life. Send me the resources, mentors, confidence, and aid that I need to remain on this path. Give me a sense of greater Purpose as I pursue these goals from now on. Give me strength when I want to quit and courage when I am scared. Most important, help me start *now*.

DAY 33:
THE MISSING LINK TO ACHIEVING
YOUR GOALS WITH PURPOSE

"Let us not pray to be sheltered from dangers but
to be fearless when facing them."

– RABINDRANATH TAGORE

One of the many benefits of our time together has been the cultivation of courage. To get this far on your journey, to look at yourself, to descend into your OI, to discover your limiting behaviors, stories, emotions, and beliefs—all this has indeed been a courageous act.

When I was a child, I fell in love with fantasy and science-fiction films. Watching movies like *Star Wars* (with an emphasis on *Empire*), *Labyrinth*, *Legend*, *The Dark Crystal*, *Willow*, and *Dune* were some of the most memorable moments of my childhood. One of my favorites was *The NeverEnding Story*, about a dreamer named Bastian who is bullied, ditches school, and finds a magical book.

Scenes from this movie are etched in my mind—The Childlike Empress, the hero, Atreyu, riding his trusty horse, Artax, on the open plains, and Artax sinking into the Swamp of Sadness after giving up. One scene that never made sense to me at the time showed one of the tests that the hero Atreyu must go through on his journey. He must stand at the Magic Mirror Gate, which will reveal his true self to him.

Atreyu's mentor, Engywook, says the following line about this test in discussion with Falcor, Atreu's luck dragon:

Engywook: Next is the Magic Mirror Gate. Atreyu has to face his true self.

Falcor: So what? That won't be too hard for him.

Engywook: Oh, that's what everyone thinks! But kind people find out that they are cruel. Brave men discover that they are really cowards! Confronted by their true selves, most men run away screaming!

I was so confused by this. How could people find out that their True Self is the opposite of what they thought they were?

This means that if you were timid before, you have come to learn that you have a great power within you.

If you were skeptical, you have found that you are a sensitive person who got hurt and decided to defend yourself with skepticism.

If you were numb, you have found that there was pain that caused you to shut down, but that that pain needed to be felt so that you could feel joy on the other side.

If you were scared to make a bold move because you didn't know how you were going to make it through, you've gone through a Divine Storm or two and realized that in every moment, you are indeed supported.

It wasn't until I got deep into teaching this work that I understood. We tend to overcompensate for what we think we are not. When we feel powerless or like we're not enough, it can easily turn into too much humility, hiding, or believing that we are more special than everyone else.

What's so interesting and paradoxical is that whatever your limiting beliefs used to be about yourself, you will come to find that the opposite is true. You may recall that as a child, I jumped on my mother to embrace her when she was fresh out of surgery. Because this hurt her, I decided as a child that when I express my love it hurts people. That was one of my limiting beliefs. But the truth is that if I don't express my love, I hurt myself, and when I do express my love, others benefit. I just didn't know this for a very long time. I didn't even know that I had developed such a limiting and untrue belief. As a result, I lived for years in the pain of my unexpressed love.

Slowly but surely I started to express my love a little here and there. As I began to love myself, truly love myself, I found that I was a very giving person and loved giving love to others. I loved it so much that I turned expressing my love into my calling, my mission, and my business.

What was the cost of believing that when I express my love I hurt people? What was the cost of holding back my heart?

Addiction.

Toxic relationships.

Toxic jobs.

Many Divine Storms.

Heartbreak.

Weighing 299 pounds at my heaviest.

Almost ruining my soul-mate relationship.

Not growing as fast as I could in my business.

Not making the kind of impact I could have made in serving others.

The emotional cost was immense. The financial cost was in the millions. Changing this belief, day by day, has been one of the greatest challenges I've ever faced. And each day, as I get better and better at expressing my love to myself, to my Higher Power, and then to others, life gets better and better as well.

As I open myself up in this way and become more empowered, I am required to take greater and greater risks, but there is always support. God always catches me. In finding this support, I become even bolder with my faith. And this cycle of faith creates greater and greater momentum in my life. As I become bolder with my faith and Purpose, it better enables me to pass on my gift to countless others.

And so it will be with you.

Your dedication, your faith, and your commitment to having courage each and every day, for the rest of your life, is the missing piece that has stopped you from fully bringing your Purpose to life.

Let Your Actions Truly Define You

Role models become role models because their actions truly define them. We are inspired by people like Martin Luther King, Jr., Gandhi, Jesus, Malala, or Oprah because of their courage in the face of adversity. You have the same power within you that any great person who has lived a courageous life has. While it is true that the systems of man are rigged to favor the few, the systems of God are not and those systems are more powerful than the rules of mankind. When you follow the truth that dwells within your own Heart and you do it with the courage of the greats who have come before you, that's when you have truly claimed your power.

Living your Purpose does not mean you have signed up for an easy life. Caroline Myss sums this up perfectly when she says, "You don't need a wishbone, you need a backbone."[26] A backbone is indeed what is required to live the spiritual life, to trust the unseen force behind your eyes

---

26   Caroline Myss, *Why People Don't Heal and How They Can* (New York: Harmony Books, 1998), 154.

and behind the great mystery of The Universe. That force sustains you and lives through you. It is the Divine force that is all around you, that is within you, and that whispers to you each and every day.

The question we face time and time again is, "Will I surrender to the Divine force within me or will I resist it?"

In each moment you have the opportunity to make this choice. It will feel like you are giving up control. Some will say you've gone mad. Others won't understand. But when you make it your aim to become a beacon of light on earth, you must abide by the rules of your Creator and not buy into the limitations of your current circumstances.

In *A Course in Miracles*, the choice we make in each moment is described this way: "If you want to be like Me, I will help you, knowing we are alike. If you want to be different I will wait until you change your mind."[27]

Your Heart waits. Your Soul waits. Your Creator waits for you to be courageous in every choice you make. To courageously tell your truth. To courageously live your Purpose. To courageously invoke risk at every turn, always knowing—not believing, but *knowing*—that you are supported. Even if it looks like there is no support, support is there.

If you wish to live the Divinely inspired life of Purpose, you must act how God acts. Your age matters not. Your circumstances matter not. Your gender, sexual orientation, religious or spiritual beliefs matter not. Nothing in this world can hold you back. Earthly limitations don't stand a chance against your Divine assignment. You will come to see that as you boldly and courageously follow your Heart and live your Purpose. Life and the material world will bend to your path.

God knows the solution to your problem before you know you have one. When you trust your own Heart, you trust in the One who speaks to you through it. Today, your job is to dedicate the rest of your life to doing this courageously.

How Will You Proceed?

The goals we set yesterday should both excite you and frighten you. Achieving these goals is not what matters most. What matters most is how you attempt to achieve them.

What you desire has been deliberately placed out of reach so that you can become the person it takes to obtain it.

---

27   Helen Schucman and William Thetford, *A Course in Miracles* (Murine Press, 2008), 96.

Your Soul chose to come here, in this time, in this space, in your body, so it could go through these challenges. Nothing has happened by mistake. Everything that you've been through is part of a larger Divine plan that you will only see when looking backward. So trust in your Heart. Then turn that trust into bold and courageous action. Make it a daily practice to find and express your courage, and let the chips fall where they may.

Do not deprive yourself of the journey that you signed up for before you came here. Do not deprive all of us of the gift of your Heart. If the world seems dark now, it is because it needs your light. And your light can be expressed only through courage. *Courage is when you align with the desires of your Heart, despite your SPs.*

Your old limiting behaviors, stories, emotions, and beliefs will surface from time to time, usually most intensely right before you are about to break through to a higher order of living. When they do, don't hold back. Stay true to the desires of your Heart and then have the courage to get out of your own way. Let's do this journaling exercise together, now.

What is the worst-case scenario I fear in my romantic life?

How am I committing to have courage in this area?

What is the worst-case scenario I fear in my business, career, or vocation?

How am I committing to have courage in this area?

What is the worst-case scenario I fear in my health and wellness?

How am I committing to have courage in this area?

What is the worst-case scenario I fear with my family?

How am I committing to have courage in this area?

What is the worst-case scenario I fear in creative life?

How am I committing to have courage in this area?

What is the worst-case scenario I fear in my financial life?

How am I committing to have courage in this area?

Today's affirmation: Each day I align with the desires of my Heart and follow them with trust.

Today's prayer: Dear God, thank You for giving me the clarity to set goals of Purpose. Now that I am clear on what I want to create in my life, give me the courage to become the person it takes to achieve these goals. I know that my Soul chose this path before I came to earth. Give me the courage to follow the calling of my Soul, to embody the ideals I hold sacred, and to shine my light into a world of darkness. May the example of my life become a lighthouse for others. As I return to You and come home, give me the perspective and desire to inspire others to come home to You as well. Give me courage daily and provide me safe passage to where You call me. I am Yours and You are mine.

DAY 34:
DEFINE YOUR SOUL'S MISSION

"I had decided to stop chasing the money,
and start chasing the passion."

– TONY HSIEH

When you look at your new goals of Purpose, do they feel like a job, a task, a to-do, or a mission? If you said anything but a mission, I encourage you to go back through the goal-setting exercise.

We've got to start looking at your future with new eyes and with a grander intention. There are obstacles ahead. You have dedicated the rest of your life to growing, to embodying courage, and to invoking the spirit of a worthy opponent, which is going to be challenging. There will be moments in your future when you doubt yourself. So what will keep you going?

When you link your efforts and your Purpose to a cause greater than yourself, it will give you the emotional intensity you need to keep going through any challenge. That means having a clear understanding of why you are doing what you are doing, and how your Purpose-driven goals align with your Soul's mission.

In other words, how will you, your Creator, and others benefit from your actions? How can you see where you're headed as your destiny, rather than just the setting and meeting of goals?

When you attach deeper meaning to your goals and actions, you will find that you are more resourceful than you ever thought possible. Viktor Frankl said this about finding your mission: "Those who have a 'why' to live, can bear with almost any 'how.'"

My Whys

Let me share with you a few of my "whys," which forever transformed the way I look at what I do and why I do it. When I first decided to coach people, I did so out of a need to survive. I had already made a choice to pursue my dream of creating TheDailyLove.com and helping other people. But after making that choice, I couch surfed for two years, staying at four different places over that time.

I didn't know where food was coming from each day. Money became a big focus. It got to a point where I was wearing out my welcome with my amazing friends and had to make a bold move. So I decided to offer coaching through my blog and website.

This one move took me from a place of poverty and having to rely on the help of others to survive, to being able to afford a $500-a-month room and food, which was a massive leap for me at the time. I was coaching because I needed a roof over my head, but that place of discomfort did not last long.

As I started talking to people and hearing their stories about how strong they were and what they had overcome, it began to change me. I now earn a living by inspiring other people to make bold and courageous choices. One of the greatest gifts of what I do is that, in the process, I get an invaluable education. I learn as much as my clients do, if not more.

I began to contemplate the freedom that my clients felt as a result of working with me and how much had to conspire for us to meet. I started to understand that all my Divine Storms had gotten stubborn little me to surrender and realize that I had a previously unused and unrecognized gift to help people heal from extreme trauma.

I've worked with veterans, abuse survivors, struggling entrepreneurs, couples who were on the brink of divorce, burned-out single mothers, overweight people, and more. Just about any type of suffering you can imagine, I've helped people who were living through it. For whatever reason, my gift helps create immediate and powerful transformation in my clients' lives. But I had no idea I could do this for a long time. That is, until I starting coaching.

Now whenever my SPs kick in (yes, they still do), whenever I want to quit, stop, or run away, I think about all the people I could still reach. I think about the abused people I could help. I think about all the incredible people who give to everyone but themselves that I could help, perhaps for the first time, find self-love. I think about the people who have denied who they really are for their whole lives, who I might be able to inspire to finally be themselves, freely and openly.

What is more valuable and worthy of stretching myself than that? Nothing.

But First, the Objections

There are a few objections people have when I ask them to turn their goals into a mission. The top two are:

1. "I see how you are helping other people, Mastin, but I don't see how I can."

2. "Even if I could, I wouldn't be very good at it. My voice doesn't matter."

Remember, it's vital to stay away from the trap of comparing or being too humble. You cannot compare your future to your past, because it hasn't happened yet. And one of the greatest realizations you will have is that there is indeed a unique and special gift that you are meant to give to the world. Only you can give it. You were made to give this gift. Your job is not to be humble about it, but to give with all your heart and effort, and then detach from the outcome.

Also remember to keep focused on your Purpose as you look for opportunities to help. There is an abundance of people whom you can serve, right here, right now, today. Just start with one.

As you begin helping people, you gain more confidence about your abilities and gift. You begin to see that there is a thread, a through line, a similarity among the kinds of people who come to you for help. And you see that you can indeed help them.

One of my favorite stories about this idea comes from the great spiritual teacher Mary Morrissey. She and her friend were going to see the Dalai Lama speak, and he said something that inspired Mary. A few moments later, on their lunch break, Mary's friend asked her for some advice, and Mary simply repeated what the Dalai Lama had said. Her friend was blown away. "I'll always remember this day and this advice," she told Mary. Mary mentioned that it wasn't her advice, but the Dalai Lama's, to which her friend replied, "I didn't hear him say it, but I heard you say it."

This is just one of many examples showing that your voice, your Purpose, your mission to serve others matters. When you doubt yourself, keep all those whom you can serve in your heart and use that as fuel to keep going.

What's Your Gift?

One more important thing to keep in mind: Many of my clients ask me, "What's my gift?" Often people worry that they don't know what their gift is.

If that's you, here's a hint: it's what comes easy to you.

We tend to doubt what comes easy to us, thinking that we must work hard and forge new skills to be successful. While it is true that hard work can create a masterful skill level, when you work hard at what you naturally want to do, hard work turns to joy.

Answer the following in your journal:

How can my perspective help others?

Who can I help right now?

How can I turn my goals into a mission greater than myself?

What is my unique and special gift that comes easily to me?

How can I give this gift to the world today and each day from now on?

How can I give myself this gift today and each day from now on?

What will the world look like when I die if I commit myself to giving my gift each and every day, with the intensity and focus of a mission?

Today's affirmation: I trust what comes easily to me.

Today's prayer: Dear God, bring me clarity on what my mission is. Show me what comes easily to me. Give me the inspiration to live for something greater than myself while still taking radical care of myself. Show me the path of my joy, my Purpose, my mission, and my destiny. You have made me perfectly. Help me accept this perfection and use my unique gifts to bring more light into the world. I allow Your Light to shine through me.

DAY 35:
A SCHEDULE FILLED WITH PURPOSE

"If you talk about it, it's a dream, if you envision it, it's possible, but if you schedule it, it's real."

– TONY ROBBINS

There are two universal objections I hear about why people can't create a life filled with Purpose:

Objection #1: I don't have enough time.

Objection #2: I don't have enough money.

The main problem with these two excuses is that you are basing what's possible for you in the future on your past or present circumstances. People who say these things are trapped by their current limitations. They are not living from a vision.

Let me address these limiting excuses individually.

First, time is a resource that we all share equally. We all have the same 24 hours in a day. However, time is a resource that appreciates in value as we get older. Meaning, the older we get, the more we value time. Why? Because there is less and less of it as we age.

When we are younger, we value money more. Why? Because we have more time and generally fewer resources. However, people who have acquired wealth know that money can only bring so much happiness and contentment, and that it's not our greatest resource. One of the most powerful questions we can ask ourselves is, "How am I going to invest my time today?"

While it's true that we never know how much time we have in life, I intend to live a long life and do what I'm doing until my last breath. To grow in my relationship, to grow in my business, and to take better care of myself, I had to look at how I was spending my time.

What I found is that my schedule was based on my old hierarchy of others, others, others, which was not a wise way to invest my time. I was allowing myself to be at the whim of others.

I love e-mail, social media, and texting. However, these mediums put pressure on us to respond quickly. You do not want your in-box or your messages to trap you. You want to create your day based on your priorities and what you need to do to bring your Purpose to life. In other words, if you don't schedule your Purpose, you'll never bring it to life.

You can use your time each day however you want. Based on your current circumstances, what you can and cannot do will vary. However, following are five important elements you need to consider when creating your new Purpose-driven schedule.

1) Sleep and recovery

People who say they don't need that much sleep do not perform as their highest level. In his book *Power Sleep*, Dr. James B. Maas says that reduced alertness due to not enough sleep costs us $70 billion per year. Maas also says that in order to achieve peak performance, we must sleep between 8 and 10 hours a night. When we do this, we do not need an alarm clock to wake us up at the right time.

For me personally, I've found that 8.5 to 9 hours of sleep is ideal. You might be thinking that that is a lot of sleep. And it is. Many people say they want to get less sleep so they have more hours in their day to get things done. However, if you are sleep deprived, your waking hours are less enjoyable, and you function in less productive and useful ways. Additionally, when you are well rested and allow your body to recover, you add more years to your life.

This is why the first thing you must do is schedule your sleep. That means blocking off enough time on your calendar each night to get a full night's rest. It may also mean you need to set boundaries at work, in your relationship, or elsewhere to ensure this happens.

Getting enough sleep is the foundation for bringing your Purpose to life. If you are not well rested, if you don't allow your body to recover, you store excess body fat, are less healthy overall, and do not have enough energy to face your forward journey.

2) Exercise and movement

Exercise is also vital to schedule. My personal routine involves waking up and warming up in a hot bath followed by cardio and weights before starting my day. I have found for my body, that is key for having energy all day long.

You don't have to lift weights or do cardio, and you don't have to exercise in the mornings like I do (although I highly suggest it). The important thing to think about is getting in some daily movement. It could be yoga, hiking, surfing, spinning, walking, and so on. It should be whatever you like to do to get your body, your endorphins, and your energy started. Whatever that is, block off time for it in your calendar each day because exercise and movement is another important pillar in your Purpose-driven life.

3) Food and water

If you are not eating well or hydrating properly, you lack the energy to fuel your Purpose. Water supports your metabolism and many other functions within the body. Dr. Philip Goglia, in his book *Turn Up the Heat*, recommends a half ounce of water per pound per day for sedentary people and one ounce per pound per day for active people.

You will need proper food as well, though everybody is different. Goglia discovered that people can roughly be divided into three metabolic types, which determine the ideal foods for your body to consume. This explains why Paleo is great for some people and not others, and why others can eat lots of carbs and still stay thin. The three types are: fat/protein efficient, carbohydrate efficient, and duel efficient. A simple lipid blood profile can determine your metabolic type. (Get Goglia's book, or go to www.pfcnutrition.com to learn more about your metabolic type.)

It's vital to schedule your food and water. If you don't schedule it, you're likely to fall into unhealthy habits, like skipping lunch and then going for that doughnut and coffee in the afternoon because your energy has dipped. Figuring out what foods are best for you and then making eating them part of your daily schedule will help you have enough energy and fuel to live your Purpose.

4) Meditation

Meditation will help you calm your mind and tune into your Heart, which is why I recommend meditating for at least 10 minutes in the morning and 10 minutes at night. If you can get up to 20 and 20, that's even better. There are all different methods for meditating, and as far as I'm concerned, there is no wrong meditation. You can use an app like Headspace to help you, or the Heart Meditation I recommended earlier. Whatever method you use, the aim is to quiet the mind so that it is obedient, clear, and calm. This allows your Soul to shine through.

5) Your Purpose goals

After you've rested, moved, meditated, hydrated, and eaten, you will be properly fueled and ready to bring your Purpose to life. How much time each day do you need to bring your Purpose goals to life? Schedule it and stick to the schedule. Be merciless about the time you have set aside each day to pursue your Purpose.

Create Your New Purpose-Driven Schedule

With these five crucial elements in mind, we are going to create your schedule. As you do, keep in mind that this is your destiny, your mission, your Purpose that we're talking about. Scheduling time to prepare yourself for and work toward your Purpose is massively important. If you use the phrase *go with the flow* as an SP to not make time for change, let's stop that today.

Begin by considering your calendar cleared so we can rebuild it from scratch. If you are someone who doesn't typically keep a schedule, remember that if it's not scheduled, it's not real. There is a big difference between being flexible and accepting what happens and not truly committing to your goals with Purpose. Once your calendar is clear, start scheduling the following elements one by one:

1. Schedule your sleep—8 to 10 hours of it. Also make sure you have enough time before bed to wind down. I am usually asleep by 9:00 p.m., so I start winding down around 7:30 p.m. If I want to be asleep when my head hits the pillow at 9:00 p.m.

each day, I've got to protect my evening time by turning off the television and logging off of social media, and not taking any more calls for the day.

2. Schedule your exercise, ideally in the morning. If you can combine cardio, resistance training, and stretching to increase your flexibility, you will get maximum results. However, the best exercise is the exercise you enjoy, because that's what you know you'll keep doing day after day.

3. Schedule your food and water. I fill all my water bottles up the night before so when I wake up, it's done. You can also prep your meals on Sunday so you know what you will be eating for the rest of the week.

4. Schedule your meditation time. If you don't already have a meditation practice, start with 10 minutes twice a day (morning and evening) and go from there.

5. Schedule your time for your Purpose goals. What you need to do here will be different for everyone, depending on what your Purpose is and how you broke down your goals on Day 32.

After you've scheduled all this, you may find that there is far less time available in your day than you thought. Any resistance you have to creating this new schedule is an old SP. Love yourself enough to schedule the time you need to bring your Purpose to life.

If you are in a job that restricts your time, then do your best to get as much in as you can. Ten minutes each of exercise, meditation, and working on your Purpose goals is better than nothing. Start small and work your way up if you have to. Remember, I started with the baby step of just making my bed each morning. You can start with baby steps too.

Finding success to live your Purpose comes back to fundamentals. Many people seem to want some fancy, complicated "secret trick" that will fast-track their growth. There isn't any such thing. It's about the fundamentals. Becoming aware of your SPs. Loving yourself when you notice them. Not pressing "Snooze." Getting to the gym. Taking time to start your day with gratitude. Setting a boundary. Eating a salad instead of a chocolate croissant.

You can see how much self-love you have by looking at your schedule. You can see what hierarchy you've been living within by looking at your schedule. Making sure that you have what you need each and every day, to bring your Purpose to life is vital, so protect your calendar. Set boundaries. Cut out meaningless activities like binge-watching TV or time on social media. A great app to help you take back your power from the Internet is called Self Control. It allows you to set times when the Internet will be turned off to help you block distractions.

If you look at your calendar and see a bunch of meetings and commitments that you do not want to keep, or don't want to keep right now, give yourself full permission to back out or reschedule. This may affect some of your relationships with people who are used to taking up a certain amount of your time. Always keep your Hierarchy of Power in mind: 1) Self, 2) Creator, 3) Others. Remember, it's okay to renegotiate your relationships when you need to, to live a more empowered life.

When you take an honest look at your life and how you are spending your time, you can reschedule, reconsider, set boundaries, change habits, and get serious about using your very precious time wisely. Each day that goes by is another day that you will never get back, so you have to always be asking yourself: *How do I want to invest my time?* The answer to that question will determine how serious you are about claiming your power and creating a new future.

On the following pages, plot out the new schedule that you will commit to going forward. When you do this, you take a massive leap toward bringing your Purpose to life.

Sleep schedule:

Evening wind-down schedule:

Exercise and movement schedule:

Meditation schedule:

Water and food prep schedule:

Purpose goals schedule:

Friends and family I am setting boundaries with:

Previous commitments I am renegotiating and rescheduling:

Boundaries I am setting with my job or career:

Boundaries I am setting in my romantic life:

Binge behavior I am cutting out:

I will use my weekend time more effectively by:

Today's affirmation: I love myself enough to create an empowered schedule, to renegotiate my commitments, and to use my precious time wisely.

Today's prayer: O Divine Creator, You have gifted me with life. Help me use my time wisely. Help me forgive myself for not soaking up every moment and for any previous misuse of the precious time You've gifted to me. Give me the power to set boundaries. Show me how to love myself enough to rest, recover, move, eat, hydrate, meditate, and set aside time for goals that will manifest Your will in my life. Show me how to best use my time. May Your will fill my schedule and all that is false fall away.

DAY 36:
PERMISSION TO THRIVE

"There are those of us who are always about to live.
We are waiting until things change, until there is
more time, until we are less tired, until we get a
promotion, until we settle down—until, until, until. It
always seems as if there is some major event that
must occur in our lives before we begin living."

– GEORGE SHEEHAN

To my surprise, one of the greatest obstacles my clients have faced in bringing their Purpose to life has been the belief that they need someone else's permission to begin, to shine, or to "be big." I call this "permission syndrome" and it happens to a lot of us. We tend to wait for permission from family members, spouses, our tribe, even God, before we feel entitled to make a change in our lives.

It took a while for me to really understand why this happens. After some time and analysis, I came to see that this feeling, like so many other limiting behaviors, can be traced back to old SPs associated with an old hierarchy. If you are coming from a hierarchy of putting your Higher Power or others first, then you haven't yet fully developed your own willpower. That is to say, you don't yet fully feel you have the freedom or perhaps the worthiness to choose to live whatever kind of life you want.

Today, we are going to find out whose permission you think you need to move forward and claim your power. We're going to identify those individuals and then strip their influence away.

Permission Syndrome

One of the common reasons why people suffer from permission syndrome is because of how they were raised. When you were a child, you probably had to get permission to go to the bathroom at school or to take days off when you were sick. Additionally, many educational systems try to fit all children into the same box. The problem that can result is that, instead of learning to think for themselves, children are taught to look to others to tell them how well they are doing and to ask for permission before they do anything on their own, even something as basic and natural as going to the bathroom.

Sir Kenneth Robinson, an innovator in the field of education, said, "The fact is that given the challenges we face, education doesn't need to be reformed—it needs to be transformed. The key to this transformation is not to standardize education, but to personalize it, to build achievement on discovering the individual talents of each child, to put students in an environment where they want to learn and where they can naturally discover their true passions."[28]

Beyond that, you may have come from a culture or community that does not fully value personal success. In fact, if you become too successful, some cultures will try to cut you down. As I mentioned, the Australians are honest about this, calling the phenomenon "tall poppy syndrome." If someone becomes too successful or "tall," he or she will be chopped down to size to match the rest.

You may have even learned to fear the jealously of others, not wanting to share your good news, improved life, or happiness with them because they are likely to react negatively to it. As a result, your natural survival pattern is to play small and not stand out. If that's the case, remember that you want to surround yourself with people who support your Purpose. That may mean renegotiating, or even terminating, some of your relationships.

If you have been taught to look to others first for permission and validation, if you have been put in a box, or if you have been encouraged to stay small so you didn't upset others, it's time to break free from that pattern.

Yes, there will be people who don't celebrate your newfound freedom and success. There will be people who tell you that you are "different now" or that they miss the "real you," referring to who you were in the past. The brutal truth is that your transformation threatens others. Their message (said or unsaid) will be: "Stay small" and "Don't shine."

In the midst of all the outside pressures and noise, here's what's true: You have permission to shine, to live big, to enjoy the fruits of your labor, to bask in the abundance of God, to play, to run, to be free,

---

28   Ken Robinson and Lou Aronica, *The Element: How Finding Your Passion Changes Everything* (New York: Viking, 2009), 238.

to build, to create, to explore, to mess up, to make mistakes, to learn lessons, and to find out, in your own way, at your own time, just how truly powerful you are.

I remember the pivotal time in my life when I first came to this realization. I had created my blog, *The Daily Love*, and it had been running for several years. My mom had been editing my blogs and working with our bloggers to help them get published on our site. Then one day, she sent me an e-mail saying that she felt she had to stop editing for us and move on to something new in her life. I was sad about her decision, but I supported it.

After that, things changed between us. I had talked to my mom every day for the 12 years since I had left Kansas to move to L.A. But, as she drifted away from working with me and the business picked up, we didn't talk as much. In fact, soon after that I had three back-to-back Enter the Heart retreats in Maui, and I didn't talk to my mom for almost a whole month. This was very strange and brand new for me.

After those retreats, I had scheduled about a dozen Enter the Heart seminars in the United States and Canada, including one in Kansas City. The plan was for my parents to come see me work, something they hadn't done yet. When the day of my K.C. seminar came around, my dad told me that my mom was too sick to make the 40-mile drive. At first I took it personally. But then I got worried.

My Heart told me to go to their house on my day off. I brought my girlfriend, Jenna, and friend Tommy Rosen with me. It was a Divine miracle that Tommy was there because he is an addiction expert. My mom had been on prescription medication my whole life to numb the pain from her broken back injury. I didn't know it at the time, but the three of us were about to have an intervention.

The intervention was one of the hardest things I had ever done. Jenna was there and so brave. Tommy was there and so clear. I was there, shaking as I broke every family rule we had. Rule number one had always been: "Don't upset Mom; she is in enough pain already."

When I saw my mom and how frail she had become, I knew I had to do something. I didn't ask permission. I followed my Heart, and Jenna, Tommy, and I said everything that needed to be said. A few weeks later, my mom checked herself into the Betty Ford Clinic to get clean. The doctors told her that based on her vitals, and a long-term mix of painkillers and benzodiazepines, she was close to death.

After my mom got clean, a miracle happened. For 30 years, I had known a mother who was always in pain. But after getting clean, she was no longer in pain. She went from bedridden to traveling the globe, something that had seemed impossible before she went to rehab.

This story has a happy ending, but when I traveled back to Kansas City with Jenna and Tommy after the intervention, I was a wreck. I felt like I had betrayed my parents, whom I loved so much. But then Tommy gave me some advice that I will never forget. He said, "Mastin, you are sober from drugs, which means this: Imagine that your whole family is a bunch of monkeys and they live inside a barrel. The barrel is all they know. But you're a monkey who got out of the barrel and saw that there is more to life than barrel living. Now you are shaking the barrel and other monkeys don't like it. You did the right thing. Keep shaking the barrel."

What Tommy shared calmed my nerves. It also made me realize something. After all that time, I was still living according to the idea that I couldn't do anything to hurt my mother. However, as a grown and sober man who understood certain insights about life, I had to break that rule, temporarily. I intentionally caused my family short-term pain with the vision of long-term happiness. In doing so, I believe I saved my mother's life.

It took all that before I realized that I didn't have to ask for my parents' permission. On that day, when I broke the rules, I didn't ask them if it was okay. But until then, I still needed their approval. I wasn't conscious of the fact that I needed it, but I did even though, no matter what, they had always supported me. That's not to say that I don't still value their opinion very much, but I now know I don't need anyone's permission, not even theirs, to follow my Heart.

The same is true for you.

Ready to Cut the Cord?

As you have been reading these words, perhaps you have already thought about whose permission you still need to live your Purpose. This person or these people may even be dead, yet you are still waiting around for them to give you permission. Or maybe there is a family or societal rule, conscious or unconscious, that you are afraid to break with your new empowered self.

It's time to cut the cord and live powerfully in your Purpose. To start doing that, in your journal, let's name the person or persons whose permission you still believe you need to thrive.

Whose permission do you need to live your dreams?

Why do you think you need this person's permission?

Are there any rules you think you will break if you live your Purpose?

What is the worst-case scenario if you break these rules?

If you had permission, what bold move would you make?

Well done! The answers to these questions will bring massive clarity. Now it's time to do something powerful to change this dynamic, something that perhaps you didn't know you needed to do.

Below, I would like you to write two letters. One is from the person whose permission *you used to need* to live your Purpose. If that person actually gave you permission, what would they say?

The second letter is from you to yourself. The deepest truth is that *you do not need anyone's permission* to live your Purpose and claim your power. The choice is wholly and truly yours. Claim it by writing a letter to yourself, giving yourself permission to live big. Ready? Go!

Letter from the person(s) whom you thought you needed permission from:

Letter to yourself, giving yourself permission to live big:

Today's affirmation: I give myself permission to thrive.

Today's prayer: Dear God, help me feel Your approval in my life. Help me forgive myself for falsely believing that I needed anyone's approval but Yours to shine, to live big, and to claim my power. You are the keeper of my Purpose, and I know that in Your eyes, I am perfect and have full permission to live as big, wholeheartedly, and abundantly as You wish for me. Bring me signs. Open doors. Send aid. Show me that You approve of my Purpose and help me find the courage to detach from the opinions of the world. For Your opinion of me is all that matters.

DAY 37:
CLAIM YOUR VISION

"Where there is no vision, the people perish."

– PROVERBS 29:18

Today is an exciting day because we get to form a vision of what you want your new empowered, Purpose-driven life to look and feel like. Then we are going to be intentional about creating an environment that will support this vision.

Here's a breakdown of what we are going to do today:

1. Create a vision board.

2. Create reminders to place around your home.

3. Make a list of past wins.

4. Consciously celebrate new small wins.

5. Create a plan for road bumps, negative feelings, and setbacks.

In other words, today we create! We envision. We step into the grandness of your Soul and your Heart and let your Purpose unfold before you. Let's take each of these one by one.

Create a Vision Board

Begin by going back to your goals with Purpose and printing them out along with a list of your next grounded action steps. Then look on Pinterest, Google Images, and elsewhere on the Internet for stunning and inspiring images, words, and quotes that represent these goals. Finally, print out your Purpose statement and your new hierarchy. These are going to be the elements that come together to make your vision board come to life. You'll also need a board of some kind—a corkboard or a large piece of thick paper—to attach your images.

When you have all these elements assembled, start creating your vision board by placing your Purpose statement, your hierarchy, and your next grounded action steps in the center. Then create a beautiful, inspiring display around them filled with images, affirmations (you can use the ones from this book or elsewhere), prayers, and quotes that evoke your top two emotions. It's also important to find images of mentors or people you want to be like.

When I created my first vision board, I had images of true Love, the Hay House logo, a picture of Oprah, a photo of Joseph Campbell, and logos from *Star Wars*, *The Matrix,* and *The NeverEnding Story.* I also had a massive logo of "The Daily Love" and the emotions that I wanted to feel in there. What's amazing is that it all came true. I met my soul mate. I am now publishing my second book with Hay House. And I was featured on Oprah's *SuperSoul Sunday* in 2012.

I don't say these things to brag or suggest that the vision board alone is what made it all happen. A lot of my clients falsely believe that the vision is enough. But you already know that that is not the case.

One of the reasons a lot of people make vision boards and fail is because they don't back it up with bold, decisive, and courageous action. It doesn't help you if you pass by it each day and glance at it but never take action. You need *both* the vision and the grounded action steps that will take you there.

After I made my vision board, I did everything I could to make it happen. I blogged, tweeted, and e-mailed daily. I made it my intention to serve, and surrendered to God the outcome of that service.

I believe in the words of Isaiah (52:13): "Look! My servant will prosper, and he will be exalted and lifted up, and will be very high." I knew that if I focused on serving and let God take care of the details, I would prosper. I also knew that I had to take bold, consistent, and courageous action to do my part.

When I wanted to quit, I would let myself quit—for 30 minutes or an hour. And then I would get right back up and keep going.

There is great abundance, joy, and prosperity that will come to you for being obedient to your Soul. But that is not why you are doing this. When you give up the need to be successful and focus on serving God from your Soul's vision, you take a quantum leap into success, abundance, and joy. However, your intention to serve must be pure.

Another reason a lot of people who make vision boards fail is because their goals were set from a place of ego, a destructive hierarchy, and the need to be the most special person around. As you humble yourself with quiet confidence and live your beliefs with action, you will rise.

So create your vision board with a sense of Purpose, surrender, and detachment from worldly success. Know that God's plans for you are greater than what you can imagine for yourself. God works best when you surrender, so allow yourself to be like clay in His hands. Once you've created your vision board, place it in a prominent spot within your home so that you will see it every day. Then step back and let your life be molded into something awe inspiring.

Create Reminders

In addition to your vision board, I believe it's important to create reminders about your top two emotions, your Purpose goals, and your new hierarchy to place around your home. You can do this by printing out or drawing the words and gathering other visual cues (via Google Image or Pinterest search, like you did before) that remind you of these things, which you can then place on your fridge, in your bathroom, in your bedroom, by the front door, in your car—really anywhere and everywhere that you spend a lot of time.

You do this to reprogram your brain. When your brain takes in these reminders on a regular basis, you internalize these ideas more and more each day and reinforce their importance in your life. The goal is to create more and more of the top two emotions you want to feel in your life, and to help you avoid any roadblocks that might get in the way of that.

Make a List of Past Wins

Next up, make a list of wins that you have had in the past. No matter what you've been through, there have been moments where you've succeeded in the past. These don't have to be massive wins. What's most important is that the wins you name bring forward your top two emotions.

Name five wins in your journal that you've had in the past that bring forward your top two emotions:

1. _____

2. _____

3. _____

4. _____

5. _____

The reason to do this is to remind yourself that you are powerful, able, and ready to create your life intentionally, moving forward. One of the best ways to do this is to remember past successes.

Celebrate Small Wins

To keep your momentum going, it's important to celebrate and give yourself credit for the small wins that you accomplish along the way. For example:

Getting to the gym or yoga center—win.
Speaking your truth—win.
Drinking enough water today—win.
Opening your Heart—win.
Meditating—win.
Scheduling time—win.
Getting enough sleep—win.
Setting a boundary—win.

When you can celebrate the small wins, you create positive energy and forward momentum. Big transformation comes as a result of many small wins over time. Make it your aim to be proud of yourself for each small win that you have every day, starting with today.

What small wins can you celebrate today? Make your list:

1. _____

2. _____

3. _____

4. _____

5. _____

Create a Setback Plan and a "Burnout" Plan

We want to get ahead of future setbacks, so the next thing we need to do is create a setback plan. That's because setbacks happen. You fall off your eating plan. You get injured and don't work out. You cave and return to a toxic relationship.

You will still face such things from time to time. What matters most when you do is how quickly you recover and regain forward momentum. That's why we're going to create a plan you can put in place right now so you can take immediate steps to get back on track, the next time you hit a bump in the road.

Start by finding one trusted friend who can hold you accountable. Tell that person about the SPs you are trying to overcome and how you have tripped up in past. Then ask the person to carry out a sacred duty for you. When they notice you slipping back into an old pattern, you want them to call you on it, to help you get out of it, and to help you get back on track. When you are accountable to someone else, you make progress faster.

You also want to have a "burnout" plan. Sometimes I go so hard that I burn myself out, so I consciously create ways to change things up when this happens. I call these things "pattern interrupts." For me, that can mean choosing to go get a massage in the middle of the workday. Sometimes I give myself permission to take a sick day or a nap. If I have overcommitted myself, I start clearing my calendar. I make time to go to a sacred place.

Two of the most sacred places I am able to spend time in are Maui and Bali. If you can design trips, small or large, where you can get away and get outside of your daily routine, you will find yourself feeling inspired, restored, and coming up with ideas that you wouldn't have in your normal routine. If you can find time to connect with nature, that is a great and powerful way to keep you in the right head space to connect with your vision.

If you can't get away, find a quiet place, download an app like Headspace to guide you to stillness, or create a sacred space in your home where you can return home to yourself. Joseph Campbell said it best, "Your sacred space is where you can find yourself over and over again."

Consciously creating pattern interrupts prevents burnout and gives the ability to keep ideas fresh. If you have any guilt about taking time out of your routine for this kind of "vacation," let me quash that guilt with a quote from Sir Richard Branson: "The places you go and the new people you meet can inspire you in unexpected ways. As an entrepreneur or business leader, if you didn't come back from your vacation with some ideas about how to shake things up, it's time to consider making some changes."[29]

So spend some time now, before you need it, thinking about how you can recover when you stumble and how you can keep yourself energized and fresh, so it's less likely that you stumble in the first place. This means doing things like designing your time off, creating space in your life, and consciously getting outside your routine.

Become Your Own Coach

Finally, one of the most powerful coaching tips I can give you for maintaining your vision is to record yourself giving the advice you need to hear to live your vision. You can do this right on your smartphone, and then watch it or listen to it any time you are down and out. No one can coach you better than yourself.

Sound silly? Well, let me tell you a story about this tip. In early 2014 I decided that it was time for me to master my fitness. I was working out, but I was also getting injured a lot. Every time I got injured it would set me back because the injury would tie me down, and I didn't know how to work out with injuries. I wanted to get a handle on these injuries so I could get into the best shape of my life. But I had no idea I was beginning a multiyear process to learn about health, fitness, and how to have maximum energy.

---

29   Laura Entis, "You Need a Real Vacation (And So Do Your Employees)," *Entrepreneur*, April 3, 2014, https://www.entrepreneur.com/article/232766.

In November of 2014, I went to Bali for our annual Writer's Mastermind and I brought my friend Adam with me, who is a personal trainer. Our deal was that he would help me get in shape and I would help him write his book. I spent a month with him and he helped me create a massive amount of momentum in my health and wellness routine. He turned me onto The Rock's Instagram page and The Rock's ritual of #AMCardio, which I still do to this day.

At the end of my time with Adam, I was in a peak state. I had lead two retreats and was really in the zone. I had been working out and eating well for six weeks, so I had never been in better shape physically. At the same time, I was scared that when I got back home, I would revert back to my old ways. So, before I returned to the United States, I got out my phone and recorded two videos in this inspired state—of everything I had to do to *stay in that state.*

In the videos I reminded myself of the importance of exercise, diet, and consistency. I warned myself about falling back into old patterns and gave myself advice as to how to get out of these patterns. Then I put the videos away, until about a month later when I needed them. I watched the videos and everything I told myself to watch out for had happened. I had returned to those same old patterns; I knew myself so well. This inspired me to keep going and to up my game. I got back on the exercise wagon and found top mentors in the fields of nutrition (Dr. Philip Goglia) and exercise (Gunnar Peterson).

Today, I am losing weight and know exactly what I need to do to get into the best shape of my life. I went through many setbacks and had a long learning curve on this topic, but my videos to myself have saved me time and time again.

Right now, you are inspired, you are clear, and you see things in a new way. So capture it. Record a message to yourself on your smart phone that you can turn to anytime you need it.

Here's what to include:

1. What your vision is.

2. What your Purpose is.

3. What your top goals and next action steps are.

4. What SPs to look out for.

5. What to do to get back up when you have a setback.

6. Why it's important to get back up.

7. Who you can turn to for help.

With this video in your pocket, as well as your vision board, reminders, a list of past wins, a dedication to celebrating future small wins, and your plan for future setbacks, you are set up to make massive progress moving forward. Any time that you get stuck in the future, you can come back to this chapter for a quick refresher on getting back to your Purpose.

Today's affirmation: I celebrate the small wins every day.

Today's prayer: Dear God, let Your vision be made manifest in my life. Help me celebrate my past wins, my small wins, and each and every miracle You have graced me with. Help me get back up when I stumble and remember that I do all this for You.

DAY 38:
CREATING BELIEFS WITH PURPOSE

"All I have seen teaches me to trust the
Creator for all I have not seen."

– RALPH WALDO EMERSON

We are well on our way to reaching a new level of sustained Purpose in your life.

Today, we are going to create empowering new beliefs that support your newfound freedom and Purpose. Remember, a belief according to Tony Robbins is "a feeling of absolute certainty about what something means."[30] We must be careful about what meanings we attach to things as we move forward.

There are two categories of beliefs that we must form to create a rock-solid foundation for your new life:

1. Beliefs about yourself.

2. Beliefs about setbacks and road bumps.

Beliefs about Yourself

Go back, way back, to when you first discovered the limiting beliefs that were covering up your OI. Do you even remember them? Look back and remind yourself what they were if you don't.

As a quick reminder: if you're at home or alone at the office working on your OI, this work might seem overwhelming and you might want to step away or go grab some sugary snacks, but sit with it for just a moment. You've got this! Those unpleasant feelings of uncertainty and fear will fade away soon enough. Keep your thoughts focused on the here and now.

---

30 "From Limitations to No Limits at All," Tonyrobbins.com, https://www.tonyrobbins.com/stories/from-limitations-to-no-limits-at-all/.

Here's what I've found to be true. Whatever your limiting beliefs were, the opposite is true in the eyes of your Creator. For example, if you used to believe that you were not powerful enough to change the lives of others, the opposite is true in the eyes of God. Your Soul, your Heart, the person you really are is more than enough to change not only your own life, but the lives of many others. You just didn't realize it.

Recall that one of my old limiting beliefs was that when I expressed my love, I hurt people, but the opposite is actually true. When I express my love, I help myself and I help others.

We can spend a lifetime letting our limiting beliefs hold us back. When you experience your first OI, you create your first limiting belief. That limiting belief then becomes the filter through which you look at the world. As you move forward, you become so attached to that world-view that you create a story to back up your belief, which ends up creating more of that belief. In short, your limiting beliefs become self-fulfilling prophecies. Back when you were dead, you kept yourself dead with your old limiting beliefs.

What's really important to understand now is that the opposite is also true. You can keep yourself alive, thriving, and on Purpose with beliefs that support your Soul.

Life is uncertain. You have a magical roller-coaster ride ahead of you with ups, downs, twists, turns, and miracles. What will keep you on Purpose, or keep you dead, is your beliefs. How you choose to see future events will determine the outcome.

Let's consciously choose beliefs with Purpose. Begin by listing your old limiting beliefs and then turn them around. What is the actual truth? What does your Soul know to be true? What beliefs to do you need to have in order to bring your Purpose to life moving forward? What beliefs do you need to have in each area of your life in order to master it? In your journal, answer the questions that follow about your beliefs in each area of your life.

My old beliefs about my romantic life were:

My new beliefs about my romantic life are:

My old beliefs about my career, vocation, or business were:

My new beliefs about my career, vocation, and business are:

My old beliefs about my health and wellness were:

My new beliefs around my health and wellness are:

My old beliefs around my financial life were:

My new beliefs around my financial life are:

My old beliefs around my spirituality were:

My new beliefs around my spirituality are:

Fantastic! Now let's create beliefs for future setbacks.

Beliefs about Setbacks and Road Bumps

In the past, what did you used to believe when you had a setback in the area or areas of life where you were dead? For example, let's say you fell head over heels in love, but then got your heart broken. As a result, maybe you decided that you would never open your heart again.

Or, perhaps you started a business and there was an unforeseen challenge that bankrupted you. Maybe you decided that meant you should never take a risk again.

Or, maybe you've tried "everything" to lose weight, but nothing worked. So you decided that you are just meant to be overweight and gave up trying to lose weight.

Let's out your old beliefs about uncertainty and setbacks. Name them here:

Great, now let's think about what your new beliefs could be when you hit a setback. For me, when I set out to get healthy but then ended up getting injured over and over again, I used to believe it was a sign that I wasn't supposed to be in shape. That held me back for a while, until I changed my belief to this: I'm discovering all the ways I need to love my body even more.

Any time you are in an argument with your significant other, an empowering belief you can adopt is, *This is a great opportunity to learn how to better communicate with my partner.*

Any time you have a setback in your business, a new belief you could choose would be, *This is preparing me for even greater challenges.*

The quality of your life really parallels the quality of your beliefs. You have the power to form meaning in your life. Whatever meaning you create will determine the circumstances in which you live. So let's work on choosing new meanings for those old beliefs you used to have about setbacks and road bumps. List your new beliefs in your journal.

Great work! If you feel inspired, add these beliefs to your vision board, leave them around the house as reminders, or if you're extreme like me, tattoo them on your arms so you see them every day. These new beliefs are the foundation on which you will live a life that most only dream about.

Today's affirmation: I choose to create empowering beliefs.

Today's prayer: O Creator, help me believe what You believe. Fill my Heart with Your love. Show me how You see obstacles, and help me understand that my future is full of Your Grace. Guide me as I walk into the unknown future. Bring me evidence that my new beliefs are true, and that all I need is within me through my connection to You. Guide my steps. May my voice be Yours. May my actions be Yours. May my choices be inspired be You. Help me see as You see and Love as You Love.

DAY 39:
PAY IT FORWARD

"You can help when no one else can. You can secure their confidence when others fail . . . Life will take on new meaning. To watch people recover, to see them help others, to watch loneliness vanish, to see a companionship grow up about you, to have a host of friends—this is an experience you must not miss. We know you will not want to miss it. Frequent contact with newcomers and with each other is the bright spot of our lives."

— THE BIG BOOK OF ALCOHOLICS ANONYMOUS

We are now nearing the end of your journey of transformation. Today we are going to talk about making it your intention to take the lessons of this book, embody them, and then let your embodiment be an example for others to follow.

What's so powerful about paying forward what you've learned is that in doing so, you will continue to heal yourself. I remember talking to my therapist Trinka when I had just finished couch surfing. I was touting my large new social media platform at the time, telling her, "I've reached millions of people." She listened to me for a while and then said to me, "Mastin, did you ever think you were so messed up that it took all those millions of people to help you heal?"

She wasn't shaming me. She was keeping me humble. I took in that lesson and never forgot it.

Could I go back to the days of being an addict and giving my power away? Yes. What keeps me sober, in my power, and living my Purpose, is serving others. When you are connected to others in a healthy way, you heal yourself. This journey will be for naught if you do not pay it forward.

When you are focused only on yourself, or are self-centered, you shrivel up. We are all inexplicably connected to one another, and as you connect with your Purpose and make it manifest on the earth, you are called to help those who have yet to walk the path you have walked. You begin to see, in a profound way, that there is abundant support for you as you do this. God knows all the suffering that there is in this world. Perhaps God sent you to earth to experience some of that suffering so that you could have the empathy, experience, and strength to overcome it and be a messenger for others.

Some Final Lessons

As you think about how you can pay forward what you've learned, here are some things to keep in mind:

1. You have come far, but always remember where you were when you started this journey, especially when dealing with others who are not in the same place that you are. Your job is not to judge others. You cannot heal or help people when you are judging them.

2. People are not inspired when they are lectured to, coerced, or forced to do or see things in a new way. What inspires others the most is your example, and by allowing them to fully see who you have become. So let the new you do all the talking. Or, if there are people you think could benefit from what you've just been through, send them a copy of this book. The idea is to inspire change, not to force it.

3. Don't wait until you feel you have this all down perfectly to help others. This is a lifelong process, and helping others is part of that journey. So start right now by answering the following questions in your journal. You've got to help who you can, with what you have, based on where you are right now.

   Who can you serve right now and how can you best serve them?

   What opportunities do you have to live your Purpose right now?

   What is your next grounded action step?

What is your next courageous choice?

How can you expand your faith even more today?

Today's affirmation: I am a lighthouse for God's love.

Today's prayer: Dear God, give me the courage to move forward in my Purpose despite my fears. When others criticize my bold new choices, help me feel that I am loved and approved of by You. Bring me support and help me grow.

DAY 40:
REPEAT THE PROCESS AND
DEDICATE YOUR LIFE TO THIS JOURNEY

"The minute you get away from fundamentals—whether it's proper technique, work ethic or mental preparation—the bottom can fall out of your game, your schoolwork, your job, whatever you're doing."

– MICHAEL JORDAN

We have come a long way together. Now all that is left to do is dedicate the rest of your life to fully living your power and Purpose.

I did not write this to be the kind of book that you simply read and then put on a shelf, where it will be forgotten. I hope this will be the kind of book you keep with you as a companion, that you return to when you stumble. Keep in mind that you can always return to this book and repeat this process whenever you need to renew your claim on your power or revitalize your sense of Purpose.

In fact, I hope this book will be something you use always because claiming your power and living your Purpose are lifelong pursuits. Dedicating yourself to living in this way is something that we all need to work toward each and every day to make happen. And what better thing to dedicate the rest of your life to than that?

Stepping into the Great Unseen

You have been called, and you have answered that call. You now know that there is great unseen support for you as you dive deeper into your calling. As you surrender and serve, you find that synchronicities and miracles become a natural occurrence in your life. As this happens, you become bolder and bolder in your faith, make bigger and bigger moves, each time trusting in your Creator to catch you. For you will be caught if you fall.

As you move forward with your Purpose, God will support you because that is why God made you. God will not be shocked by this, but you will be—as you realize that this has, is, and always will be true. As you continue to walk this path that you are really just beginning, you will see that your Creator has never failed and will never fail you. You have been brought to earth to grow as a Soul and to learn lessons, sometimes very difficult lessons. And yet in the midst of these lessons, there is God's Grace.

When all seems lost, lean on your faith and know that every struggle, every moment of pain, every hard lesson comes bearing an equal or greater gift. These gifts arise from Divine Intelligence and not human logic. You will find, in your own intuitive way, what gifts are coming your way. It may feel lonely to be awake in a world that seems asleep to these principles. But you will find your support tribe and together you will become stronger.

This new life you are living is within the sunlight of your Soul. Think of yourself as a full moon. You shine because of the light of greater power. And yet you can still create light where there is darkness.

Do not dim your light for fear of rejection, persecution, or hate.

Do not let the fear of losing love or approval run your life.

Do not fear criticism.

Step boldly into your Purpose and know that from God's perspective, you are already loved, already approved of, and perfectly made. There is no flaw in you. When you own it, live it, and then help others do the same by your example, you know you are truly powerful and free.

Today's affirmation: As I step into the unseen, I become stronger.

Today's prayer: Dear God, May my life be an example of Your light. Shine through me, as me. Show me the way. May I fulfill the potential that You planted in my heart and as I rise, as I shine, help me lift others out of darkness and back to Your Light. May my life be light in the world, and may I participate joyfully in its sorrows. I am here to heal myself and then share that healing with others. I am Your servant. I am Your beacon. I am Your humble vessel. Use me as You will, and may I make my mark on this world, making it a better place than when I arrived.

REFERENCE MATERIAL

Books & Media

Brené Brown, *Daring Greatly: How the Courage to Be Vulnerable Transforms the Way We Live, Love, Parent, and Lead* (New York: Avery, 2015).

Brené Brown, *The Gifts of Imperfection: Let Go of Who You Think You're Supposed to Be and Embrace Who You Are* (Center City, MN: Hazelden, 2010).

Candace Pert, *Molecules of Emotion* (New York: Simon & Schuster, 2010).

Caroline Myss, *Advanced Energy Anatomy: The Science of Co-Creation and Your Power of Choice*, Audiobook (Boulder, CO: Sounds True, 2001).

Caroline Myss, *Why People Don't Heal and How They Can* (New York: Harmony Books, 1998).

Caroline Myss, *Sacred Contracts: Awakening Your Diving Potential* (New York: Harmony Books, 2003).

Mastin Kipp, *Daily Love: Growing into Grace* (New York: Hay House, 2014).

Other Resources

My online course to accompany this book:
www.ClaimYourPowerBook.com/40.

Kris Carr, www.kriscarr.com.

Tony Robbins, https://www.tonyrobbins.com.

Eckhart Tolle, https://www.eckharttolle.com.

ABOUT THE AUTHOR

Mastin Kipp is a #1 best-selling author and the creator of Functional Life Coaching™ who specializes in a strategic, no-B.S. approach to accelerate his clients' lives and businesses. Mastin has been recognized by Oprah Winfrey on her Emmy-award winning show *SuperSoul Sunday* as a "spiritual thinker for the next generation." Mastin appears alongside Tony Robbins, Eckhart Tolle, Deepak Chopra, Dr. Brené Brown, and many others as a part of Oprah's SuperSoul 100, a collection of awakened leaders who are using their voices and talent to elevate humanity.
Website: mastinkipp.com

Hay House Titles of Related Interest

YOU CAN HEAL YOUR LIFE, the movie,
starring Louise Hay & Friends
(available as a 1-DVD program, an expanded 2-DVD set, and an online
streaming video)
Learn more at www.hayhouse.com/louise-movie

THE SHIFT, the movie,
starring Dr. Wayne W. Dyer
(available as a 1-DVD program, an expanded 2-DVD set, and an online
streaming video)
Learn more at www.hayhouse.com/the-shift-movie

■ ■

BRIGHT LINE EATING: The Science of Living Happy, Thin & Free, by
Susan Peirce Thompson, Ph.D.

*DESTRESSIFYING: The Real-World Guide to Personal Empowerment,
Lasting Fulfillment, and Peace of Mind,* by davidji

*THE MOTIVATION MANIFESTO: 9 Declarations to
Claim Your Personal Power,* by Brendon Burchard

*BREAKING THE HABIT OF BEING YOURSELF: How to Lose Your Mind
and Create a New One,* by Dr. Joe Dispenza

All of the above are available at your local bookstore,
or may be ordered by contacting Hay House (see next page).

■ ■

We hope you enjoyed this Hay House book. If you'd like to receive our online catalog featuring additional information on Hay House books and products, or if you'd like to find out more about the Hay Foundation, please contact:

Hay House, Inc., P.O. Box 5100, Carlsbad, CA 92018-5100
(760) 431-7695 or (800) 654-5126
(760) 431-6948 (fax) or (800) 650-5115 (fax)
www.hayhouse.com® • www.hayfoundation.org

Published and distributed in Australia by: Hay House Australia Pty. Ltd.,
18/36 Ralph St., Alexandria NSW 2015 • *Phone:* 612-9669-4299
Fax: 612-9669-4144 • www.hayhouse.com.au

Published and distributed in the United Kingdom by: Hay House UK, Ltd.,
Astley House, 33 Notting Hill Gate, London W11 3JQ • *Phone:* 44-20-3675-2450
Fax: 44-20-3675-2451 • www.hayhouse.co.uk

Published and distributed in the Republic of South Africa by:
Hay House SA (Pty), Ltd., P.O. Box 990, Witkoppen 2068
info@hayhouse.co.za • www.hayhouse.co.za

Published in India by: Hay House Publishers India, Muskaan Complex,
Plot No. 3, B-2, Vasant Kunj, New Delhi 110 070 • *Phone:* 91-11-4176-1620
Fax: 91-11-4176-1630 • www.hayhouse.co.in

Distributed in Canada by: Raincoast Books, 2440 Viking Way, Richmond, B.C.
V6V 1N2 • *Phone:* 1-800-663-5714 • *Fax:* 1-800-565-3770 • www.raincoast.com

Access New Knowledge.
Anytime. Anywhere.

Learn and evolve at your own pace with the world's leading experts.

www.hayhouseU.com

Free e-newsletters
from Hay House, the Ultimate Resource for Inspiration

Be the first to know about Hay House's dollar deals, free downloads, special offers, affirmation cards, giveaways, contests, and more!

 Get exclusive excerpts from our latest releases and videos from *Hay House Present Moments*.

 Enjoy uplifting personal stories, how-to articles, and healing advice, along with videos and empowering quotes, within *Heal Your Life*.

 Have an inspirational story to tell and a passion for writing? Sharpen your writing skills with insider tips from *Your Writing Life*.

Sign Up Now!

Get inspired, educate yourself, get a complimentary gift, and share the wisdom!

http://www.hayhouse.com/newsletters.php

Visit www.hayhouse.com to sign up today!

 HAYHOUSE RADIO *radio for your soul*®   HealYourLife.com